Johannine Christianity

Johannine Christianity

ESSAYS ON ITS SETTING, SOURCES, AND THEOLOGY

Dwight   xxx

BY D. MOODY SMITH

University of South Carolina Press

Copyright © University of South Carolina 1984

Published in Columbia, South Carolina, by the
University of South Carolina Press

First Paperback Printing, 1989

Manufactured in the United States of America

Library of Congress Cataloging in Publication Data

Smith, D. Moody (Dwight Moody)
   Johannine Christianity.

   Includes bibliographical references and index.
   1. Bible. N.T. John—Criticism, interpretation,
etc.—Addresses, essays, lectures. I. Title.
BS2615.3.S64 1984   226'.506   84-19595
ISBN 0-87249-672-4 (pbk.)

TO JANE ALLEN SMITH
ὃ ἐποίησεν αὕτη λαληθήσεται
εἰς μνημόσυνον αὐτῆς

CONTENTS

I n the process of collecting and reflecting upon these essays, I have happily been able to see some coherence and lines of development in my own thinking. While I can claim no major breakthrough or discovery for myself, my own work has paralleled and reflected the advance of Johannine scholarship in interesting ways.

One speaks of the advance of Johannine scholarship only with hesitancy. Amidst the plethora of conflicting views on Johannine Christianity, it sometimes seems that "chaos" is the more fitting term. Nevertheless, there is a main line of Johannine research, defined more by the issues than by agreement upon them, and it is very clearly not where it was a generation or so ago. The first article in this collection indicates where that line stood less than a decade ago, and it still serves reasonably well as an indication of what problems and issues are being discussed.

The major issues of research were raised or focused by Rudolf Bultmann's great commentary on the Gospel of John (1941) and subsequent scholarship can in large measure be understood as a coming to terms with this commentary. My own earliest work, dealing as it did with the literary problems of the Fourth Gospel and Bultmann's resolution of them, taught me how the most technical aspects of Johannine research may be integrally related to the problem of understanding and interpreting the text. The sources, setting, and theology of Johannine Christianity are closely related matters,

ix

as I hope these essays will attest. From the sources my interest moved to the setting, with the goal of getting a better grasp of the theology of John. But the question of sources, particularly as regards the Fourth Evangelist's possible knowledge and use of the synoptic gospels, I have never been able to leave behind. The earliest and most recent essays in this volume deal with the problem of John and the synoptics.

The initial essay, which gives the book its title, was the result of an effort to bring together and relate certain dominant emphases of Johannine research in order to show a pattern of perspectives on Johannine Christianity that seemed to be clearly emerging. In this regard my own thinking had been much informed by the seminal works of Raymond E. Brown, J. Louis Martyn, and Wayne A. Meeks, and by the research of my own former student R. Alan Culpepper. The emergent pattern is one now shared by a large number of scholars in this country and abroad. I like to think that I perceived something that was less obvious when this article was first presented as a paper before the Johannine Seminar of the Society for New Testament Studies than it is today.

Of the articles on sources the first, which appeared in *New Testament Studies* twenty years ago, goes over some of the ground covered much more intensively in *The Composition and Order of the Fourth Gospel* (1965). It is still useful, especially since the book is now out of print. The two articles dealing with the question of a Johannine miracle source appeared more than a decade later. Under the influence of Robert Fortna (*The Gospel of Signs*) I have become less skeptical of the *semeia*-source hypothesis than I was in 1965. That John had narrative sources or traditions other than the synoptic gospels is, in my opinion, scarcely in doubt. In these two 1976 articles on narrative sources I propose or entertain hypotheses about their origin and character. The conclusions of the two articles may seem to point in different directions, but they are actually not incompatible.

In the Davies *Festschrift* contribution I revive and elaborate Bultmann's proposal that the milieu (and purpose) of the Johannine miracle source (or tradition) was the effort to win disciples of John the Baptist to Jesus. In particular, I underscore what this implies about the Jewish or Jewish-Christian character of the source and note how this may fit into a growing consensus regarding Johannine origins. The other article supports the case for a pre-Johannine gospel, culminating with a passion narrative, as a necessary stage in the dialogue with (or within) the synagogue. If both proposals are correct, one stage—that of the miracle source or cycle directed to Baptist sources—would obviously have preceded the other, directed to any Jews who would hear. The obvious implication that the Johannine circle or school had roots in the Baptist movement is a view now widely shared in Johannine scholarship (Bultmann, Cullmann, Raymond E. Brown). My point is that a miracle source alone might have had a decisive impact among followers of the Baptist, whose leader, apparently *not* a miracle worker (John 10:4), had also been executed. On the other hand, once a missionary effort was directed to Jews generally, presumably a later development, the problem of the crucifixion of the messianic claimant would have to be addressed. At that point the addition of, or combination with, a passion narrative would have been a logical and necessary step.

Although we can scarcely attain certainty in such matters, the evidence favoring the Johannine miracle-source and passion-source proposals has seemed to me to be substantial, notwithstanding the fact that it is, in the nature of the case, circular and circumstantial. That is, the primary evidence is contained in the extant document itself, and one must judge among the discernible possibilities. I concede that a more primitive form of the gospel might have contained dialogue as well as signs. Moreover, we cannot exclude the possibility that at some point in the tradition history preceding the gospel, individual signs were used as the basis for such discourses as we now find in the Fourth Gospel without (or prior to) being incorporated into a gospel-like framework. Yet I continue to be impressed by several considerations which favor a miracle-source proposal: first, John did not derive his narrative, especially miracle, tradition from the synoptics; second, the discourses presuppose the signs and other narratives, but the reverse is scarcely true; third, the discourses and certain statements within the basic narratives are easily understood as the result of later composition or editing; fourth and finally, statements such as 2:11; 4:54; 12:37; 20:30 (cf. 2:23) are best understood as indications of some collection or coupling of signs narratives prior to the composition of the present gospel. Certainly dogmatism and presumption of "proof" is inappropriate, and it may be that the source situation was more complex than we have imagined; i.e., such alternative possibilities as have just been mentioned may not be mutually exclusive.

The beginning point for all narrative-source proposals is, of course, the recognition that John did not base his account upon the synoptics, whether or not he knew them. The independence of the Fourth Gospel from the synoptics is, however, presently being severely challenged. Obviously I belong in that tradition of scholarship that sees in the Gospel of John the principal literary legacy of a distinct form and community of early Christianity rather than a midrash on the synoptic gospels. Such a position does not necessarily entail the view that John could not have known the other gospels at all, but it makes such a circumstance understandable. It accepts the burden of explaining why, if he knew them, he did not make greater and more obvious use of them.

The question of the relationship of John to the synoptics is, of course, not only basic but ancient. A longtime fascination with the subject is reflected in the fact that my earliest scholarly publication is the article about John and the synoptics on the triumphal entry in this volume. Despite an increasing awareness of the complexity of the problem, my opinion on this and related issues has not fundamentally changed, as the later essays will attest. The next article, on B. W. Bacon's view of the relationship between John and Mark, was a labor of love, Bacon having been a distinguished predecessor of one of my chief mentors, Paul Schubert, late Buckingham Professor of New Testament Criticism and Interpretation at Yale. Bacon's views, while distinctly Baconian in their expression, are altogether typical of an earlier day. Rightly or wrongly, Bacon takes for granted John's dependence on Mark, a matter that is now very much the subject of discussion and debate among Johannine scholars. His work nicely illustrates how much presuppositions affect the nature of argument in our field. The piece following is a long review of two recent major works on John and the synoptics, both in French and both by Roman Catholic scholars. There the similarity ends. The Neirynck book is an extended and minute examination and evaluation of the work of M.-E. Boismard, who in three large volumes has developed an elaborate theory of gospel origins and relationships. In order to review Neirynck, I had to come to terms with Boismard. Both are fully conversant with recent source and redaction criticism of the Fourth Gospel. Monsignor de Solages' book is quite different in that respect as well as in others. Rather conservative, it is nevertheless an interesting effort to quantify, or get some statistical fix on, the Johannine-synoptic relationship. My *New Testament Studies* article on the same subject, originally a paper delivered at a plenary session of the Society for New Testament Studies in Durham, England, is a provisional effort to make an assessment and general statement about this entire matter. Perhaps I lean over too far backward to be open to differing views, but it should be clear that my difficulties in understanding how the Fourth Evangelist could have known and utilized the other canonical gospels remain sizable. Despite my willingness to concede that John may have known one or more of the synoptics (a possibility which I think I have never denied), I remain essentially unconverted to the position of Neirynck, whose efforts to understand John as essentially derivative from the synoptics seem to me to be much more plausible in the case of certain episodes from the passion and resurrection narratives than on consideration of the gospel as a whole. Thus I cannot accept his description of me as semi-converted (cf. *NTS* 30 [1984]: 161); I fear I remain at most among the *sebomenoi* in the weaker sense of that term!

The essays on Johannine theology are less technical than the others, but certainly not by intention less serious. I should perhaps reiterate that my interest in the setting and sources of the Gospel of John has had a theological goal in view. It is important to know as much as possible about a document's milieu, and thus about what its author would have likely taken for granted, if one is to understand it historically. I remain committed to the importance of historical understanding and historical theology as tasks laid upon us by our scholarly discipline and by the character of Christian theology. So the question of sources becomes significant, and particularly the question of whether the Fourth Evangelist knew the other canonical gospels. Did he presuppose and accept the synoptic view of Jesus, or did he ignore, reject, or simply remain ignorant of it? How one reads John's Gospel will depend importantly on how that question is decided.

At the same time, it is impossible to ignore the hermeneutical advances now being made as interpreters apply the insights and perspectives of literary-critical theory to the New Testament. In this connection, one thinks first of the seminal work of R. Alan Culpep-

per, *Anatomy of the Fourth Gospel* (Fortress, 1983). According to
his analysis, the distillation of an *implied* author and an implied
reader are all—or the most—the text per se can be made to yield.
For the purpose of understanding the text as such, the reader does
not need to know more. At the same time, however, in precisely this
respect Culpepper's conclusions are largely congenial with his own
earlier work on the Johannine school and with a fairly broad consensus of recent Johannine scholarship. To me this is an encourag-
ing result, particularly for the interests of the historian and Christian
theologian. In view of, and in the terms of, this literary-critical approach, the crucial question for the Christian exegete may be that
of the relationship of the narrative world of the text to the Christian
world in which it was produced and to the world of Jesus which it
purports to describe.

It is illuminating in this connection to apply Culpepper's literary-
critical terminology to the historical proposals of J. Louis Martyn.
On Martyn's terms the implied author projects the struggle of his
community onto the narrative world of Jesus in the confidence that
the two are at bottom the same. Thus the narrative world of the text
and the worlds of both the author's community on the one hand
and Jesus on the other are intrinsically and inextricably connected.
The implied reader will recognize this and respond accordingly. The
literary analysis of Culpepper is not incongruent with the historical
proposals of Martyn, although it might accommodate other, similar
hypotheses. Given these terms, it seems to me that the Christian
exegete has something at stake in the proposition that the narrative
world of the text, the world of the Johannine community, and the
world of Jesus do, in fact, overlap significantly, even if they are not
exactly congruent. The point may perhaps be stated more sharply
by putting the matter negatively: finding that the implied author is
unrelated to a real author in that he does not represent an actual
interest in, or a relationship to, a real world—whether that of the
Johannine community or of Jesus—would undercut the status of
the text as a witness to the gospel which seems to be proclaimed in
or through it. At least this would be the case if we are justified in
assuming that the Christian gospel is based upon Jesus and in its
written form is genuinely addressed to a believing community. Otherwise, the written gospel is something less than an authentic word-
event in the fullest, historically pregnant, sense of that expression.

In this connection it is worth observing also that on the basis of Culpepper's analysis one could argue for John's knowledge of the other gospels. The implied reader knows the story of Jesus, or major aspects and parts of it (pp. 222f.). As *we* read John, we know these things from the synoptic gospels. Whether John's first readers knew them from that, or another, source is a good, and moot, question.

The essay on Jesus in the Fourth Gospel deals with a matter which is, of course, of general historical and theological interest. I do not seek to make a new contribution so much as to underline certain aspects of John's portrayal which, it seems to me, are sometimes ignored or played down. The final essay, entitled "Theology and Ministry in John," is a somewhat abbreviated version of lectures originally delivered to an audience consisting of ministers rather than academic biblical scholars. It is the only one of the collection that has been edited for this volume, not so much to bring it up to date as to remove redundancies in view of the other articles. Obviously it lacks something in scholarly refinement, not to mention comprehensiveness. Yet because it deals with matters not otherwise treated, which are important and worth emphasizing at this time, I have included it. Coming as it does at the end of the book, it constitutes a kind of provisional statement about the character and theology of John's Gospel in relation to the church life and social setting out of which it arose.

No effort has been made to make bibliographical information in the footnotes reflect more recent English translations. Thus in earlier essays Bultmann's commentary, *Das Evangelium des Johannes* is cited in the original German, but in later ones in English translation. Through 1965 the most comprehensive bibliography is Edward Malatesta, *St. John's Gospel: 1920–1965*, Analecta Biblica 32 (Rome: Pontifical Biblical Institute, 1967), a work devoted entirely to bibliography. The fullest recent bibliographies are found in the two-volume English translation of Ernst Haenchen's commentary, *John 1* and *John 2*, trans. Robert W. Funk and ed. Ulrich Busse (Philadelphia: Fortress, 1984), esp. *John 2*, pp. 254–346.

ACKNOWLEDGMENTS

The journals and publishers holding rights to these articles have graciously consented to allow me to publish them here. The articles and the original publishers who have granted permission are as follows:

"Johannine Christianity: Some Reflections on its Character and Delineation," *New Testament Studies* 21 (1976): 222–48.

"The Sources of the Gospel of John: An Assessment of the Present State of the Problem," *New Testament Studies* 10 (1964): 336–51.

"The Milieu of the Johannine Miracle Source: A Proposal," *Jews, Greeks, and Christians, Religious Cultures in Late Antiquity, Essays in Honor of William David Davies*, eds. Robert Hamerton-Kelly and Robin Scroggs. Leiden: Brill, 1976, pp. 164–80.

"The Setting and Shape of a Johannine Narrative Source," *Journal of Biblical Literature* 95 (1976): 231–41.

"John 12:12 ff. and the Question of John's Use of the Synoptics," *Journal of Biblical Literature* 82 (1965): 58–64.

"B. W. Bacon on John and Mark," *Perspectives in Religious Studies* 8 (1981): 201–18.

"John and the Synoptics," *Biblica* 63 (1982): 102–13.

"John and the Synoptics: Some Dimensions of the Problem," *New Testament Studies* 26 (1980): 425–44.

"The Presentation of Jesus in the Fourth Gospel," *Interpretation* 31 (1977): 367–78.

"Theology and Ministry in John," *A Biblical Basis for Ministry*, eds. Earl E. Shelp and Ronald Sunderland. Philadelphia: Westminster, 1981, p. 186–228.

About this last article I should say also that its substance was presented in lecture form, first in 1980 at the Institute of Religion in Houston, Texas, and subsequently as the 1981 Earl Lectures at Nazarene Theological Seminary in Kansas City, Missouri. I wish to express appreciation and thanks to Dr. Ronald Sunderland, then Director of the Institute, and Dr. Earl E. Shelp, his associate, for their encouragement and help, and also to several colleagues at the Nazarene Seminary, especially Professors Paul Bassett and Alex Deasley, who received me so warmly and well.

Mr. Kenneth J. Scott of the University of South Carolina Press, long-time friend and editor, has invited me to collect and publish these essays. I am grateful to him for his encouragement and support. My thanks also to Professors W. D. Davies, Franklin W. Young, and John H. Schütz, who read most of these articles before they were first published, offering helpful criticism and advice, and to Dean Dennis M. Campbell who counseled me concerning the composition of the volume and made available ample secretarial assistance. Frank Thielman and Robert G. Hall, my student assistants, rendered invaluable help at several points, especially in composing the index and reading proof.

The dedication of this book expresses a special debt of gratitude I owe my wife. Twenty years ago I first dedicated a book to her. In the interval our children have been reared and educated. Her devotion to this traditionally important task issued in a significant commitment to public education in the city school system of Durham, North Carolina. The dedication takes note of this, as does the reference to Jesus' word in Mark 14:9, which, while uttered under vastly different circumstances, seems somehow appropriate.

D. Moody Smith
May, 1984

ABBREVIATIONS

AB	Anchor Bible
ALBO	Analecta lovaniensia biblica et orientalia
AnBib	Analecta biblica
ATR	*Anglican Theological Review*
BBB	Bonner biblische Beiträge
BETL	Bibliotheca ephemeridum theologicarum lovaniensium
BHTh	Beiträge zur historischen Theologie
BJRL	*Bulletin of the John Rylands Library*
BWANT	Beiträge zur Wissenschaft vom Alten und Neuen Testament
BZ	*Biblische Zeitschrift*
BZNW	Beihefte zur ZNW
CBQ	*Catholic Biblical Quarterly*
ConNT	Coniectanea neotestamentica
EBib	Etudes bibliques
EKKNT	Evangelisch-katholischer Kommentar zum Neuen Testament
ExpT	*Expository Times*
FRLANT	Forschungen zur Religion und Literatur des Alten und Neuen Testaments
HAW	Handbuch der Altertumswissenschaft
HibJ	*Hibbert Journal*
HNTC	Harper's New Testament Commentaries
HTR	*Harvard Theological Review*
HTS	Harvard Theological Studies
ICC	International Critical Commentary
Int	*Interpretation*
JAAR	*Journal of the American Academy of Religion*
JBL	*Journal of Biblical Literature*
JTS	*Journal of Theological Studies*
NICNT	New International Commentary on the New Testament

NovT	*Novum Testamentum*
NovTSup	Novum Testamentum, Supplements
NTS	*New Testament Studies*
RB	*Revue Biblique*
SBLDS	Society of Biblical Literature Dissertation Series
SBS	Stuttgarter Bibelstudien
SBT	Studies in Biblical Theology
SC	Sources chrétiennes
SNTSMS	Society for New Testament Studies Monograph Series
StANT	Studien zum Alten und Neuen Testament
ThBl	*Theologische Blätter*
ThR	*Theologische Rundschau*
ThZ	*Theologische Zeitschrift*
TLZ	*Theologische Literaturzeitung*
TU	Texte und Untersuchungen
UNT	Untersuchungen zum Neuen Testament
WMANT	Wissenschaftliche Monographien zum Alten und Neuen Testament
WUNT	Wissenschaftliche Untersuchungen zum Neuen Testament
ZNW	*Zeitschrift für die neutestamentliche Wissenschaft*
ZTK	*Zeitschrift für Theologie und Kirche*

Introduction | Johannine Christianity

T he ever-increasing volume of scholarly publications dealing with Johannine problems encour-
ages the hope that a solution of what Harnack
called the Johannine riddle is at last in sight. Yet a survey of the
literature may leave the impression that scholars, like so many prov-
erbial horsemen, are riding off in different directions through a
trackless morass. Such an impression is not entirely accurate, however, for significant patterns and points of coincidence are emerging
from what at first appears to be a complex and rather confused
picture. The purpose of this essay, therefore, is to point to several
well-trodden pathways through the wilderness of Johannine problems which others have hewn out, and by clarification, summary,
and assessment of some of the more important evidences bearing
upon Johannine origins to suggest why these paths are well chosen
and where they may be leading us.[1]

1. In this article "John" and "Johannine" may be taken to refer to the Fourth
Gospel and the Johannine Epistles as well as to their authors, but not to the Apocalypse unless so specified. Nothing is thereby intended or implied about the identity
of the author(s). To friends and colleagues too numerous to mention, who have
read this paper or heard it along the way and offered helpful, critical comment and
encouragement I wish to express my thanks, as well as to the John Simon Guggen-
heim Foundation for a fellowship grant which enabled me to have a year's leave
to work on problems of Johannine origins.

I

THE CHURCH IN JOHN AND JOHN IN THE CHURCH

A consideration of Johannine Christianity is, of course, to be distinguished from an investigation of the concept of the church in the Johannine writings and from the much discussed question of the use of those documents, particularly the Gospel, in the early church. Yet these closely related matters must not simply be overlooked, since if they are not of fundamental importance to our subject they may at least shed important light upon it.

There are, however, reasons for not beginning with them or attempting to treat them in detail in this essay. The communal images of the Gospel (e.g. the shepherd and the flock, the vine and the branches), the prayer for unity (John 17), and the underlying assumption of the farewell discourses that the disciples of Jesus are to constitute a continuing community after his death (an assumption that receives confirmation in 1 John) allow us to speak of a Johannine conception of the church, despite the disuse of the term *ecclesia* in the Gospel and Epistles. Yet there are problems in attempting to construct the Johannine conception of the church directly from the relevant texts. It is, of course, possible to deduce a Johannine conception of the church from the texts, particularly when one reckons with what appear to be John's serious omissions as well as with what he says. A certain understanding of the church thereby comes to expression, and the kind of understanding that emerges has already been well articulated, particularly by Eduard Schweizer in his essay on the church in the Johannine literature.[2] But it is worth asking whether by this means one can determine with great confidence an organization and conception of Christian community that underlies and informs the document. Everyone knows that it is a methodological error to assume for John the Pauline or deutero-Pauline, much less the early catholic, doctrine of the church. On the other hand, a residual element of uncertainty remains when one extrapolates from the implications and omissions of a document that does not deal explicitly with ecclesiology a doctrine of the church.

2. "The Concept of the Church in the Gospel and Epistles of St John," *New Testament Essays: Studies in Memory of Thomas Walter Manson*, ed. A.J.B. Higgins (Manchester: Manchester University Press, 1959), pp.230–45; with which compare the same author's *Church Order in the New Testament*, SBT 32 (London: S.C.M., 1961), pp. 117–36.

Therefore, Raymond Brown's criticism of Schweizer's approach should no more be dismissed as a product of his Catholicism than should Schweizer's interpretation be credited to his Protestantism.[3] We can agree that something like Schweizer's description of Johannine ecclesiology is a reasonable inference from the exegesis of the relevant texts, while admitting that it is not the only possible inference. What the evangelist might have written had he intended to comment directly upon ecclesiological questions and how he might have responded had he been asked them are moot questions. If it be maintained that he was, in fact, writing to deal with certain ecclesiological issues, as well as problems disturbing contemporary churches, one must concede that in the broadest sense this is doubtless so. Yet because his treatment of them is oblique rather than direct, precisely what they were remains, in my opinion, a question for discussion rather than a well-established presupposition for further investigation.[4] Thus while the concept of Christian community, or of the church, in the Johannine literature is certainly not irrelevant for the definition and understanding of the concrete and specific historical reality of Johannine Christianity, the clarification of this concept may not be possible on the basis of exegesis alone. Exegesis will lend some support to more than one interpretation, as the divergent views of Schweizer and Brown, to name only two examples, show.

Nevertheless, it can probably be agreed that on any reading of the Gospel and Epistles there appears a sectarian consciousness, a sense of exclusiveness, a sharp delineation of the community from the world. Although this sensibility is sharper in 1 John (e.g. 2:15–17) than in the Gospel (cf. 3:16–17; 12:47; 17:21, 23), it is present there as well (e.g. 17: 9–14).[5] Comparisons with community consciousness in Qumran, which is likewise related to a fundamental

3. R. E. Brown, *The Gospel According to John (i-xii)*, AB 29 (Garden City, N.Y.: Doubleday, 1966), pp. cv-cxi.

4. E. Käsemann, *The Testament of Jesus,* trans. G. Krodel (Philadelphia: Fortress, 1968), has, of course, drawn far-reaching conclusions about the nature of Johannine Christianity and the Johannine church from an analysis of the theological bearing or direction of relevant texts, esp. John 17.

5. The difference between the First Epistle and the Fourth Gospel, with its stronger missionary interest, has been set forth by F. Hahn, *Mission in the New Testament,* SBT 47; (London: S.C.M., 1965), pp. 152–63. On the Fourth Gospel cf. Bultmann,

dualism, are entirely apposite and to the point. If this sectarian or quasi-sectarian self-consciousness is not a matter of dispute, its roots, causes, and social matrix nevertheless are. What thereby comes to expression? A Christian sense of alienation or separation from the world generally? From the synagogue? From developing ecclesiastical orthodoxy? Can the sense of exclusiveness be isolated within the Johannine corpus by means of tradition- or source-critical analysis? That is, can it be correlated with literary strata or historical stages of development? The definition of Johannine ecclesiology is set within certain limits by the documents themselves, but they in turn raise as many questions as they answer.

The important and complex question of the use of Johannine writings, particularly the Gospel, in the early church must remain for the most part beyond our purview, although there may be important things to be learned about Johannine Christianity from an investigation of this problem. We limit ourselves to a brief statement of where the question seems presently to stand. In an important work published more than a generation ago, J. N. Sanders attached great importance to the Gospel's use among Gnostics and what he understood to be its consequent relative disuse among the second century fathers until the time of Irenaeus.[6] F. M. Braun's more recent study of John's Gospel in the ancient church is in large measure directed against Sanders' point of view and attempts to demonstrate the widespread use of the Gospel among the earliest orthodox fathers.[7] Braun's arguments and assessment of the evidence have not, however, proved conclusive. Recently M. R. Hillmer has, in my opinion, rather successfully disputed Braun's position, bringing into

---

The Gospel of John: A Commentary, trans. G. R. Beasley-Murray et al. (Philadelphia: Westminster, 1971), pp. 509—10. The missionary aspect of John's Gospel is not denied by Käsemann (*The Testament of Jesus*, p. 70), although he scarcely emphasizes it.

6. *The Fourth Gospel in the Early Church: Its Origin and Influence on Christian Theology up to Irenaeus* (Cambridge: Cambridge University Press, 1943). Cf. W. von Loewenich, *Das Johannes-Verständnis im zweiten Jahrhundert*, BZNW 13 (Giessen: Töpelmann, 1932), pp. 60—115. Although von Loewenich does not adumbrate Sanders' thesis, his findings are not irreconcilable with it.

7. *Jean le théologien et son évangile dans l'église ancienne*, EBib (Paris: J. Gabalda, 1959), esp. pp. 65—66.

consideration the recently discovered Coptic Gnostic texts of Nag Hammadi.[8] While Hillmer does not intend a defense of Sanders' position, his research certainly tends to vindicate it.[9] A similar view of the disuse of the Fourth Gospel in orthodox ecclesiastical circles of the second century, concomitant with its popularity among Gnostics, had in fact already been advanced by Walter Bauer.[10] While such an assessment of the early Gnostic associations of the Fourth Gospel may well be correct, it is still difficult to move from our fragmentary knowledge of the use of the Gospel in the second century church to conclusions about the church situation in which it was composed. The heretical use of the Gospel in the second century may reflect its own genuinely heretical tendencies, yet Irenaeus' efforts to claim the Gospel for the catholic church and thus to oppose both the heretics and, possibly, the opponents of the Gospel surely had basis and justification in the text itself.[11]

There are issues of obvious importance to our purposes involved in the discussion of the use and disuse of John's Gospel in the second century, particularly with regard to the question of use by Gnostics. Nevertheless, it does not at the moment seem possible to book a through ticket from the churches of the second century which used John to the church in which it was actually written. To state matters differently, if there was in Christian antiquity a Johannine line of

8. "The Gospel of John in the Second Century" (unpublished Th.D. thesis, Divinity School, Harvard University, 1966). Hillmer draws upon insights of H. Köster, *Synoptische Überlieferung bei den apostolischen Vätern,* TU 65 (Berlin: Akademie Verlag, 1957), concerning the impossibility of showing literary dependency upon the canonical gospels in instances where neither quotation formulas nor materials or characteristics peculiar to a particular evangelist are present.

9. "This hesitating and gradual acceptance of John on the part of the Apologists and at the same time the extensive use of it in Gnostic writings, such as the Excerpta ex Theodoto and the Naassene Fragment, suggests that it was in Christian-gnostic circles that John was preserved and first recognized as important" ("The Gospel of John in the Second Century," p. 171).

10. See *Orthodoxy and Heresy in Earliest Christianity,* trans. and ed. R. A. Kraft and G. Krodel et al. (Philadelphia: Fortress, 1971), pp. 187, 206–12, for John's disuse among the orthodox, particularly at Rome.

11. To attempt to bring John under the categories of either orthodoxy or heresy is, however, anachronistic, as Stephen Smalley has noted in his recent article, "Diversity and Development in John," *NTS* 17 (1971): 276–92.

development,[12] it has not yet proved possible to identify it clearly in the second century and thus to follow it back into the first.

Related to this state of affairs is the difficulty of tracing the tradition—if, indeed, there was such—behind the statements of Irenaeus. It is quite possible, and even likely, that Irenaeus does not represent the genuinely Johannine line of development, which may have continued to exist outside the realm of emergent institutional orthodoxy, although he may see in the Fourth Gospel points of genuine theological agreement. If we have lost track of the connecting links between the evidences of the use of the Fourth Gospel in the second century and its earlier origins, we are not necessarily left without a clue. If knowledge is not augmented by future manuscript discoveries, it may be advanced by further assessment and clarification of data already known.

JOHANNINE CHRISTIANITY IN THE NEW TESTAMENT

If we are looking for the surest way into the Johannine problem we begin with some simple and obvious, but nevertheless germane, observations about the boundaries of Johannine Christianity within the New Testament. Naturally, the New Testament cannot be taken to be entirely representative of first century Christianity, but it provides an indispensable access to it. Moreover, to the extent one can delineate Johannine Christianity cleanly and without overlap in the New Testament, something significant is thereby implied about its position, whether theological, spiritual, or geographic, in early Christianity.

To plot the coordinates of Pauline, Matthean, Lucan or Marcan Christianity within the New Testament is not a very difficult task. For Paul there are, of course, the genuine letters, which give us a mass of information, a considerable amount of which at least invites correlation with Acts; the deutero-Paulines (Ephesians, Colossians and 2 Thessalonians) and the Pastorals; and traces of Paul in other non-Pauline books such as James, 2 Peter, perhaps 1 Peter, perhaps Hebrews, as well as 1 Clement and Ignatius. If we know anything at all about the New Testament churches we know the Pauline churches. The gospels cannot be pinned down quite so precisely.

12. The term is, of course, that of J. M. Robinson and H. Köster, *Trajectories Through Early Christianity* (Philadelphia: Fortress, 1971).

Nevertheless, Luke has a point of contact with Pauline Christianity, however much he may have misunderstood Paul's theology. There is also clear evidence of contact with Mark, who in large measure provides Luke's narrative framework, and with a sayings tradition (Q) shared with Matthew. Moreover, Luke provides a prologue in which he sets forth an understanding of his own historical position and purpose vis-à-vis his predecessors. Similar if less extensive coordinates might be plotted in the cases of Matthew and Mark.

John, however, presents a rather different situation. The critical orthodoxy of an earlier generation which assumed John's knowledge of and dependence upon Paul and the synoptic gospels—or at least one of them—can no longer be our starting point.[13] While it cannot be claimed that such assumptions are no longer defensible, it is precisely the point that today they require defense. And those who would defend them would probably not want either to interpret John in terms of alleged divergences from the synoptics or to attempt to understand the evangelist theologically as the successor of Paul, much less a pioneer in the hellenization of Christianity.[14] Despite some residual disagreement on the question of Johannine and synoptic relationships, few would today defend the view that John's Gospel is based principally upon the synoptics or that they were his chief written sources.[15] In my own view, John can be adequately explained without presupposing dependence upon the syn-

13. For the view that John drew upon Paul, see, e.g., A. Barnett, *Paul Becomes a Literary Influence* (Chicago: University of Chicago Press, 1941), pp. 104–42, esp. 104–5. For the once generally held assumption that John knew and used the synoptic gospels, see E. C. Colwell, *John Defends the Gospel* (Chicago: Willett, Clark, 1936), esp. pp. 7ff.

14. Contrast A. Schweitzer, *The Mysticism of Paul the Apostle* (New York: Henry Holt, 1931), p. 349: "The Hellenistic conception of redemption through union with Christ is set forth with admirable completeness in the Gospel of John."

15. J. Blinzler, *Johannes und die Synoptiker: Ein Forschungsbericht,* SBS 6 (Stuttgart: Katholisches Bibelwerk, 1965), pp. 31–32, with some reason challenged my earlier statement, *NTS* 10 (1964): 349, about an emerging consensus (e.g., Gardner-Smith, Goodenough, Bultmann, Dodd) on John's independence of the synoptics. Since a statistical count of scholars would surely not yield a sweeping consensus on Johannine independence, there was justification for Blinzler's refusal to agree that one existed. Nevertheless, the positions taken by Brown, esp. p. xlvii; R. Schnackenburg, *The Gospel According to St. John,* Vol. 1: *Introduction and Commentary on Chapters 1–4,* Herder's Theological Commentary on the New Tes-

optics (or any one of them) or upon the Pauline corpus, although we cannot be entirely certain that he had knowledge of neither. Since it is no longer possible to date John's Gospel well into the second century, it cannot be presumed that he was familiar with many or most of the other New Testament writings. The chronology which made John's knowledge of, and dependence upon, other New Testament writers a likelihood, if not a virtual certainty, has broken down. For this among other reasons Johannine dependence upon other expressions of early Christianity has become problematic, if not dubious; that is, it has become difficult to explain the conceptual, stylistic, and theological *Eigenart* of the Johannine literature in terms of a departure from, or development of, earlier strains of Christian thought represented in the New Testament.

To suggest that some further explanation of the Johannine mood has not for some time been invoked would, of course, be misleading. For example, the view that the distinctiveness of Johannine Christianity in relation to other forms of early Christianity known to us stemmed from its hellenizing character was an earlier result of the application of research in the comparative study of the history of religions to the New Testament. This same sort of investigation certainly has a right to continue, although the view that John is "Hellenistic"—if by that is meant Greek rather than Jewish—is certainly now very dubious. Moreover, the function of such investigations can no longer be to explain John's departures from the synoptic view of Jesus or from Paul's theology, as though these provided the base line or foundation of Johannine thought. Rather, they may shed light on distinct and peculiar features of Johannine style and thought as these have developed in independence of other dominant forms of early Christianity. In other words, the history-of-

---

tament (New York: Herder & Herder, 1968), pp. 1–43; J. N. Sanders, *A Commentary on the Gospel According to St. John,* ed. B. A. Mastin, HNTC (New York: Harper, 1968), pp. 8–12; L. Morris, *The Gospel According to John,* NICNT (Grand Rapids: Eerdmans, 1971), pp. 49–52; and R. T. Fortna, *The Gospel of Signs: A Reconstruction of the Narrative Source Underlying the Fourth Gospel,* SNTSMS 11 (Cambridge: Cambridge University Press, 1970), pp. 8–11, 226ff., all espousing Johannine independence of the synoptics, lead me to believe that I was certainly pointing to a very significant direction of scholarship, whether or not that deserves to be called a consensus.

religions problem of the Fourth Gospel (or of the Gospel and Epistles) is not to explain how it came to differ from the synoptics or
Paul, but how and why Johannine modes of conceptuality and speech
attained such distinctiveness alongside other developments in early
Christianity.

It is difficult to narrow down the cultural and religious milieu of
the Fourth Gospel or of the Johannine literature, even if here and
there we seem to be standing very close to some important aspect
of it. Research into the general religious background of the Fourth
Gospel has proved by itself an inadequate (although by no means
irrelevant) approach to the resolution of Johannine problems, partly
because the themes and symbols of John are found in such a large
number of religious documents of Jewish as well as pagan origin.
Moreover, the origin and dating of materials alleged to be part of
the background is itself often problematic, so that appeal to them
may seem tantamount to attempting to explain the earlier by the
later or the known by the unknown. While investigations of this
sort are certainly not illegitimate and wrong or destined to futility,
they may prove to be more fruitful if they are focused or controlled
as much as possible with respect to the questions asked, the sources
employed, and the answers expected. It is, of course, possible that
the Johannine evangelist deliberately drew upon the language and
symbolism of more than one religious tradition in order to speak in
terms that would be universally understood.[16] But even the recognition of this possibility need not preclude the search for the vantage
point from which the evangelist put it all together. Although general
religionsgeschichtliche factors will not be irrelevant in the search
for such a vantage point, it is surely to be sought first of all within
the spectrum of early Christianity, and probably very near its nexus
with Judaism.

EVIDENCES OF THE EXISTENCE OF A JOHANNINE
COMMUNITY IN THE JOHANNINE LITERATURE
AND ELSEWHERE

The raising of the question of the substantial independence of the
Fourth Gospel from the synoptics has followed upon the impact of

16. As has been suggested by G. W. MacRae, "The Fourth Gospel and *Religionsgeschichte,*" CBQ 32 (1970): 13–24, esp. pp. 22–23.

form criticism on the investigation of the synoptic gospels. Although these scholarly developments arose independently, they are not unrelated. By its presuppositions, methods, and results, form criticism called attention to the church setting and traditional character of the material of the synoptic tradition. Bultmann's famous dictum that the gospels and their traditions are primarily sources for the situations from which they arose and only secondarily sources for the historical situations they describe[17] not surprisingly evoked widespread dismay and disagreement. Yet what he affirmed—as distinguished from what he seemed to deny—has gained very widespread assent. The gospels and the traditions behind them, when subjected to critical analysis, reveal or suggest a great deal about the circles in which they arose. A better understanding of the churchly milieu of the synoptics seems also to be an emerging by-product of redaction criticism as well as form criticism. The relative ease with which redactional material can be separated from sources or tradition in Matthew and Luke, and to a lesser degree in Mark, has greatly facilitated the redaction-critical task; and thus enables us to see those gospels more clearly against their churchly backgrounds.

It is therefore reasonable to ask whether one may also better understand the Fourth Gospel by attempting a more precise definition of its setting in early Christianity carried out in part by means of an analysis of its components. We are already in a fairly good position to undertake such a task, for we possess also letters with strong stylistic and conceptual affinities with the Gospel and an Apocalypse with at least some points of contact[18] if also wide-ranging differences, which is associated with the other documents by tradition. These documents may be considered relevant to the analysis of the Gospel. Moreover, the application of redaction-critical and

17. See Bultmann's article of 1926, "The New Approach to the Synoptic Problem," reprinted in *Existence and Faith: Shorter Writings of Rudolf Bultmann*, ed. S. M. Ogden (New York: Living Age Books, 1960), pp. 35–54, esp. p. 38. Bultmann ascribes the enunciation of this principle to Wellhausen and, although he states it in general terms, obviously regards it as particularly applicable to the gospels.

18. These were recognized long ago by scholars convinced on linguistic and conceptual grounds that the Apocalypse could not be the work of the evangelist. See, e.g., the discussion of R. H. Charles, *A Critical and Exegetical Commentary on the Revelation of St. John*, ICC (Edinburgh: Clark, 1920), 1, xxix-xxxiv, esp. xxxii-xxxiii.

related modes of analysis to the Johannine documents, particularly the Gospel, has already been pursued forcefully and with considerable success.[19] The distinctive character of the Johannine narrative material within the Gospel strongly suggests a principal source (or sources) and one independent of the synoptics. This general viewpoint is supported by a phalanx of scholars of diverse methods and interests.[20] It cannot, of course, be said that the narratives of John are at no point influenced by, or related to, those of the synoptics. The passion narrative is the most obvious example, although there are others (1: 19ff.; 2:13ff.; 4:46–54; 6:16–21 etc.). But precisely in those passages which have obvious synoptic parallels the extent of divergence is considerable, and difficult to account for on the basis of clear Johannine interests. At the least it seems necessary to predicate other narrative sources than the synoptics, sources which the evangelist seems to have treated with greater care and seriousness. The existence of such an independent narrative tradition is prima facie evidence, on form-critical grounds, for the existence of a traditioning community. Moreover, the Johannine narrative material, when subjected to literary analysis, yields pericopes that fit

19. Especially, but not only, by R. Fortna, *The Gospel of Signs,* and also "Source and Redaction in the Fourth Gospel's Portrayal of Jesus' Signs," *JBL* 89 (1970):51–66. For other recent forms of a sign-source theory see E. Bammel, "John Did No Miracle: John 10: 41," in *Miracles: Cambridge Studies in their Philosophy and History,* ed. C.F.D. Moule (London: Mowbray, 1965), pp. 179–202, and "The Baptist in Early Christian Tradition," *NTS* 18 (1971): 95–128, esp. 108–13, 122–26; also J. Becker, "Wunder und Christologie: zum literarkritischen und christologischen Problem der Wunder im Johannesevangelium," *NTS* 16 (1970):130–48. Severe strictures against Fortna's work have been advanced by B. Lindars, *Behind the Fourth Gospel,* Studies in Creative Criticism (London: S.P.C.K; 1971), pp. 28ff. Yet he nevertheless regards the possibility of separating out the synoptic-like (narrative) material in the Fourth Gospel as more promising than the task of reconstructing a discourse source (p. 27), since, as he thinks, narrative sources of some sort do, in fact, underlie the Fourth Gospel. The Johannine passion narrative represents a distinct set of problems, now treated comprehensively by A. Dauer, *Die Passionsgeschichte im Johannesevangelium: eine traditionsgeschichtliche und theologische Untersuchung zu Joh 18:1–19:30,* StANT 30 (Munich: Kösel, 1972), who concludes that the Johannine passion has been influenced by the synoptics in its development but nevertheless represents a basically independent form of the tradition.

20. See nn. 15 and 19 above.

the form-critical categories derived from the synoptic tradition.[21] While the narrative tradition was probably fixed in written form prior to its incorporation into the Gospel, it doubtless had a tradition history.

That there may also have been a Johannine tradition of dominical sayings or similar materials is less obvious but nevertheless a real and significant possibility. Efforts to show the existence of an independent oral tradition throughout the Gospel have been no more successful than comprehensive source theories,[22] but are not for that reason completely unfounded. Projections of what may be an iceberg appear on the surface: sayings of John the Baptist with synoptic parallels; the Johannine version of traditional words about the seed falling into the earth, saving one's life and losing it, and following Jesus (12:24–26); apparently traditional sayings in 4:35–38; and perhaps scattered parabolic forms.[23] Certainly the love commandment (13 34; 15: 12; 1 John 2:7–8., etc.; 2 John 5) is in a real sense also traditional, as the references in the Epistles clearly show.[24] On the other hand, in Matthew 11: 27; Luke 10: 22 (Q) a saying with a markedly Johannine ring has found a place in the synoptic tradition.[25] Moreover, the prologue belongs to a distinct genre of early Christian expression and may be based upon an earlier hymn.[26]

21. On the form-critical analysis of the Fourth Gospel see esp. C. H. Dodd, *Historical Tradition in the Fourth Gospel,* pp. 5–9 and passim; also Fortna, *The Gospel of Signs,* pp. 14–15.

22. E.g., B. Noack, *Zur johanneischen Tradition: Beiträge zur Kritik an der Literarkritischen Analyse des vierten Evangeliums* (Copenhagen: Rosenkilde og Bagger, 1954); cf. Bultmann's review, *TLZ* 80 (1955):521–26.

23. Dodd, pp. 366–87, observes parabolic forms in 12:24; 16:21; 11:9–10; 8:35; 10:1–5; 3:29, and, by way of an appended note (p. 386 n. 2), 5: 19–20a. For a more extensive presentation of 5: 19–20a as a parable see B. Lindars, "Two Parables in John," *NTS* 16 (1970): 318–29, esp. 318–24. He also discusses 3: 29 (pp. 324–29).

24. On the conscious development of the concept of tradition in 1 John see H. Conzelmann, "Was von Anfang war," *Neutestamentliche Studien für Rudolf Bultmann zu seinem siebzigsten Geburtstag am 20. August 1954,* BZNW 21 (Berlin: Töpelmann, 1957), pp. 194–201.

25. J. Jeremias, *New Testament Theology, Part One: The Proclamation of Jesus,* trans. J. Bowden (London: S.C.M., 1971), pp. 56–61, argues that Matthew 11: 27/Luke 10: 22 must be considered an authentic word of Jesus and disputes the contention that the logion is Johannine. Nevertheless, he grants that it is the kind of logion from which Johannine theology grew (p. 59). M.J. Suggs, who doubts the

Recent research has shown a marked tendency to enlarge consid-
erably the range of material in the discourses which may be considered traditional. The identification of such materials, like the isolation
of literary sources, remains a task beset with difficulties and uncertainties. Yet efforts to show the traditional character of substantial
portions of the Johannine discourses, or of their form, have made it
increasingly difficult to think of explaining them as though they
were the creations of the mind of a single theological genius.[27] If

---

authenticity of the saying, carefully places it within the horizon of Jewish and
Jewish-Christian reflection upon wisdom; cf. *Wisdom, Christology, and Law in Matthew's Gospel* (Cambridge, Mass.: Harvard University Press, 1970), pp. 71–97,
esp. p. 83 n. 51. J.T. Sanders, *The New Testament Christological Hymns: Their
Historical Religious Background*, SNTSMS 15 (Cambridge: Cambridge University
Press, 1971), pp. 133–39, suggests that the New Testament christological hymns,
including the Johannine prologue, have their "formal matrix" (p. 136) within the
thanksgiving of the wisdom school. Thus Matthew 11:27/Luke 10: 22 may be an
important bit of evidence in the search for Johannine origins. Does this logion stem
from the same sort of reflection upon widsom in which Johannine Christology originated?

26. J. T. Sanders, pp. 20–24, 29–57, summarizes the arguments and evidence
brought forward in earlier research.

27. For obvious reasons the works in question cannot be summarized and eval-
uated here, but some important form- and tradition-historical analyses may be
noted very briefly. H. Leroy, *Rätsel und Missverständnis: ein Beitrag zur Formgeschichte des Johannesevangeliums*, BBB 30 (Bonn: Hanstein, 1968), investigates
the Johannine misunderstandings against the background of the form and function
of the riddle in antiquity, and attributes to them a setting and function in a community establishing its distinctiveness and identity over against the Judaism from
which it has emerged. K. Berger, *Die Amen-Worte Jesu: eine Untersuchung zum
Problem der Legitimation in apokalyptischer Rede*, BZNW 39 (Berlin: Walter de
Gruyter, 1970), makes a somewhat analogous inquiry into the setting and functioning of amen-words, including those in the Fourth Gospel (esp. pp. 95–120).
Somewhat earlier was P. Borgen, *Bread from Heaven: An Exegetical Study of the
Concept of Manna in the Gospel of John and the Writings of Philo*, NovTSup, 10
(Leiden: Brill, 1965), whose investigation posits Jewish midrashim as a milieu of
the Fourth Gospel. Precursor to these studies in seeing in John traditional form and
substance arising from a Jewish setting was S. Schulz, *Untersuchungen zur Menschensohn-Christologie in Johannesevangelium; zugleich ein Beitrag zur Methodengeschichte der Auslegung des 4. Evangeliums* (Göttingen: Vandenhoeck &
Ruprecht, 1957); cf. the same author's *Komposition und Herkunft der johanneischen Reden*, BWANT 81 (Stuttgart: Kohlhammer, 1960). E. Schweizer's well-
known monograph, *Ego Eimi: die religionsgeschichtliche Herkunft und theolo-

Bultmann's attribution of much of that material to a single pre-Christian revelation discourse has gained few followers, B. Noack's attempt to break up the discourses into small units of oral tradition proved inapposite to the discursive character of the Johannine sayings and speeches.[28] But now in the wake of Bultmann new efforts to identify a substratum or substrata in the discourses appear. These are of at least two varieties. On the one hand, there are efforts to see John against a Jewish milieu (Leroy, Berger, Borgen, Schulz), accompanied by attempts to identify traditional forms arising either out of the Jewish background (Borgen's midrashic homily) or out of a Johannine Christian community (Leroy, Berger) with Jewish roots or contacts. On the other, there are attempts to distinguish literary or traditional strata on the basis of the identification of diverse theological or churchly interests (Richter, Becker). Neither procedure can be excluded in principle, and they are not mutually exclusive. The separation of strata or the identification of materials on the basis of criteria obtained from outside the Gospel itself (Leroy,

---

gische Bedeutung der johanneischen Bildreden, zugleich ein Beitrag zur Quellenfrage des vierten Evangeliums, FRLANT 56; 2. Aufl. (Göttingen: Vandenhoeck & Ruprecht, 1965), is concerned principally with the conceptual background of the Johannine material, but in the very nature of the case also with the form; the same may be said of the less known but nonetheless important work of K. Kundsin (Kundzins), "Charakter und Ursprung der johanneischen Reden," Latvijas Universitates Raksti (Acta Universitatis Latviensis): Teologijas Fakultates Serija 1, 4 (1939), 185–301. Strata within the Gospel arising out of a putative Johannine Christian environment have been isolated by G. Richter, Die Fusswaschung in Johannesevangelium, Biblische Untersuchungen 1 (Regensburg: Pustet, 1967), who sees in the two interpretations of the feet-washing different strata of different origin. Cf. also Richter's article, "Zur Formgeschichte und literarischen Einheit von Joh 6:31–58," ZNW 60 (1969): 21–55, in which he argues against Borgen's assignment of vv. 51b–58 to the original discourse on the basis of Borgen's own criteria governing the form of a midrashic homily. Immediately following the article of Richter on John 6:31–58 there appeared in the same journal an article by J. Becker, "Aufbau, Schichtung und theologiegeschichtliche Stellung des Gebetes in Johannes 17" (pp. 56–83), in which he challenged the usual assumption of the literary unity of John 17, mainly on the basis of the isolation of diverse theological or ecclesiastical interests. He followed this shortly with a similar analysis of the farewell discourses, "Die Abschiedsreden Jesu im Johannesevangelium," ZNW 61 (1970): 215–46.

28. As Bultmann pointed out, TLZ 80 (1955): 521–26.

Borgen especially) seems, however, to be more easily controllable and less subject to the danger of arbitrariness in objectifying one's own standards of consistency and coherence. Of course, an important creative role for the evangelist (or for an author) in the composition of the discourses can scarcely be denied. Yet it is quite likely that such passages as those instanced above, in which traditions or sources clearly break the seemingly even surface of the Gospel's style and thought, are not exceptional but indicative of a tradition history underlying much of the material in question.[29]

Of course, the greater part of the discourse or sayings material in John has a distinctly Johannine ring. Indeed, with the similar material of 1 John it forms the basis for determining what is Johannine. Moreover, the Jesus who speaks there is scarcely the historical figure who can be discerned in and behind the synoptic tradition, but in large part a Jesus distilled from the confession and controversies of the Johannine church. Such considerations do not necessarily militate against the traditional nature of the material, however, since the questions of historical authenticity and traditional character are altogether distinct, and certain modes of expression may typify a community as well as an individual.

Precisely in this connection, it may be of considerable significance that the Paraclete of the Fourth Gospel is said to recall (14:25-26) and expand upon (16:12-15) what Jesus taught in his earthly ministry. From this observation to the conjecture that the words of Jesus in the Fourth Gospel, so obviously spoken from the standpoint of a spirit-inspired postresurrection community (cf. John 7:39; 20: 22), are to be regarded as the fulfillment of the promise of the Paraclete rather than words of the historical Jesus is but a short

29. The language question is related to the investigation of the history of the Johannine tradition. On Johannine language see S. Brown's useful summary and assessment, "From Burney to Black: the Fourth Gospel and the Aramaic Question," *CBQ* 26 (1964): 323–39. The appropriate question may no longer be whether John was composed in Aramaic, but at what stratum or point in the history of its development Aramaic (or Semitic) sources or influences had their impact. M. Black, *An Aramaic Approach to the Gospels and Acts,* 3rd ed. (Oxford: Clarendon Press, 1967), pp. 149–51, referring to Bultmann's discourse-source theory, suggests that we may be dealing with an Aramaic source of Jesus' sayings, transformed by what he calls a "targumizing" process. This suggestion (which already stood in the 1954 edition of Black's work, pp. 257–58) accords rather well with the direction of much recent investigation.

step.[30] Not irrelevant to this is the fact that Christ speaks through the spirit to the churches in Revelation 2 and 3.[31] That the words of Christ in the Apocalypse differ somewhat in form and content from most of the words of Christ in the Fourth Gospel need not imply that the two are unrelated in any way. They differ presumably as the purposes and certainly as the literary contexts of the Gospel and Apocalypse differ. That one type of saying appears in an apocalyptic work while the other sounds Gnostic can no longer be taken to mean that they are of entirely unrelated origin.[32] If the author of 1 John demands that his fellow Christians should not believe every spirit but test the spirits, since there are now many false prophets (4:1), may he not reflect a situation in which spirit-inspired prophets uttering words of the risen Lord have become a distinct problem in the church?[33] If so, this would be exactly the development one might have anticipated. The burgeoning of this sort of Christ prophecy, which may find a parallel in the sayings *ex ore*

30. On the Spirit-Paraclete's actual functioning in the Johannine community, see G. Johnston, *The Spirit-Paraclete in the Gospel of John*, SNTSMS 12 (Cambridge: Cambridge University Press, 1970), esp. pp. 127-48. Leroy, p. 180, regards the authoritative figure of Jesus in John as really the exalted Lord, speaking by means of the Spirit through inspired prophets. Moreover, he sees no contradiction between such charismatic activity and an interest in tradition. On Jesus, Spirit and the Johannine community note also Käsemann, *The Testament of Jesus*, esp. pp. 36 ff., as well as A. Kragerud, *Der Lieblingsjünger im Johannesevangelium* (Oslo: Osloer Universitäts Verlag, 1959), esp. pp. 93-112, to whom Käsemann refers.

31. Kundsin, pp. 268-84, already saw a close formal relationship between the I-words of Revelation and the sayings of the Fourth Gospel. Precisely this relationship accords with the view that the saying of Jesus in the Fourth Gospel and in Revelation stem from similar, prophetic phenomena in early Christianity.

32. G. W. MacRae, "Some Elements of Jewish Apocalyptic and Mystical Tradition and their Relation to Gnostic Literature" (unpublished Ph.D. dissertation, Cambridge University, 1966), has impressively argued that the concepts of the divine name, heavenly veil, and wisdom, found in both Jewish and Gnostic texts, are related, and that the direction of influence is from Judaism to Gnosticism. Kundsin, while seeing apocalyptic as an important factor in the development of the Fourth Gospel, nevertheless agrees that with respect to world view the standpoint of the author may be described as Gnostic (pp. 287-88).

33. Cf. H. Frhr. von Campenhausen, *Kirchliches Amt und geistliche Vollmacht in der ersten drei Jahrhunderten*, BHTh 14;2. Aufl. (Tübingen: Mohr, 1963), pp. 203-4.

Christi in the Odes of Solomon, would seem to account, by way of reaction, for the emphasis upon tradition and the traditional commandment which prevades 1 John (1:1-4; 2:7-8 passim). This is not to suggest that the Johannine tradition of Jesus' speech was entirely spirit-prophetic. This seems, in fact, not to have been the case (see below). But that such a phenomenon was an element constitutive of the Johannine *Eigenart* is, it seems to me, entirely likely.

The adduction of evidence from 1 John necessarily raises the question of the relation of the Epistles to the Fourth Gospel, a question not unimportant for any attempt to understand or reconstruct Johannine Christianity. Although it has long been customary to use the Epistles, especially 1 John, to interpret the Gospel and vice versa,[34] this is at best a methodologically questionable procedure. Despite undeniably impressive theological, lexical, and stylistic similarities noted by critics from ancient to modern times, the differences between the Gospel and the Epistles are real and not insignificant.[35] Theological differences alone give one pause, although there are others. It is well known, for example, that while the Gospel is not without a future eschatological reference, on almost any assessment the traditional apocalyptic framework is more evident in 1 John. Perhaps most significant is the emphasis upon tradition and confession in 1 John, noted as a distinguishing feature by Conzelmann. Thus in the last several decades we have witnessed a significant shift away from the once universally held position of common authorship. Typical of this shift is Bultmann. Having once in his *Theology of the New Testament* cited Epistles

34. See, e.g., Bultmann, *Theology of the New Testament, II, 3:* "Whether the Epistles were written by the author of the Gospel himself or simply came out of his 'school' can here be disregarded."

35. C. H. Dodd, "The First Epistle of John and the Fourth Gospel," *BJRL* 21 (1937): 129-56, made the case for separate authorship on stylistic and conceptual grounds. There followed the brief but significant article of H. Conzelmann, "Was von Anfang war," in which he pointed to the significant shift in the meaning of ἀρχή from Gospel (preexistence of logos) to First Epistle (beginning of the tradition) as typical of the distinguishing churchly, traditional interest of the author of the Epistle (*Neutestamentliche Studien für Rudolf Bultmann*, pp. 194-201). Conzelmann's insights have been developed farther by G. Klein, "Das wahre Licht scheint schon — Beobachtungen zur Zeit und Geschichtserfahrung einer urchristlichen Schule," *ZTK* 68 (1971): 261-326.

and Gospel indiscriminately together, he now takes the position that the Epistles are the work of at least two authors, neither of whom is the Fourth Evangelist.[36] If the evidence so far adduced in the scholarly discussion does not preclude the traditional view of common authorship, it has certainly deprived it of the status of a foregone conclusion which it once enjoyed. Particularly in view of other lines of evidence which indicate the existence of a peculiarly Johannine strain of thought, presumably indigenous to a school or to certain early Christian circles or churches, the case for multiple authorship appears stronger. But even if the older view of common authorship is maintained, the Epistles nevertheless presuppose the existence of such a Johannine orbit in which a special tradition and confession, as well as certain leaders, held sway.

The question of the authorship of the Apocalypse is, of course, another matter. But although the seer is scarcely the author of any of the other extant Johannine documents, the question of a relationship between Revelation and the other writings is nevertheless real. One important connection (i.e. charismatic or prophetic utterance) has already been observed. That there are others is undeniable,[37] although efforts to understand them have not been entirely successful. Perhaps a relation between Jewish apocalyptic and Gnostic motifs is now coming to light in the investigation of the Nag Hammadi documents.[38] If so, this will suggest new solutions to an old problem. The apocalypticism of Revelation and the Gnostic-like conceptuality of the Gospel and Epistles of John may not stem from entirely different worlds.

Further indication of the traditional character and social matrix behind the name John in the New Testament is the evidence of the redaction of the Gospel, if not of the First Epistle as well. ("Re-

36. *Die drei Johannesbriefe,* Kritisch-exegetischer Kommentar über das Neue Testament 14. Abt., 7. Aufl. (Göttingen: Vandenhoeck & Ruprecht, 1967), pp. 9-10.

37. See above, n. 18; cf. nn. 30,31.

38. See n. 32, above, and cf. R. McL. Wilson, *Gnosis and the New Testament* (Oxford: Blackwell, 1968), p. 132. That there are several treatises from Nag Hammadi bearing the title apocalypse may not in itself be a decisive factor, however, since these are typically revelation discourses of the redeemer. The whole question of the nature and relation of apocalyptic and apocalyptic form is thereby raised.

daction" is an ambiguous term, since it can refer to editorial work at any stage of the development of a document; I use it here to designate editorial work by a hand other than the author's, accompanying or just prior to the publication of a work.) At the very least John 21, which is certainly a later addition to the Gospel, attests the existence of a constituency for which the Gospel was published. This would hold true even if the appendix had been added by the original author, which I think it was not. The most obvious implication of 21:20-23 is that such a constituency exists. The establishment of the secondary character of chapter 21 warrants the search for other redactional additions. A reasonable skepticism about the precise delineation of these and the perception of their motivation does not allay the suspicion that they exist. Probably the problem of the false ending of the farewell discourses at 14:31 has been occasioned by the addition of chapters 13–16(17).[39] While excisions of material as redactional on the basis of apocalyptic eschatological and sacramental content have rightly met with some skepticism, subsequent exegesis has frequently been found in substantial agreement with the judgment that 6:51-58 is secondary.[40] Other instances of possible redactional activity can be cited.[41] To the extent that the Gospel of John betrays evidence of redaction as well as tradition, there is added reason to suspect that it is the product of a distinctively Johannine church which played a contributive role in its inception and development. The redaction of a document likely takes place in a community in which that document is already valued or regarded as authoritative. Given other evidence for the origin of the Fourth Gospel in a Johannine community and tradition, it is natural to see in the latest redactions the continuing influence of that community.

39. This view has become fairly common. See, e.g., R. E. Brown, *The Gospel According to John (xiii-xxi)*, AB 29A (Garden City, N.Y.: Doubleday, 1970), pp. 583ff., 608ff.; also Becker, ZNW 61 (1970): 217-18.

40. This was, of course, the position of Bultmann, Bornkamm, E. Lohse, and, at one time, Jeremias. On the subsequent discussion between Borgen, who regards these verses as genuine, and Richter, who dissents from his arguments, see n. 27 above.

41. E.g. the translations in 1:38ff.; ὕδατος καὶ in 3:5; the qualification of the statement that Jesus baptized in 4:2, as well as the note that John had not yet been cast into prison in 3:24.

Finally, the figure of the Beloved Disciple must have some significance for the problem of Johannine origins. In chapter 21 he is presented as a historical figure whom people knew, and it is difficult to accept the view that an entirely symbolic figure from chapters 1–20 has been historicized by a redactor.[42] If this presentation is not a fabrication, then we have to reckon with a figure who is at least thought to be associated with the distinctly Johannine tradition from the beginning, as little as we may know about him, and as unconvincing as we may find the arguments, ancient or modern, that he is John the son of Zebedee. If this is the case, then we must conjure with the probability that Johannine circles held and cultivated the belief that their tradition extended back to Jesus himself. To grant this does not necessarily imply a great deal about the historicity of the figure Jesus in the Gospel. Although John doubtless contains chronological and topographical material worthy of historical scrutiny, it presents a picture of Jesus which, when placed alongside that of the synoptics, can be regarded as historical in only the most rarefied sense of the word.

If the Johannine community which produced the Gospel saw itself in traditional continuity with Jesus, we are in a position to perceive in the "we" of the prologues of both Gospel and Epistle, not the apostolic eyewitness per se, but a community which nevertheless understood itself as heir of a tradition based upon some historical witness to Jesus. As little as the symbolic character of the Beloved Disciple precludes the existence of some actual personage, so little does the Johannine theologizing upon the concept of seeing and the insistence upon faith without sight (20:29) preclude the view that "we have beheld his glory" has as a part of its

42. As Bultmann, *The Gospel of John*, pp. 483-84, holds. Among the recent works on the Beloved Disciple, note esp. J. Roloff, "Die johanneische 'Lieblingsjünger' und der Lehrer der Gerechtigkeit," *NTS* 15 (1968): 129-51; R. Schnackenburg, "Der Junger, den Jesus liebte," *Evangelisch-Katholisches Kommentar* (Vorarbeiten 2), pp. 97-117; as well as "On the Origin of the Fourth Gospel" in *Jesus and Man's Hope* (Pittsburgh: Pittsburgh Theological Seminary, 1970), I, 223-46, esp. pp. 233-43; and T. Lorenzen, *Der Lieblingsjünger im Johannesevangelium: eine redaktionsgeschichtliche Studie*, SBS 55 (Stuttgart: Katholisches Bibelwerk, 1971), who finds that the Beloved Disciple appears in passages that are the composition of the evangelist, but nevertheless, with Roloff and Schnackenburg, regards him as a historical figure.

meaning the obvious one: at the beginning of the community and of its tradition stands someone who had seen Jesus. Moreover, the tenor of 1 John points to a community leaning quite heavily upon a tradition, on the basis of which the author believes he has an acknowledged right to make theological and ethical discriminations and judgments. If 1 John and Revelation certainly, and the Gospel probably, reflect a polemical situation in the church, such a finding accords entirely with the existence of a tradition. Particularly in a community marked by charismatic utterance, the tradition could easily become the occasion of dispute as to its extent, meaning, and proprietorship. Furthermore, in such a polemical situation an appeal to tradition, and thus to the past, would scarcely be made unless it were at least believed that the appeal could not be falsified.

While certainty in such matters is scarcely attainable, the cumulative effect of a variety of evidence makes it appear highly probable that the Johannine writings emerged from a tradition, from a particular strain of early Christianity. Moreover, we shall not badly mislead ourselves if we think of a community (or communities) with some stability, with which it had been endowed in part by its continuity with the past. It is likely, if not certain, that the Johannine community was coterminous with specific Christian congregations who lived both *in* it and *from* it. The rather small extent of clear literary relation and other evocations of contact between the Johannine literature and the rest of the New Testament suggests that the Johannine *Eigenart* reflects the existence of distinctly Johannine communities, rather than communities in which the Johannine option was one of several. If possible relationships to such documents as Revelation, the letters of Ignatius,[43] and the Odes of Solomon, not to mention the Qumran Manual of Discipline, remain to some extent problematic, the affinities are probably best explained by the diffusion of "Johannine" tradition or influence at the boundaries of such communities rather than by any direct literary dependence involving the Fourth Gospel and the Johannine Epistles. Moreover, the relative independence of the Johannine material

43. Hillmer, "The Gospel of John in the Second Century," pp. 8-27, argues persuasively against direct literary dependence of Ignatius upon the Johannine Gospel and Epistles.

suggests also that geographic provenance may be a major factor in the distinctiveness of John.

The question of the place of origin of the Johannine tradition is difficult and complex, with something to be said for Asia (Ephesus), Judea, Samaria, Galilee, Syria, and Egypt. Tradition, of course, points to Ephesus, and the Asian provenance of Revelation can be taken to support this view, although it is far from decisive. The relative isolation and independence of the Johannine material in language and conceptuality may militate against the traditional viewpoint, since Ephesus was a major Christian center. Yet the Gospel could have been published in Ephesus without its tradition having originated there. Possibly history-of-religions considerations provide a sort of vector which can help identify the most likely point of origin (and development) along the geographic spectrum. Affinities with Ignatius and the Odes of Solomon have recently led many scholars to favor Syria.[44] The affinities of John with Qumran and features traced to Samaria[45] comport well enough with this location, although they do not necessarily demand it. John's relative isolation from other streams of tradition in the New Testament seems to bear witness to a place of origin somewhat off the beaten track, and this possibility may perhaps be combined with the suggestion of Syria generally, although scarcely with Christian Antioch.[46] If the Johannine Gospel or tradition actually originated in a rather remote corner of the Christian map, its distinctive character as well as its difficulty in finding acceptance in the emerging catholic church become more intelligible. Nor is such an origin incompatible with John's Gospel's having rather early made friends among Christians later branded heretical.

44. See Kümmel, *Introduction*, p. 175, who cites Jülicher, Fascher, Burney, Bauer, Schweizer, and Haenchen.

45. See esp. W. Meeks, *The Prophet-King: Moses Traditions and the Johannine Christology*, NovTSup 14 (Leiden: Brill, 1967), pp. 216-57.

46. We know, of course, that Antioch was an important center for Christian missionary activity before Paul became connected with it, and it is frequently suggested as the place of origin of the Gospel according to Matthew; cf. Kümmel, p. 84; B. F. Streeter, *The Four Gospels: A Study in Origins* (London: Macmillan, 1936), pp. 500-27. That John also came from that area is not, however, impossible, although that view would carry with it the corollary that Antioch was a center harboring several diverse strands of Christianity. In fact, echoes of John as well as Matthew are found in Ignatius of Antioch, although the latter predominate.

COMPONENTS OF HISTORY OF THE JOHANNINE TRADITION

Obviously the problems of the origins of the Johannine literature can be fruitfully approached in a variety of ways. The possibilities for productively coordinating several approaches or methods of analyzing the material have already been noted and explored. Louis Martyn's proposal for utilizing and combining insights and results from source criticism, the comparative history of religions, and the development of early Christian theology suggests the factors and issues with which any effort to understand and reconstruct the development of Johannine Christianity must deal.[47]

If it can be granted that the evidence discussed in the earlier part of this essay points to the existence of Johannine Christianity as a fairly discrete and identifiable entity with its own history, tradition, and self-consciousness, it becomes possible and even necessary to ask about its development and shape. This problem and task may be aptly termed the history of the Johannine tradition. Certainly the task of reconstructing such a tradition-history cannot be undertaken here. But to indicate some further factors with which such a reconstruction will have to deal may prove worthwhile and helpful.

One may begin, in agreement with Louis Martyn and others, with a recognition that a polemical situation within the synagogue and later between the Johannine community and the synagogue is almost certainly a significant, if not *the* central, milieu of the Johannine material, particularly the Fourth Gospel.[48] Although some of the distinctive points of Martyn's thesis, including the proposed deliberate two-level hypothesis with its implications regarding the topography of the city in which John was written, may be problematical, he has forcefully and persuasively called attention to a wide range of evidence for such a setting. Martyn's proposals are not entirely new, nor does he claim that they are. But probably his work has had a greater impact, especially in America, than have previous efforts to place John against a background of Jewish-

47. "Source Criticism and *Religionsgeschichte* in the Fourth Gospel", in *Jesus and Man's Hope*, I, 247-73.

48. See J. Louis Martyn, *History and Theology in the Fourth Gospel* (New York: Harper, 1968), for a full and detailed statement of this position. Martyn's central thesis was adumbrated by W. Wrede, *Charakter und Tendenz des Johannesevangeliums*, 2nd ed. Sammlung gemeinverständlicher Vorträge (Tübingen: Mohr, 1933), pp. 40 ff.

Christian debate.[49] Future Johannine interpretation will have to conjure with his thesis and with the strong element of polemic with real Jews in the Fourth Gospel. In this regard it is very interesting that Bultmann some years ago suggested a similar milieu for the Fourth Gospel, without however making use of the proposal for purposes of historical reconstruction or interpretation.[50]

We have also already noted agreement, in principle at least, with the identification of an independent Johannine narrative tradition, if not a Gospel of Signs (Fortna), and we have pointed to mounting evidence for the existence of a Johannine discourse tradition as well. It may now be possible to suggest how both these traditions relate to the important Jewish milieu of which Martyn is a leading proponent.

Fortna has already noted the possibility of connecting the interest in miracles of his Gospel of Signs to the Jewish-Christian opponents of Paul described in 2 Corinthians 10–13 (cf. esp. the mention of τὰ σημεῖα τοῦ ἀποστόλου in association with "signs, wonders, and miracles" in 2 Corinthians 12:17).[51] This proposal is to some extent dependent upon the thesis of D. Georgi regarding the character of Paul's opponents,[52] which itself admits of some further discussion, since the question of the number and nature of Paul's opponents in Corinth is a complex one. When all cautions and reservations are allowed for, however, it is still tempting to see in Paul's Jewish-Christian Corinthian opponents, with their charis-

49. Among works particularly worth mentioning are K. Bornhäuser, *Das Johannesevangelium: eine Missionschrift für Israel*, Beiträge zur Förderung christlicher Theologie 2, 15 (Gütersloh: Bertelsmann, 1928); T. C. Smith, *Jesus in the Gospel of John* (Nashville: Broadman, 1959); J. A. T. Robinson, "The Destination and Purpose of St. John's Gospel," *NTS* 6 (1960): 117-31, and "The Destination and Purpose of the Johannine Epistles" *NTS* 7 (1960): 56-65; W. C. Van Unnik, "The Purpose of St John's Gospel," in *Studia Evangelica: Papers Presented to the International Congress on "The Four Gospels" in 1957*, ed. K. Aland et al., TU 73 (Berlin: Akademie Verlag, 1959), pp. 382-411.

50. See, e.g., *Theology of the New Testament, II, 5; The Gospel of John*, p. 335.

51. *The Gospel of Signs*, p. 224. Cf. also D. L. Balch, "Backgrounds of I Cor. 7; Sayings of the Lord in Q; Moses as an Ascetic θεῖος ἀνήρ in II Cor. 3," *NTS* 18 (1972): 351-64.

52. *Die Gegner des Paulus im 2. Korintherbrief: Studien zur religiösen Propaganda in der Spätantike*, WMANT 11 (Neukirchen: Neukirchener Verlag, 1964), esp. pp. 282-92; pp. 292ff. will also bear scrutiny for their possible pertinence to the Johannine milieu.

matic excesses, their interest in miracles, and possibly their conviction that the heavenly world was already opening out before them, close relatives of those early Christians responsible for the miracle tradition of John's Gospel. It is perhaps sufficient and most important to identify a type, phenomenologically speaking, within early Christianity without at this point attaching great significance to our ability or inability to show some tangible historical connection. As I see it, there is not sufficient evidence either to demonstrate or to falsify the conjecture that a Johannine Gospel of Signs originated among the specific group of opponents Paul confronts in 2 Corinthians 10–13. Through the identification of such a type, the putative gnosticizing tendencies of Paul's opponents and of the Johannine literature may be mutually illumined. For just such a combination of Jewish and quasi-Gnostic elements has been shown, on other grounds, to be a distinct possibility for our period.[53] Wherever or whenever the origins of Gnosticism may lie, its early and close relation to certain modes or forms of Judaism and Jewish Christianity appears to be a likelihood. Of course, there are real difficulties in postulating "Gnosticism" as the conceptual basis or presupposition of the thought of Paul's opponents (Schmithals) or of the Gospel and Epistles of John (Bultmann). But we may in fact have in the Johannine writings an instance of that rejection of Judaism and correlative rejection of the world and development of myth that has come to be associated with Gnosticism. If so, then the present form of the Gospel of John may represent neither anti-Gnosticism (Bultmann) nor pro-Gnosticism (Käsemann, Schottroff[54]), but an early stage in the emergence of motifs that had a later flowering in Gnosticism.

53. See nn. 32, 38 above. Note also C. K. Barrett, *Das Johannesevangelium und das Judentum: Franz Delitzsch-Vorlesungen 1967* (Stuttgart: Kohlhammer, 1970), pp. 54ff., who points out that the opponents of Ignatius had both Jewish and Gnostic characteristics.

54. *Der Glaubende und die feindliche Welt: Beobachtungen zum gnostischen Dualismus und seiner Bedeutung für Paulus und das Johannesevangelium*, WMANT 37: (Neukirchen; Neukirchener Verlag, 1970). Luise Schottroff accepts the existence of a *semeia*-source behind the Fourth Gospel and attempts to show that the Gospel's correction of that source, that is, its devaluation of the miraculous per se, is related to its fundamentally Gnostic perspective, on the basis of which she understands the Johannine dualism.

While Martyn has rightly seen the Johannine community in conflict with a synagogue of a Pharisaic-rabbinic type, this extension of his thesis suggests connections through a sort of Jewish Christianity with less orthodox forms of Jewish life and thought. Whatever one makes of the possibility of working out this proposal in great detail or with a high degree of probability, one must acknowledge that it points in a direction whose general correctness is confirmed by a variety of considerations. The Johannine form of Christianity emerges from a Jewish matrix whose existence can be confirmed from several sides. And elements within this Jewish matrix may prove very suggestive in accounting for the language and conceptuality of the Johannine discourses.

That the Qumran scrolls attest a form of Judaism whose conceptuality and terminology tally in some respects quite closely with the Johannine is a commonly acknowledged fact. The frequently voiced opinion that the scrolls somehow demonstrate the early date, Palestinian origin, and historicity of the Fourth Gospel is surely misplaced, but the alleged affinities are not without some substance. Particularly noteworthy are the Manual of Discipline's terminological similarities and fundamental dualism.[55] The latter apparently found concrete expression in the life-style and self-consciousness of the sect. Precisely the notes of separation and exclusiveness that appear in Qumran are echoed in the community consciousness of the Johannine literature.[56]

Another link between John and Judaism has been seen in John the Baptist, perhaps a close relative of the Essenes, in whom the Fourth Gospel manifests a peculiar interest, which is probably to be understood as a reaction to claims of a Baptist sect concerning their martyred leader (cf 1: 6-8, 15, 19ff.; 3: 2cff.; 4:1; 5:33ff.;

55. See esp. J. H. Charlesworth, "A Critical Comparison of the Dualism in 1QS 3: 13-4: 26 and the Dualism Contained in the Gospel of John," in *John and Qumran*, ed. Charlesworth (London: Geoffrey Chapman, 1972), pp. 76-106, previously published in *NTS* 15 (1969): 389-418; also the earlier work of O. Böcher, *Der johanneische Dualismus im Zusammenhang des nachbiblischen Judentums* (Gerd Mohn: Gütersloher Verlagshaus, 1965).

56. In this connection see also the important article of W. Meeks, "The Man from Heaven in Johannine Sectarianism," *JBL* 91 (1972): 44-72, esp. 49-50, 69ff. Meeks (p.49 n. 16) calls attention to his agreement with Leroy, *Rätsel und Missverständnis*, as to the rather exclusive self-understanding of the Johannine churches.

10:40-42). The many affinities with the Odes of Solomon, which partly overlap with those of Qumran,[57] are not easily explained as the result of the odist's use of the Johannine literature. If the opposite is difficult to demonstrate as well, the points of similarity are nevertheless worthy of some explanation. The fact that the Odes are replete with Jewish or Jewish-Christian motifs is scarcely insignificant in this connection. The adumbrations of Johannine thought and expression in Ignatius are likewise difficult to explain as the result of copying or direct borrowing in either direction, yet it is striking that Ignatius seems to be involved in controversy with other Christians of Gnostic-docetic, as well as Jewish, bent.[58]

Looking somewhat farther afield, the Johannine interest in Samaria has recently been brought forcefully to our attention through Wayne Meeks's demonstration of remarkable links connecting Samaritan prophetic-messianic expectation, Moses speculation in late Judaism, and Johannine Christology.[59] Although Meeks' own position is set forth against the background of his rejection of Bultmann's proposals defining a Gnostic background for the Fourth Gospel from Mandaean sources, it nevertheless calls to mind the patristic attribution of the origin of the Gnostic heresy to Simon Magus and Samaria.[60] Meeks seems correct in regarding Mandaean parallels as less useful for his line of investigation than Philonic, rabbinic and Samaritan sources. Certainly the Mandaean question is beset with difficulties, largely because of the obscurity of the sources themselves. Yet, in my opinion, the terminological and symbolic similarities to John in the Mandaean sources do not allow us to dismiss them lightly.[61] Moreover, a significant body of scholarly opinion sees in the Mandaeans a sectarian offshoot from Judaism which left the motherland and migrated eastward at the time

57. See Charlesworth, "Qumran, John and the Odes of Solomon," in *John and Qumran*, pp. 107-36.

58. As Barrett, *Das Johannesevangelium und das Judentum*, pp. 54ff., has noticed.

59. *The Prophet-King*, pp. 216ff.

60. See E. Haenchen, "Gab es eine vorchristliche Gnosis?," in *Gott und Mensch: Gesammelte Aufsätze* (Tübingen: Mohr, 1965), pp. 265-98, reprinted from *ZTK* 49 (1952): 316-49.

61. The parallels are now conveniently available in English in the translation of Bultmann, *The Gospel of John*.

of the origin of Christianity or somewhat later.[62] That Mandaean parallels prove the Gnostic character of John is a dubious proposition, since there is some question as to the Gnostic character of the Mandaeans.[63] That, however, is another, if not unrelated, issue, and perhaps not the most important one for Johannine studies. While the present state of our knowledge does not allow us to speak of Mandaean influence on the Johannine Christianity, neither does it allow us to claim the opposite. The Mandaean affinities of John's Gospel and the best guess as to Mandaean origins combine to suggest again that the Johannine literature is related to sectarian, perhaps gnosticizing, Judaism. To speak of gnosticizing Judaism or Jewish Gnosticism—they are not necessarily the same thing—raises a host of issues with which few scholars are able to deal. In this connection one recalls that H. Odeberg long ago set out and commented upon Jewish mystical and speculative texts which he thought were related to the Mandaean materials and of great significance for understanding the milieu of Johannine thought.[64] More recently G. Scholem has adduced from the same and similar sources evidence for what he calls Jewish Gnosticism.[65] At the least such materials

62. See Robinson, *Trajectories Through Early Christianity*, p. 263, for a key quotation from K. Rudolph, in which the latter marshals the support of "the two best authorities on Mandaean literature, Lady Drower and R. Macuch". Also p. 264 n. 56 for further references. A helpful introduction to the Mandaeans and the present state of the investigation of them is Rudolph's "Die Religion der Mandäer," in *Die Religionen Altsyriens, Altarabiens und der Mandäer,* Die Religionen der Menschheit 10, 2 (Stuttgart: Kohlhammer, 1970), pp. 403-58, in which he brings together in summary form results of his earlier investigations.

63. That the Mandaean literature is not Gnostic is argued by E. Yamauchi, *Gnostic Ethics and Mandaean Origins* (Cambridge, Mass.: Harvard University Press, 1970), on the basis of the Mandaeans' positive sexual ethic.

64. *The Fourth Gospel: Interpreted in its Relation to Contemporaneous Religious Currents in Palestine and the Hellenistic-Oriental World* (Uppsala: Almqvist & Wiksells, 1929); see pp. 5-6 for Odeberg's rationale for undertaking the work: "During his studies in early Jewish mysticism the writer found a strangely close correspondence between the Jewish mystical sources and certain strata of the Mandaean literature." It is, of course, precisely the language and conceptuality of Jewish mysticism which Odeberg finds echoed also in the Fourth Gospel.

65. *Jewish Gnosticism, Merkabah Mysticism, and Talmudic Tradition* (New York: Jewish Theological Seminary of America, 1960). On the terminological question of Gnosticism, see esp. pp. 2-3. Perhaps "Jewish proto-Gnosticism" would better accord with the phenomenon Scholem describes.

attest the existence within Judaism of an intellectual or spiritual milieu whose affinities with the Johannine world seem as great as their distance from the interests commonly associated with the Pharisaic and rabbinic strains of Judaism.

Perhaps the most obvious Jewish parallels to Johannine Christology lie in the realm of wisdom speculation, as was long ago noted.[66] That virtually everything said of the logos in the prologue of John had already been predicated of wisdom in Judaism is a widely acknowledged fact, the significance of which has perhaps been somewhat obscured in the controversy over whether John was influenced directly by wisdom speculation or both John and wisdom sources stood under the influence of a Gnostic myth. In view of the many threads connecting John with Judaism, it seems unlikely that wisdom influence was not also mediated through that milieu, regardless of what may be the disposition of the Gnostic question. To grant this allows one once again to connect the Johannine conceptuality with Paul's Corinthian situation, where the question of wisdom Christology seems very much alive (1 Cor. 1–4; there must also have been at least some relation between the problems which surface there and those connected with the presumed interlopers dealt with in 2 Cor. 1–13.)

This only partial enumeration of the variety of connections between John and Judaism may, of course, be nothing more than an exercise in scholarly eclecticism. I am of the opinion, however, that such lines of research as have been mentioned constitute a series of rather well-established vectors pointing inward toward a common center. That center is a matrix or milieu within Judaism or at its periphery from which Johannine Christianity (understood as a tradition-bearing community) developed.

If this is a correct insight, it may suggest something about the reasons for the conflict with Pharisaic Judaism which is widely mirrored in the Gospel. That is, the heterodox Jewish germinal ground of the Johannine tradition would have provided ready conceptual categories (e.g., qualified dualism, Merkabah, and wisdom speculation) and an impetus for the development of Christology along

66. See, e.g., Bultmann's article of 1923, "Der religionsgeschichtliche Hintergrund des Prologs zum Johannesevangelium," now reprinted in *Exegetica*, pp. 10–35; and Rendel Harris, *The Origin of the Prologue of St. John's Gospel* (Cambridge: Cambridge University Press, 1917).

lines that would likely lead to collision with the Pharisaic Judaism which became predominant after the Roman War. The possibility of such a conflict would have been enhanced as elements already given in the originating matrix were combined with the preaching of Jesus as the Christ. This process was likely accompanied by the appearance of elements we have come to associate with Gnosticism, which entered either from the originating matrix (i.e. through or from Judaism) or perhaps from elsewhere.

We have already noted that charismatic prophetic activity likely played a significant role in the development of the Johannine tradition. How might such activity relate to the sort of milieu we have just suggested? If sectarian Judaism was the germinal ground of the Johannine tradition, spirit-inspired prophecy may well have provided the specific occasion for the emergence of Johannine Christian affirmation in the form of words of Jesus. It is, of course, not only in the Johannine literature and Revelation that we find evidence of charismatic prophetic activity, but across a rather broad spectrum of early Christianity. We find such evidence for example in Acts (e.g. 13:1;19: 6), Paul's letters (1 Cor. 12:28-29;14), Ephesians (2:20; 3:5), Ignatius (Phil. 7), the Pastorals (1 Tim. 1:18; 4:14), the Didache (11–13), and Hermas, not to mention the synoptic apocalypses, where we read of false prophets who do signs and wonders (Mark 13:22) and say ἐγώ εἰμι (Mark 13:6). Moreover, the words of Jesus in Matthew 11:25-27 (Luke 10:21–22) and the many words apparently attributed to Christ in the Odes of Solomon, as well as the I-sayings of certain Revelation discourses in the Nag Hammadi texts,[67] have a "Johannine" ring, and may also be related to this sort of activity. One thinks also of Melito of Sardis' paschal homily, in which "I am" sayings similar to John's are elaborated,[68] Celsus' description of the Samaritan prophets, and the self-predications widely attributed to the Samaritan Simon Magus. Can it be also that the popularity of John among the Mon-

67. To which G. W. MacRae has called attention in his article, "The Ego-Proclamation in Gnostic Sources," in *The Trial of Jesus: Cambridge Studies in Honour of C. F. D. Moule*, ed. E. Bammel, SBT, 2d ser. 13 (London: S.C.M., 1970), pp. 122-34.

68. O. Perler, ed., *Méliton de Sardes sur la pâque et fragments: Introduction, texte critique, traduction et notes*, SC 123 (Paris: Éditions du Cerf, 1966); see paragraphs 100–103 of the sermon (pp. 120 ff.).

tanists and the corresponding opposition in some orthodox circles have a bearing on the actual origin of John?[69]

If in fact the formulation of some revelation discourses of Jesus originated in such charismatic activity, it naturally does not follow that every saying in John has had such an origin directly. Once a pattern was provided, sayings of this sort might become constitutive of a tradition and eventually would be *self-consciously* composed by authors. Thus, for example, it is possible that the Fourth Evangelist may have adapted some such sayings to the controversy with the Jews that developed in his community, while composing others that fitted the situation that had arisen.

From the perspective just set forth one may now see in the Paraclete sayings of 14:5-6 and 16:12-15 the enunciation of a theory concerning the phenomenon of spirit-inspired utterance intended on the one hand to ground it in Jesus' own historic ministry, and thus to validate it (14:26), and on the other to set some control over it by placing it within the context of a portrayal of Jesus, who was not only the word become flesh, but one who spoke words with the irrevocable status of divine commandments. When in 1 John one sees traces of the same problematical aspect of the Johannine process of spirit-inspired creativity, one finds that author reiteratively invoking the tradition (1:1-4) as the touchstone of belief and enjoining his readers to test every spirit (4:1-6).

THE COHESION OF THE JOHANNINE TRADITION

We have attempted to indicate some principal components of a history of Johannine tradition. But how did such seemingly disparate entities as originating eyewitness, miracle tradition, passion narrative, controversy with the synagogue, incipient Gnosticism or quasi-Gnosticism, and charismatic prophecy come to lodge under the same roof? In conclusion we shall sketch the outline of a provisional answer to that question.

The proclamation of Jesus as the Jewish Messiah, crucified but risen from the dead, in and by a community with roots among Jesus' own disciples, was augmented by miraculous proofs of his dignity. Although there are grounds for questioning Fortna's view

69. On Montanist use of the Fourth Gospel see Bauer, *Orthodoxy and Heresy in Earliest Christianity*, pp. 141, 145, 187, 225.

that the original narrative source, the Gospel of Signs, consisted of a passion-resurrection narrative as well as miracle stories,[70] certainly inclusion of the passion and resurrection fits the Christian-Jewish milieu that has been posited by Fortna. The proclamation that a crucified insurgent was, in fact, the Messiah of Israel would have raised the most serious questions among Jews, so that emphasis upon his miracle-working activity could have scarcely made headway until this stumbling block had been removed or interpreted in a theologically satisfactory way. Accordingly, the use of the Old Testament to explain the crucifixion of Jesus goes back to a primitive state of the tradition and presupposes a Jewish audience.[71]

That the miracle tradition of John embodies a θεῖος ἀνήρ Christology and that it existed in the form of a pregospel collection which has a right to be called an aretology may be the case.[72] (The debate over the appropriateness of the technical terms scarcely puts into question the realities to which they point.) What cannot be doubted, however, is the independence of the Johannine miracle

70. Enumerated by Robinson, *JAAR* 39 (1971):344ff.; cf. Lindars, *Behind the Fourth Gospel*, pp. 38-39f: "Bultmann and Becker are well justified in refusing to regard this [the passion narrative] as part of the same source as the signs."

71. See Lindars, *New Testament Apologetic: The Doctrinal Significance of the Old Testament Quotations* (Philadelphia: Westminster, 1961), pp. 265-72, esp. pp. 269ff.; cf. pp. 98, 104ff., 113-14f., 122-27. Given the need to explain the crucifixion of Jesus in a Jewish context, which was certainly the most primitive context of the preaching of the gospel, what Lindars calls the "passion apologetic" (*New Testament Apologetic,* pp. 75-137), must have soon resulted in the development of passion accounts. That that happened early and in a Jewish milieu is to be inferred from the integral relation of Old Testament testimonia to the passion accounts of our present gospels. Thus Fortna's proposal of a Sign Gospel makes a certain sense in view of the *Sitz im Leben,* as well as the functioning of the document which he has in view, and that general setting accords well with the present thrust of Johannine studies.

72. For evidence for the aretalogical forms, H. Köster, "One Jesus and Four Primitive Gospels," *HTR* 61 (1968): 203-47; note also M. Smith, "Prolegomena to a Discussion of Aretalogies, Divine Men, the Gospels, and Jesus," *JBL* 90 (1971): 174-99; P. Achtemeier, "Gospel Miracle Tradition and the Divine Man," *Int* 26 (1972): 174-97; and D. L. Tiede, *The Charismatic Figure as Miracle Worker,* SBLDS 1 (Missoula, Mont.: Society of Biblical Literature, 1972), a 1970 Harvard doctoral dissertation under Köster. Certainly the existence in earliest Christian circles of a collection of miracle stories apart from a passion narrative (or sayings) is a possibility.

tradition and its importance to Johannine Christianity. Probably the original reason for its importance, and the sine qua non for further developments, which there doubtless were, was the fact that Jesus actually had been a miracle worker. As such, he was neither the first nor the last of his type. When the evangelist took this miracle tradition up into his gospel he may be presumed to have endorsed its validity, however much he may have qualified and interpreted it.

Also interesting is the fact that the recitation of the miracles, excepting the raising of Lazarus, is bracketed on the one side by the witness of John at the beginning of the Gospel and on the other by the statement that John worked no miracle (10:41). The latter occurs in a transitional passage that was possibly the end of the Book of Signs at one stage of the composition history of the Gospel.[73] A primitive purpose or function of the miracle tradition of John may, in fact, be suggested by 10:41; i.e.; Jesus' miracle-working activity differentiates him from the Baptist.[74] At a later stage, or in another connection, it must have received a broader use, principally in the mission to, and debate with, the Jewish synagogue. At that stage, or in that connection, the miracle narratives seem to have become the foundation for the organization of the discourse materials. The shape of these discourses is, of course, determined internally not only by the signs, but by the opposition of the Jews. That these Jews are the contemporaries of the late first-century Johannine community is altogether probable (Martyn). In the context of such debate with the synagogue a passion and resurrection narrative would have become a necessity in order to justify the continued proclamation of a crucified criminal as the Messiah. If the inner Jewish or Jewish-Christian setting of the Johannine com-

73. So Lindars, *Behind the Fourth Gospel*, pp. 62-63, 70-71, and Brown, *The Gospel According to John (i-xii)*, p. 414; cf. E. Bammel, *Miracles*, pp. 200-201, and *NTS* 18 (1971): 109, who sees in 10: 41-42 the conclusion of Z, the Johannine miracle source.

74. See Bammel, *NTS* 18 (1971): 112, esp. nn. 4 and 5. Cf. R. E. Brown, "Jesus and Elisha," *Perspective* 12 (1971): 85-104. That Jesus' signs may also bear some relation to Moses' signs before Pharaoh, particularly in view of the frequent pairing of Jesus and Moses in the Fourth Gospel, must of course remain a possibility. The bearing of such considerations is not to exclude the possibility that Jesus in the Fourth Gospel is assimilated to the figure of the divine man of late antiquity, since some of the best examples of such a figure seem to appear in Jewish sources.

munity and tradition antedates the Roman War, as I think altogether possible, and even probable, then a passion narrative or something comparable would seem a likelihood for that earlier period.

The fact that discourses through chapter 12 are largely organized around the signs does not, of course, mean that all of the discourse material is dependent on the debate concerning the signs, although much of it obviously is. Conceivably some of this material grew up alongside the signs, partly on the basis of Jesus tradition analogous to the synoptic, but very largely out of words uttered by early Christian prophets. That polemic vis-à-vis the Baptist sect or the synagogue generally could have given rise to such prophetic utterance is not unlikely. Expressly polemical situations provide the setting for the words of the exalted Jesus transmitted via the Spirit to and through the prophet in the seven letters of the book of Revelation.

Nevertheless, the "christological" character of these words of Jesus in the Fourth Gospel suggests as its explanation something more than the synagogue debate.[75] The claims of Jesus are calculated not so much to answer the Jews' questions and arguments as to fulfill all their worst fears and suspicions. At this point the peculiarities of sectarian Judaism or of forms of Jewish reflection which died out or were suppressed in the aftermath of the Roman War and Jamnia may provide some basis for understanding the intellectual and religious conceptual matrix from which the Johannine discourse material and its christological thought developed.[76] In this connection the possibility that Gnosticism may have arisen from, at the boundary of, or in rejection of Jewish thought, expectation, and practice is intriguing. The kind of Jewish conceptual world that is suggested from many sides by a variety of scholarly perspectives and interests may provide an explanation for the Gnostic affinities of the Gospel and Epistles.

To say this is not to minimize, much less to discount, an original and seminal Christian element in the Johannine Christology. Moreover, it may still be true that in a certain sense John makes explicit

75. So also Martyn, *Jesus and Man's Hope*, pp. 266; cf. *History and Theology in the Fourth Gospel*, p. 117 n. 173.

76. Cf. Martyn, *Jesus and Man's Hope*, p. 268, esp. the long quotation from Odeberg, *The Fourth Gospel*, pp. 268-69.

and clear what is implicit or inchoate in the other gospels or in other forms of early Christian preaching. Yet Christians and those influenced by Christian tradition perceive what has in fact been made explicit in the light of a history of theological and dogmatic language that owes much to John. Therefore, one should not too easily suppose that John, at the end of the first century, said what some inexorable theological logic made it necessary for him to say, nor that such a theological rationale alone suffices to explain John's language and conceptual world.

So, although it may seem that investigations of diverse originative milieus of the Johannine literature have cast up some very strange— if not uncongenial—bedfellows, closer inspection reveals that they may, surprisingly, fit into the same bed. Whether that bed is actually procrustean is a matter which will require some time to adjudicate. At the moment, however, the prospects for their coexistence seem favorable.

If the origin of Johannine Christianity and the development of its traditions are to be understood as processes centering in Judaism and Jewish Christianity, it nevertheless does not seem possible to explain the entire history of the Johannine tradition against such a background. Nor is it clear that the Gospel or Epistles in their present form are addressed entirely (or even primarily) to the Jewish-Christian controversy which underlies them. There are motifs in the Johannine literature that go beyond the controversy with Judaism and reflect a later stage in the development of the Johannine church. The farewell discourses of the Gospel appear to represent principally an inner Christian development, and to raise christological, eschatological, and ecclesiological issues arising apart from or subsequent to a break with the synagogue. Naturally, it cannot be assumed that inner Christian developments were always subsequent to any controversy with Judaism. A similarly Christian perspective is reflected in the passion narrative, where Jesus is made to say that his kingdom is not of this world (18:36) and the Jews that they have no king but Caesar (19:15). This last statement reflects their complete rejection of Jesus and their abdication of their role as people of God in the eyes of the evangelist. Such statements imply that the relation of John to Judaism had become a hostile one, defined by the characteristic dualism of the Gospel, so that in this sense the Jews do represent the world that rejects

Jesus. Likewise, the letters reflect a situation within a church that was presumably beyond the struggle with Judaism and well into questions of orthodoxy, heresy, and church order. On the other hand, the letters to the seven churches in the book of Revelation evidence a continuing controversy with Jews and Jewish-Christians (cf. also John 8:31ff.), with some indication of Judaizing (and gnosticizing?) heresy, and may emanate from an earlier stage. Finally, the extent to which the widely perceived universalism of the Gospel is rooted in the intention of the evangelist seems to me also to be a question worthy of further reflection, but one which cannot be discussed here.

Part I	Sources

<table>
<tr><td>I</td><td>

The Sources of the Gospel of John

</td></tr>
</table>

F or more than one hundred years scholars have endeavored to discover and separate the sources or literary strata believed to be embedded in the Gospel of John. Previous attempts to explain the origin of the Fourth Gospel by theories of a *Grundschrift* or literary sources and redaction, not to mention rearrangement, found their culmination and were probably superseded when, over a generation ago, Rudolf Bultmann set forth a comprehensive literary theory in his magisterial *Das Evangelium des Johannes.*[1] Bultmann's work has given a measure of unity to the subsequent discussion of the literary

1. Kritisch-exegetischer Kommentar über das Neue Testament, begründet von H. A. W. Meyer, 2. Abt., 15. Aufl. (Göttingen: Vandenhoeck & Ruprecht, 1957). Bultmann's interest in the source problem of John antedates the publication of his commentary by at least two decades. He first analyzed the prologue in "Der religionsgeschichtliche Hintergrund des Prologs zum Johannes-Evangelium," *Eucharisterion, Studien zur Religion und Literatur des Alten und Neuen Testaments* [H. Gunkel Festschrift], ed. H. Schmidt (Göttingen: Vandenhoeck & Ruprecht, 1923), pt. II, pp. 3–26. Later he made a source-critical study of 1 John and discovered there a discourse source similar to the one he subsequently traced through the Gospel ("Analyse des ersten Johannesbriefes," *Festgabe für Adolf Jülicher zum 70. Geburtstag* [Tübingen: Mohr, 1927], pp. 138–58). In another early study, "Die Bedeutung der neuerschlossenen mandäischen und manichäischen Quellen für das Verständnis des Johannesevangelium," *ZNW* 24 (1925): 100–46, he did important background work for the development of his discourse source theory. For a description of earlier investigations and theories see W. F. Howard, *The Fourth Gospel in Recent Criticism and Interpretation,* rev. ed. by C. K. Barrett (London: Epworth, 1955), pp. 61ff.; also W. Bousset, "Ist das vierte Evangelium eine literarische Ein-

problem where it has been taken into account. Those who sharply disagree with Bultmann have found it a convenient benchmark by which to gain a perspective on the problems of the Gospel. His theory, worked out in most minute detail, involves the evangelist's use of sources, the presumably accidental disruption of the original textual order, and the (incorrect) restoration and editorial expansion of the text by an ecclesiastical redactor. Any discussion of recent developments in this area will naturally and appropriately begin with his work.

This article will not deal with every aspect of Bultmann's theory. I shall only attempt to indicate the influence of his source hypothesis upon subsequent investigation and discussion of the problem of the composition of the Fourth Gospel. Although the discussion which Bultmann's source theory has stimulated may have been somewhat overshadowed by the enormous interest that has been shown in other aspects of his work, it is of some importance. While it has not produced a clear solution of the problem, it has served to better define the limitations and possibilities which confront further research.

THE SOURCE THEORY OF RUDOLF BULTMANN

Aside from the work of the redactor Bultmann discerns four principal literary sources or layers in the Gospel.[2] First of all, he discov-

heit?," *ThR* 12 (1909): 1 ff., 39 ff. There is also a good review of three recent decades of Johannine research: E. Haenchen, "Aus der Literatur zum Johannesevangelium, 1929–56," *ThR*, n.s. 23 (1955): 295–335. W. G. Kümmel's excellent survey and assessment of the literature since 1940 in his revision of the Feine-Behm *Einleitung in das Neue Testament*, 12 Aufl. (Heidelberg: Quelle and Meyer, 1963), esp. pp. 135–49, unfortunately appeared too late to be taken into account in this essay.

2. The problem of redaction, as well as that of the dislocation and rearrangement of the text, involves the stages of development following the completion of what Bultmann regards as the original Gospel, and we shall not deal with it here. The source theory provides Bultmann's answer to the question of how the Gospel was originally composed.

In a doctoral dissertation presented to the Graduate Faculty of Yale University I have attempted to make a much more extensive examination of Bultmann's work. The citation of some literature omitted here because of limitation of space was included in that volume. See *The Composition and Order of the Fourth Gospel: Bultmann's Literary Theory* (New Haven: Yale University Press, 1965).

ers in the prologue a *Vorlage* which the evangelist is said to have drawn from a written discourse source employed at many other points in the Gospel.[3] Bultmann refers to this source as the revelation discourses (*Offenbarungsreden*). These discourses are identified by their peculiar rhythmic structure, the Semitic cast of their language, and their mythical, Gnostic motifs. They often function as "texts" for the evangelist's own preaching, in which case both the texts and the preaching usually appear as words of Jesus.[4] The narratives of chapters 1–12, especially the miracle stories, are also said to have been drawn by the evangelist from a written source, the hypothetical *semeia*-source.[5] It is upon this source rather than the synoptic gospels that the evangelist relied for most, although not all, of his narrative material. As might be expected, the third major source comprises the passion and resurrection narratives.[6] Although this portion of the Gospel is perhaps closest to the synoptic tradition, Bultmann believes, and is able to argue persuasively, that the similarities and parallels are best accounted for on the hypothesis that John drew upon a separate source rather than upon the synoptic Gospels. A fourth and final element of the original text of the Gospel, although not a "source", is the work of the evangelist himself. This somewhat enigmatic figure is said to have been an adherent of the rival Baptist sect before he came over to Christianity, bringing with him the *Offenbarungsreden* and perhaps other Baptist tradition.[7] He is much more than a mere editor or purveyor of tradition. His literary skill and theological insight are manifest not only in the sections of the Gospel which he composed, but also in the manner in which he wove the three principal written sources and other traditional materials into a harmonious whole, making of them a vehicle for his own theological thought. Bultmann identifies the hand of the evangelist by means of contextual, stylistic, and theological criteria.[8] Although the Gospel contains certain Semitic

3. Ibid., p. 4 n. 5.
4. Ibid., p. 93.
5. Ibid., p. 78.
6. Ibid., pp. 489ff.
7. Ibid., p. 76.
8. The stylistic characteristics which Bultmann attributes to the evangelist include Semitisms of one sort or another, the epexegetical ἵνα'-clause, the οὐ(κ) ...

features, these are to be attributed largely to the sources. Bultmann regards it as certain that the evangelist himself wrote in Greek.

THE DISCUSSION OF BULTMANN'S PROPOSAL

While Bultmann's source theory has had its effect on subsequent Johannine research, it has by no means won universal, or even wide, assent. Soon after the publication of the commentary Jeremias, Dibelius, and Menoud expressed doubts about the adequacy of the evidence for the sources.[9] Among scholars in the English-speaking world, C.H. Dodd did not take the source theory into account (the commentary was unavailable when his book was written), and C.K. Barrett, while giving it some consideration, rejected it completely.[10] On the continent Oscar Cullmann continues to go his separate and independent way, while some of Bultmann's students, among others, have their own doubts and reservations. There have been at least two systematic analyses and criticisms of Bultmann's source theory. A decade after his work was completed E. Ruckstuhl, a Swiss Catholic, published a thoroughgoing critique of both the source and redaction theories entitled *Die literarische Einheit des vierten Evangeliums*. This was followed in 1954 by another treatment of the source proposal in B. Noack's *Zur johanneischen Tradition*.[11]

ἀλλά construction, emphatic ἐκεῖνος, and other such traits often regarded as typical of the Gospel as a whole. In contexts where the *Offenbarungsreden* appear, the evangelist's prosaic style is said to distinguish his hand from the source material. Moreover, according to Bultmann, the evangelist's theological perspective often differs from that of his sources, and this fact is helpful to the perceptive source critic.

9. J. Jeremias, "Johanneische Literarkritik," *ThBl* 20 (1941): 33–46, esp. 39–43; M. Dibelius, "Ein neuer Kommentar zum Johannes-Evangelium," *TLZ* 67 (1942): 257–63; Ph.-H. Menoud, *L'Évangile de Jean d' après les recherches récentes*, Cahiers théologiques de actualité protestante 3, 2d ed. (Neuchatel: Delachaux & Niestlé, 1947), pp. 12–26.

10. C. H. Dodd, *The Interpretation of the Fourth Gospel* (Cambridge: Cambridge University Press, 1953), p. 121 n. 2; C. K. Barrett, *The Gospel According to St. John* (London: S.P.C.K., 1956). The importance of Bultmann's commentary, especially his source theory, was recognized by B. S. Easton, who reviewed the commentary and produced an English translation of the *Offenbarungsreden* source (*JBL* 65 [1946]: 73–81, 143–56).

11. Ruckstuhl, *Die literarische Einheit des Johannesevangeliums, Der gegenwärtige Stand der einschlägigen Forschungen*, Studia Friburgensia, n.s. 3 (Freiburg

Of the two, Ruckstuhl's is the most extensive and the least sympathetic. As the title implies, he really sets out to defend the literary unity of the Fourth Gospel against the onslaught of Bultmann's source and redaction analysis. The presumption is that if his carefully conceived and documented theory is untenable, the Gospel's unity must be unimpeachable. Recalling that Bultmann himself once asserted that the prime requisite for the source criticism of the Gospel was a set of suitable stylistic criteria,[12] Ruckstuhl proposes to inquire whether Bultmann has really been able to derive such criteria from the Gospel and thus convincingly support his hypothesis.

As a result of his investigation Ruckstuhl claims that Bultmann is able to bring forth an impressive set of stylistic criteria only for the evangelist. The stylistic characteristics of the sources do not distinguish themselves sufficiently from those of the evangelist and are fewer in number. This deficiency cannot be ascribed to Bultmann's negligence, for he has assiduously scoured the text for all sorts of stylistic characteristics. But he has made the methodological error of ascribing the passages with the more distinct stylistic features to the evangelist, leaving the more stylistically neutral or colorless passages to the alleged sources. Moreover, the characteristics of the evangelist are not uniquely his own, for they appear also in sections which Bultmann assigns to the sources. To ascribe such characteristics to the evangelist when they appear in the midst of a source, as Bultmann often does, is, according to Ruckstuhl, a very arbitrary procedure.[13] Futhermore, some of Bultmann's stylistic characteristics are said to indicate only differences of content—namely, narrative or discourse material—rather than real differences of style.[14]

The rhythmic criterion which Bultmann utilizes to identify the *Offenbarungsreden* is attacked by Ruckstuhl as too unstable to serve as a basis for source separations. On Bultmann's own showing the verses of the discourses are of very irregular length and rhythm. Ruckstuhl also calls attention to the fact that while the *Offenba-*

---

in der Schweiz: Paulusverlag, 1951), pp. 20–134, 180–219, 267 ff.; B. Noack, *Zur johanneischen Tradition, Beiträge zur Kritik an der literarkritischen Analyse des vierten Evangeliums* (Copenhagen: Rosenkilde og Bagger, 1954), pp. 9–42.

12. Ruckstuhl, p. 39. He refers to Bultmann's article in *Die christliche Welt* 41 (1927): 502–11.

13. Ruckstuhl, p. 62 n. 2. E.g., the resumptive οὗτος or ἐκεῖνος (αὐτός) occurs six times in material which Bultmann otherwise assigns to the *Offenbarungsreden*.

14. Ibid., pp. 104–6.

rungsreden rhythm sometimes seems to be deficient in the material ascribed to that source, it not infrequently appears in passages Bultmann leaves to the evangelist.[15] Ruckstuhl also casts doubt upon the significance of the evidence of narrative sources, especially the *semeia*-source, which Bultmann has adduced. The various narrative sources do not differ markedly in style, according to Ruckstuhl, and the narratives of John differ stylistically from those of the synoptics only as the Gospel as a whole differs from the synoptic gospels.[16]

As a coup de grace, Ruckstuhl employs a version of the style-statistical method developed by E. Schweizer to test the stylistic grounds for Bultmann's source separations.[17] Schweizer had compiled a list of thirty-three frequently recurring Johannine stylistic characteristics and had shown that they appear at random throughout the various hypothetical sources which Spitta, Wendt, and Hirsch had distinguished. Thus their Johannine source theories were, if not disproved, at least called into question. Ruckstuhl expands this list to fifty and, like Schweizer, finds that none occur repeatedly with

15. Ibid., pp. 43–54. Ruckstuhl contrasts the divergent rhythmic patterns found in 1:1–2; 3:8; 3:12; 8:50; 8:54a; 12:47–48; 15:2; 5:21; 15:4a; 15:5; 5:39–40; 8:12; 11:9–10; 12:49–50; 1 John 1:6–7—all of which Bultmann assigns to the *Offenbarungsreden*. Remarkable differences are indeed apparent. As Käsemann and Jeremias had already pointed out, Bultmann is not able to trace the distinct rhythmic pattern of the prologue through the speeches of the *Offenbarungsreden*. Ruckstuhl also refers to some eighty doublets in the style of the *Offenbarungsreden* which Bultmann assigns to the evangelist. As examples of these he cites 4:32, 38; 8:47; 9:41; 13: 20 (p. 48). While I agree that it is difficult to draw a sharp line between the style of the evangelist and that of the *Offenbarungsreden*, the examples which Ruckstuhl adduces from the material assigned to the evangelist are not well chosen. 13:20 is a synoptic variant which occurs in very similar form in Matt. 10:40 and Luke 10:16. Bultmann actually assigns 8:47a to the *Offenbarungsreden* rather than to the evangelist (*Johannes*, p. 245 n. 4) and suggests that a tradition may lie behind 4:38 (p. 147 n. 4). 4:32 is too brief to be very impressive. Although 9:41 may be regarded as the evangelist's application of the *Offenbarungswort* of 9:39, it is the most clear-cut instance of the style of the source in the evangelist's compositions.

16. Ruckstuhl, pp. 98–104.

17. Ibid., pp. 180–219, esp. 212–16. Cf. E. Schweizer, *Ego Eimi . . . Die religionsgeschichtliche Herkunft und theologische Bedeutung der johanneischen Bildreden, zugleich ein Beitrag zur Quellenfrage des vierten Evangeliums*, FRLANT, ed. R. Bultmann, n.s. 38, entire ser. 56 (Göttingen: Vandenhoeck & Ruprecht, 1939), pp. 103–5.

others in well-defined patterns or groupings which would indicate the existence of corresponding sources.[18] He then proceeds to test Bultmann's source theory against this new set of criteria. The results are about as clear-cut as Schweizer's. The characteristics are scattered indiscriminately through Bultmann's sources, indicating that his theory gains as little support from this sort of testing as those of Spitta, Wendt, and Hirsch. Although Ruckstuhl's method parallels Schweizer's quite closely, his conclusions depart in a striking and significant way. Schweizer only claimed to have proved a certain stylistic unity which he thought discouraging for future attempts to identify sources behind the present text of the Gospel. He did not deny that such sources could have existed.[19] Ruckstuhl, on the other hand, regards not only Bultmann's source (and redaction) theory as disproved, but all efforts to separate sources, either already undertaken or contemplated. Even the possibility of the existence of such written sources is denied.

Aside from these rather too far-reaching conclusions, Ruckstuhl's work does not, it seems to me, do justice to Bultmann's substantial reasons for undertaking source analysis in the first place. His book leaves the impression that Bultmann's method of dealing with the Fourth Gospel is rather perverse, or uncalled for, which it is not, regardless of whether it is right or wrong. The persuasiveness of Ruckstuhl's book is indeed somewhat vitiated by his seeming reluctance to take seriously the evidence which has led many scholars to question the literary unity of the Gospel. That this conservatism is not to be attributed to his Catholicism is revealed by the criticism of his work by another Roman Catholic scholar, R. Schnackenburg.[20] Schnackenburg rightly grants the effectiveness of many of Ruckstuhl's strictures against Bultmann's position, but denies that the evidence for a marked degree of overall stylistic unity carries with it the right to make a categorical judgment against any alleged

18. Among the criteria gathered by Schweizer and Ruckstuhl are the ἵνα epexegeticum, οὐ...ἀλλ' ἵνα, ἐκεῖνος (cf.n. 8 above), οὖν historicum, τότε οὖν, καθώς ...καί, etc. — stylistic characteristics which also figure in Bultmann's source analysis. Ruckstuhl does not, however, confine himself to the characteristics which Bultmann uses.

19. Schweizer, pp. 108ff.

20. "Logos-Hymnus und johanneischer Prolog," *BZ* 1 (1957): 69–109.

source at any point in the Gospel. Rather, he contends that the style-critical criteria must be used on specific passages to determine whether or not we may in certain cases distinguish between the hand of the evangelist and other material. Schnackenburg then supports his contention with a style-critical examination of the prologue, which offers some surprisingly strong, although not complete, support for Bultmann's reconstruction of a prologue source.[21] So while it must be conceded that Ruckstuhl has succeeded in putting a very large question mark over Bultmann's hypothesis, he has not been able to sweep the field as cleanly of source criticism as he desired. If Bultmann goes further than the evidence warrants in defining extensive sources down to the most minute detail, Ruckstuhl goes too far in concluding from a demonstrable stylistic unity of the Gospel that such sources not only cannot be proved but, in fact, never existed at all.

In his monograph Noack argues that oral traditions rather than written sources lie immediately behind the Fourth Gospel and proposes to break the text down into its smallest components in order to show this. But he realizes that before he can set forth a defensible account of his own position he must come to terms with Bultmann's literary analysis and source theory. He carefully examines a number of the stylistic characteristics which Bultmann employs as criteria for the identification of the hand of the evangelist.[22] Like Ruckstuhl, he discovers that sometimes the characteristics which Bultmann attributes to the evangelist turn up in the sources, in which case they are sometimes assigned to the evangelist, but sometimes not. Moreover, to account for stylistic similarities between the *Offenbarungsreden* and the evangelist, Bultmann claims that the latter has been influenced by the style and content of his source. But Noack maintains that such explanations only indicate that we are on very unsure footing in attempting to distinguish between source and evangelist.[23] Like Ruckstuhl, Noack points out that at some points there are far greater disparities in rhythm between different segments of the *Offenbarungsreden* source than between certain pas-

21. Schnackenburg's source is found in vv. 1, 3, 4, 9, 10, 11, 14, and 16 (ibid., pp. 81, 85ff.). Bultmann's includes at least parts of vv. 1, 2, 3, 4, 5, 9, 10, 11, 12, 14, 16.

22. Noack, pp. 18–34.

23. Ibid., pp. 31ff.

sages assigned to the source and others assigned to the evangelist. Again like Ruckstuhl, he observes that the stylistic characteristics of the evangelist are much more numerous and clearly defined than those of the source. Against the *semeia*-source Noack objects that such a document, containing stories but no sayings, is without historical precedent and that Bultmann's case for it is weakened by his inability to ascribe to it all the narratives of the Gospel. Neither does Noack believe that the enumeration of a first and second sign (2:11; 4:36) and the mention of signs in the conclusion of the gospel (20:30–31) point to the use of a *semeia*-source.[24] He argues that the narratives, like the sayings, were composed from oral tradition. The prevalence of parataxis in the narratives, like the characteristic asyndeta of the discourses, indicates that the author was writing down his material from memory, not from documentary sources.[25] In support of his position Noack also adduces evidence involving the evangelist's use of the Old Testament.[26] He shows that John usually quotes the Old Testament inexactly, thereby giving the impression that he is drawing upon his memory rather than copying a text. His quotations as a whole cannot be traced to any single Old Testament text nor explained as variants of Old Testament passages in the synoptics. (Had they been taken from a testimony source designed for polemical use against the Jews, they would have doubtless adhered more faithfully to some known text.) On the other hand, since no *Tendenz* can be observed in the quotations it is unlikely that they were deliberately altered. According to Noack, the evidence indicates that John quotes the Old Testament from memory. If this is really the case, he would scarcely have been more meticulous in his use of other sources, if he had any at all. The difficulties thus raised for source criticism are obvious.[27]

24. Ibid., pp. 112–14.
25. Ibid., p. 124.
26. Ibid., pp. 71–89.
27. Coincidentally with the publication of Noack's book, and quite independently of it, C. Goodwin published an article in which he made a similar investigation of the Johannine Old Testament quotations and arrived at essentially the same conclusions ("How Did John Treat His Sources?" *JBL* 73 [1954]: 61–75). According to Goodwin, John quoted the Old Testament from memory, and therefore probably would not have scrupulously copied other sources. If this is the case, the possibility of recovering such sources as he may have drawn upon is rather slim.

Bultmann lost no time in replying to Noack.[28] In a review of his book Bultmann firmly rejects as self-evidently impossible Noack's attempt to break the Johannine text into small fragments wherever possible and trace their origin to oral tradition. The Johannine material obviously cannot be handled in this way. The evidence that the evangelist quoted the Old Testament from memory and did not use the synoptic gospels is valid, but it does not prove that he did not use other sources. (In his commentary Bultmann had already minimized and all but denied the evangelist's use of the synoptics.) Bultmann protests that while Noack tests his criteria in isolation from one another, he himself always uses them together so that they offer mutual support and confirmation. He also continues to insist that the overlapping of stylistic characteristics of different strata can be explained as the result of the evangelist's having annotated and imitated his sources. It is, however, certainly arguable that the evidence of the Old Testament quotations cannot be dismissed as of no significance for the source question. Moreover, continual recourse to the explanation of annotation and imitation only shows how well integrated any hypothetical sources must be, and therefore how difficult the task of source criticism is.

But if there was any remaining doubt about Bultmann's continued adherence to his source theory, it was dispelled with his publication in 1956 of the late Hans Becker's dissertation on the revelation discourses.[29] Indeed, in the foreword he explicitly states that the appearance of such books as those of Hoskyns, Wikenhauser, Barrett, Dodd, and Noack (all of which reject or ignore his source theory) by no means makes Becker's work superfluous. Becker, who studied under Bultmann, attempts to support his teacher's proposed *Offenbarungsreden* source by systematically adducing evidence from ancient Gnostic and quasi-Gnostic literature. In the Mandaean literature, the Odes of Solomon, the Pseudo-Clementines, etc., Becker discovers a common revelation discourse pattern, which he finds

28. "Zur johanneischen Tradition," *TLZ* (1955): 521–26.

29. *Die Reden des Johannesevangeliums und der Stil der gnostischen Offenbarungsreden*, FRLANT, ed. R. Bultmann, n.s. 50, entire ser. 68; (Göttingen: Vandenhoeck & Ruprecht, 1956). In addition, note Bultmann's review of C. H. Dodd's book, "The Interpretation of the Fourth Gospel," *NTS* 1 (1954–55): 77–91; also his article "Johannesevangelium," *Die Religion in Geschichte und Gegenwart, III* ed. K. Galling, et al., 3d ed. rev. (Tübingen: Mohr [Siebeck], 1959), 840–50.

also in the Gospel of John. He believes that the existence of this common pattern in John and other ancient documents confirms the hypothesis of a revelation-discourse source underlying the Gospel. On the basis of his *religionsgeschichtliche* investigations he proceeds to isolate this source in John. With minor deviations the source he produces coincides to an amazing degree with Bultmann's *Offenbarungsreden*. That Becker shows the strong affinities of the Johannine discourses with a type of Gnostic revelation discourse is clear enough. What is not really clear is that this proves the existence of a Johannine discourse source which the evangelist copied out. Could not the evangelist himself have composed the discourses of the Gospel? This possibility is, or so it seems, very difficult to deny in view of the affinities with Gnosticism and other ancient ways of thinking which Bultmann and others readily affirm.[30]

Not all Bultmann's students, however, have been disposed to defend his views. One of the most significant criticisms of Bultmann's source hypothesis has arisen within the circle of his own pupils. It is based on theological considerations; but the theological considerations involved are historical and exegetical. That is, they have to do with the fundamental intention and theological perspective of the evangelist himself. Ernst Käsemann, who has brought these con-

30. Becker's thesis involves a very controversial aspect of Bultmann's treatment of John—and indeed, the entire development of New Testament theology—namely, his understanding of its relation to Gnosticism. Becker, like Bultmann, and others, believes that although most of the extant Gnostic documents assumed their present form after the emergence of Christianity, Gnosticism itself, including the Gnostic doctrine or myth of the redeemer, is a pre-Christian phenomenon. The revelation discourses of John are the product of such a pre-Christian Gnosticism. Although scholars such as F. C. Burkitt, R. P. Casey, and C. H. Dodd, to mention only a few, have rejected the theory of a pre-Christian Gnosticism, it is still widely held and there is yet no real consensus on the Gnostic problem. Thus the theory of the evangelist's use of a collection of such revelation discourses may not be rejected out of hand on the grounds that no pre-Christian Gnosticism, and specifically no Gnostic redeemer myth, ever existed. Fortunately, discussion of the question of the sources of John does not have to await the final solution of the Gnostic problem. While the refutation of the theory of a pre-Christian Gnosticism might preclude the kind of source which Bultmann proposes, it would not necessarily eliminate altogether the possibility of a discourse source. At the same time, not even the conclusive proof of a Gnostic redeemer myth, of a characteristic revelation discourse style, or of the existence of such a style in John would necessarily mean that the evangelist used a discourse source in the composition of his gospel.

siderations to light, first questioned the necessity of the source theory in a review of the commentary published soon after World War II.[31] In later articles he expressed doubt that a Christian evangelist would have relied so heavily on a Gnostic document such as the *Offenbarungsreden* and criticized Bultmann's identification of a discourse source, closely related to the Gospel source, in 1 John.[32] Subsequently, in an important study of the prologue he has raised questions about the theology of John which threaten to undermine the source theory by denying the assumption upon which it is based.[33]

Käsemann's analysis of the prologue is not completely unlike Bultmann's. He thinks that the evangelist used an earlier Christian hymn as its basis, but not a pre-Christian Gnostic Hymn, as Bultmann supposes. While Bultmann identified the *Vorlage* in vv. 1, 2(?)–5, 9–12, 14, 16, Käsemann finds it only in 1 (2?)–5, 10–12.[34] Most important, he assigns vv. 14–18 without exception to the evangelist. Reiterating his earlier reservations about the possibility of satisfactorily showing the connection between the rhythmic *Vorlage* of the prologue and Bultmann's hypothetical discourse source extending throughout the Gospel, Käsemann points out that even in the prologue one can hardly discern the same rhythmic structure in vv. 14–18 which is found in the earlier portion. Moreover, in v. 14 there is a significant transition from the third person to the confessional first person singular. In developing and applying the rhythm criterion Bultmann relies to a considerable extent upon the conjectured Aramaic origin of the prologue source, a hypothesis which at one or two points gets him out of serious difficulty. In Käsemann's judgment, however, this hypothesis is not well enough established to play a fundamental role in the analysis of the prologue and to serve as the basis for other theories. He regards as

31. "Rudolf Bultmann, Das Evangelium des Johannes," *Verkündigung und Forschung, Theologischer Jahresbericht,* 3 (1942–46): 182–201.

32. "Ketzer und Zeuge, Zum johanneischen Verfasserproblem," *ZTK,* 48 (1951): esp. p. 306 n. 2; also "Neutestamentliche Fragen von Heute," *ZTK* 54 (1957), 15–16.

33. "Aufbau und Anliegen des johanneischen Prologs," *Libertas Christiana, Friedrich Delekat zum 65. Geburtstag,* ed. E. Wolf and W. Matthias (Munich: Chr. Kaiser, 1957), pp. 75–99.

34. Ibid., pp. 85ff.

especially questionable the use of the conjectured Aramaic original to rescue the rhythm of the source.[35]

Most important, however, is Käsemann's criticism of Bultmann's interpretation of 1:14, which he (against Bultmann) assigns to the evangelist. Whereas Bultmann, along with many earlier exegetes and a long tradition of Christian theological interpretation, has seen the point of emphasis in the καὶ ὁ λόγος σάρξ ἐγένετο, Käsemann asserts that this is merely the necessary presupposition of the ἐθεασάμεθα τὴν δόξαν αὐτοῦ. Bultmann, taking his cue from the ὁ λόγος σάρξ ἐγένετο, understands the Fourth Gospel as the gospel of the revelation of the Word in the man Jesus and renders a Kierkegaardian interpretation of the incarnation as the incognito of the revealer. From the perspective proposed by Käsemann, however, Bultmann has thus obscured the *Leitmotiv* of the Gospel, namely, the glorious character of the incarnation as the presence and activity of God upon earth in the person of Jesus.[36]

This view of the Christology of the Gospel, which is really the obverse of Bultmann's, has some important implications for source criticism. Bultmann's source analysis enables him to assign the cruder mythological and miraculous elements of the Gospel to the speech and sign sources, which the evangelist is supposed to have used in a very artful way, employing their language, narrative, or imagery so as to express his own more sophisticated point of view. This disposition of the miraculous and mythical elements, which puts a certain distance between their original meaning and the use to which they are put in the Gospel, is precisely what is demanded if Bultmann's theological interpretation is to stand.[37] But the effect

35. Ibid., p. 78; cf. "Rudolf Bultmann, Das Evangelium des Johannes," p. 188. In fairness to Bultmann it should be noted that in the most recent comprehensive investigation of the problem of Aramaisms in the New Testament Matthew Black concludes that Aramaic sources or traditions probably underlie the prologue, the Baptist sayings in chap. 3, and, most important, many of the sayings of Jesus (*An Aramaic Approach to the Gospels and Acts*, 2nd ed. rev. [Oxford: Clarendon Press, 1954], pp. 207–9). While this confirms the plausibility of Bultmann's speech source proposal, it does not go very far toward demonstrating the validity of the *Offenbarungsreden* theory in the form in which he presents it.

36. *Libertas Christiana*, pp. 90–94.

37. *ZTK* 57 (1957): 15–16: "Bultmanns Deutung, mit der ich mich hier allein befasse, steht und fällt mit der Theorie, dass der Evangelist eine heidnische Quelle von Offenbarungsreden benutzt, überarbeitet und kommentiert habe und sich

of Käsemann's interpretation of the prologue, especially v.14, is to remove the inner theological justification and motivation of the source theory. Given Käsemann's understanding of the evangelist's perspective, the source theory, which for Bultmann was a key to the proper understanding of the Gospel, becomes superfluous. If the evangelist's thought followed the lines laid down by Käsemann, he could easily have composed the speeches of Jesus in the Gospel as the definitive expression of his Christology. It would not then be necessary to suppose that he adopted a document whose conceptions he took seriously but not literally. The hypothesis of a *semeia*-source, or something like it, is perhaps not quite so seriously affected. In Bultmann's commentary it may seem to serve the purpose of putting some distance between the evangelist and the boldly miraculous elements of the Gospel (and allow him to assign a less sophisticated understanding of *semeia* to pre-gospel tradition), yet it is not to be discounted for that reason alone. The evangelist obviously got his narrative tradition from somewhere, and he could have employed such a document, believing the events recounted to be necessarily historical and at the same time using them for his own theological purposes. This is, in fact, the way in which Käsemann suggests that John handled the miracle stories.[38] While there may be alternative explanations of the narrative material in John the *semeia*-source proposal is surely not implausible.

Käsemann's far-reaching objection to Bultmann's understanding of the Fourth Gospel and its implications for the source question, together with the more specific and technical criticisms advanced by Ruckstuhl and Noack, have brought to light the difficulties involved in Bultmann's elaborate source theory. By attacking the stylistic grounds of the theory Ruckstuhl and Noack have con-

gleichzeitig einer Zeichenquelle bediene, um mit Wundern die Gabe und den Anspruch des Offenbarers zu illustrieren. Nur so kann Bultmann sowohl das unbestreitbar im Evangelium vorliegende mythologische Gut wie den krassen Mirakelglauben vom Evangelisten distanzieren. Nur so kann er daran festhalten, dass die Fleischwerdung des Wortes das Thema des Evangeliums sei, im Sinne Kierkegaards die Fleischwerdung das Inkognito des Offenbarers wahren und mit diesem Inkognito das Ärgernis der Welt erregen lassen."

38. Cf. also E. Haenchen, "Der Vater, der mich gesandt hat," NTS 9 (1962–63): 208–16.

firmed what Schweizer had already indicated, namely, the extreme difficulty of separating extensive sources with any degree of certainty on account of the pervasive stylistic unity of the present form of the Gospel. By questioning Bultmann's conception of the theology of the evangelist and his sophistication, Käsemann has really asked whether the source theory is a necessity or whether it is the modern exegete's way of quite unconsciously discovering a theological brother under the skin in the ancient writer. Bultmann's admiration for the Fourth Gospel and his extensive appropriation of its message as he understands it in the development of his own theological position do not need to be described here. It is worth pointing out, however, that Bultmann's interpretation of John is closely related to his theory about the evangelist's method of composition, particularly his use of sources. The source theory is in this respect really much more important than the assignment of certain passages (e.g. 5: 28–29 and 6:51c–58) to the ecclesiastical redactor. The existence of this redactor, who absorbs those passages which are embarrassingly inconsistent with the main theological thrust of the Gopel, becomes credible only if the evangelist himself is conceived as the kind of subtle, sophisticated, and consistent theological thinker Bultmann believes him to be, and this conception of the evangelist is developed by Bultmann in his commentary along with the source theory. As Käsemann has so astutely discerned, the source theory and Bultmann's interpretation of the evangelist's theology go hand in hand. Only when this interpretation is established can it be convincingly claimed that such-and-such an idea or statement is impossible for the evangelist and therefore should be assigned to the redactor.

TWO RECENT INVESTIGATIONS OF THE PROBLEMS OF JOHANNINE ORIGINS

Rightly or wrongly, the most recent investigations of problems pertaining to the origin and composition of the Fourth Gospel have rejected Bultmann's elaborate source theory, have demurred at accepting it, or have ignored it completely. Perhaps one reason for this state of affairs is the relative inaccessibility of much of his argumentation in the footnotes of the commentary. Also Noack and Ruckstuhl are frequently cited as having disproved the source theory,[39] but at least Bultmann himself has not conceded that this is the case.

In fact the work of two younger scholars shows that Bultmann's proposals and the subsequent discussion have not been without their effect. W. Wilkens and S. Schulz set out in very different directions in their recent monographs and articles, but both take cognizance of the evidence which has led Bultmann and others to propose source theories to explain the origin and composition of the Fourth Gospel. Wilkens argues on the basis of intense literary criticism that in the process of transforming the document from a rather simple *Urevangelium* (Wellhausen) into what he describes as a passion gospel, the evangelist wrote or rewrote it three times.[40] The traces of an editing or reworking of the Gospel have led some scholars to propose sources or a *Grundschrift;* the stylistic unity of the Gospel has led others to deny such proposals. Now Wilkens presents a theory which attempts to account for both phenomena. According to him the evangelist, so to speak, wrote his own sources. Interestingly enough, portions of sources which Bultmann isolated (e.g. the *"Lichtrede"* discourse from the *Offenbarungsreden*) sometimes turn up as separate literary units in the intermediate stage of Wilken's revisions of the Gospel. That Wilkens' theory is as ingenious as it is elaborate cannot be denied. Yet it stumbles over its own elaborateness and ingenuity.[41] One can scarcely believe that an author's successive revisions of his work could be successfully reconstructed in the detail which Wilkens attempts. But in view of

39. P. Niewalda, *Sakramentssymbolik im Johannesevangelium? Eine exegetisch-historische Studie* (Limburg: Lahn Verlag, 1958), p. 2; J.A.T. Robinson, "The New Look on the Fourth Gospel," *Studia Evangelica*, Papers Presented to the International Congress on "The Four Gospels in 1957" Held at Christ Church, Oxford, 1957, ed. K. Aland, et al. (Berlin: Akademie-Verlag, 1959), p. 341; F.-M. Braun, *Jean le Théologien et son évangile dans l'église ancienne*, EBib (Paris: Librairie Lecoffre, J. Gabalda et Cie., 1959) pp. 11; P. Parker, "Two Editions of John," *JBL* 12 (1956): 304; S. Mendner, "Johanneische Literarkritik," *ThZ* 8 (1952): 422; E. Haenchen, "Johanneische Probleme," *ZTK* 56 (1959): p. 53 n. 2.

40. *Die Entstehungsgeschichte des vierten Evangeliums* (Zollikon: Evangelischer Verlag, 1958).

41. Cf. J. M. Robinson, "Recent Research in the Fourth Gospel," *JBL* 78 (1959): 242ff.; C. K. Barrett, "Die Entstehungsgeschichte des vierten Evangeliums," *TLZ* 84 (1959): 828–29f.

the acknowledged literary unity of the Gospel the suggestion that the present text of the Fourth Gospel is the result of the author's own revising and editing is not impossible. Wilkens himself has shown that the removal of seemingly secondary elements from a passage cannot be counted on to produce a non-Johannine core.[42] Even where one is able to separate tradition and redaction, he finds "Johannine" elements in each. Whether this indicates a unity of authorship or only a development within a school or circle of tradition and interpretation is, however, a question worth asking. If Wilkens has perhaps overdeveloped and overstated his case in this initial monograph, the line which he is pursuing certainly merits consideration.

In contrast to Wilkens, Schulz has given up literary criticism— along with numerous other methods which he identifies and describes extensively and in detail—as a primary means of investigating the text of John in favor of a combination of *Traditionsgeschichte* and *Religionsgeschichte* methods which he calls *Themageschichte*. Schulz intends to look behind the text of the Gospel for earlier traditions centering in specific themes. In an initial monograph[43] he attempted to recover the Son of Man and related traditions of the Gospel, which, when isolated, he traced to Jewish apocalyptic origins. Much of the material which Bultmann assigned to the redactor because of its futuristic eschatology (e.g. 5:28–29) Schulz now ascribes to primitive tradition. In a second study[44] Schulz deals with the prologue and the predicative *ego eimi* sayings with their related images (shepherd, vine, etc.). By means of a variety of methods he seeks to isolate the traditional units and relate them to their proper background in the religious landscape from which Christianity emerged, principally in the Jewish sectarian and Mandaean Gnostic groups of first-century Palestine and neighborhood. Frequently he finds that originally Jewish traditions have undergone what he calls Gnostic reinterpretation before being incorporated into the Gospel. Sometimes even the

42. "Die Erweckung des Lazarus," *ThZ* 15 (1959): 23–39.

43. *Untersuchungen zur Menschensohn-Christologie im Johannesevangelium, Zugleich ein Beitrag zur Methodengeschichte der Auslegung des 4. Evangeliums* (Göttingen: Vandenhoeck & Ruprecht, 1957).

44. *Komposition und Herkunft der johanneischen Reden*, BWANT, ed. K. H. Rengstorf and L. Rost, 5th ser. 1, entire ser. 81; (Stuttgart: W. Kohlhammer, 1960).

ultimate origin of a tradition or concept (e.g. the logos title) is said to be Gnostic.

Although in contrast to Bultmann, and perhaps in opposition to him, Schulz abjures the quest for literary sources extending through all or most of the Gospel, his own ambitions are obviously far from modest and his goals hard to achieve. The lines between tradition, later interpretation, and the evangelist's own work are difficult to draw with any degree of objectivity, and when one has isolated a traditional segment with some degree of certainty he may not even then be sure of its provenance. The latter problem is all the more acute in view of the extensive mixing of religious ideas and themes of various origins which was evidently characteristic of later antiquity. Nevertheless, Schulz's research is highly suggestive in that it points so clearly to the possibility that the stuff of the Johannine literature had a long—perhaps preliterary and pre-Christian—history before taking the form in which we find it in the Fourth Gospel. In principle Schulz's work does not necessarily conflict with that of Wilkens or Bultmann, inasmuch as he purports to deal with an earlier stage of the Gospel's development. In fact, however, it does, for often the explanations offered by Schulz make those advanced by Wilkens and Bultmann superfluous.

A FEW EMERGING POINTS OF AGREEMENT?

Departing from Bultmann, Johannine research, as exemplified by the work of Wilkens and Schulz, is finding new directions and producing new theories. While it may be presumptuous to regard Bultmann's proposals as moribund, they do not in fact constitute a widely accepted hypothesis on the basis of which present and future research may proceed. The study of the Fourth Gospel is not, however, advanced by the recognition of serious and well-founded objections to Bultmann's source theory. Certainly if such a literary theory could have been adequately established it would have been a great boon to Johannine study, which is now plagued with a morass of conflicting views. One can well agree with J.A.T. Robinson's observation that "the effect of reading too much on the Fourth Gospel is to make one feel either that everything has been said about it that could conceivably be said or that it really does not matter what one says, for one is just as likely to be right as anyone else."[45] But perhaps even now it is possible to discern certain trends, if not agreements, in Johannine study which indicate that we are about to move from a state of chaos toward a measure of consensus. While it cannot be claimed that Bultmann's work on the source problem has exercised a determinative influence, the extent to which some of his general perspectives, if not his detailed hypothesis, are represented in such agreement as is now emerging is remarkable.

There is, in the first place, the question of the relationship of John and the synoptic gospels. Scholars such as Wilkens and Noack, as much as they may differ with Bultmann (and each other), would agree that John did not use the synoptic gospels as his narrative source, if indeed he knew them at all. And while E. Haenchen has recently indicated disagreement with Noack, Wilkens, and Bultmann, he has nevertheless also argued that John did not draw his narrative material from the synoptics.[46] As a matter of fact, the view that John did not use the synoptics had already been set forth in England by P. Gardner-Smith (1938) and in America by E. R. Goodenough (1945).[47] C. H. Dodd voiced his substantial agreement with Gardner-Smith in his magnum opus,[48] and although C. K. Barrett still believes that John knew at least Mark and perhaps Luke, he readily grants that we cannot speak of these as his sources.[49]

45. "The Relation of the Prologue to the Gospel of St. John," NTS 9 (1962–63): 120.

46. "Johanneische Probleme," ZTK 56 (1959): 19–54. Wilkens, in his turn, has now objected to Haenchen's contention that the Johannine narrative material comes from a literary source which can be shown to be later than the synoptics ("Evangelist und Tradition im Johannesevangelium," ThZ 16 [1960]: 81–90). Wilkens insists that although the evangelist used tradition, he so thoroughly assimilated it as to preclude an analysis like Haenchen's, which proceeds by distinguishing exactly between non-Johannine source and Johannine embellishment.

47. P. Gardner-Smith, Saint John and the Synoptic Gospels (Cambridge: Cambridge University Press, 1938); E. R. Goodenough, "John a Primitive Gospel," JBL 64 (1945): 145–82, esp. 150–60, 169–70.

48. The Interpretation of the Fourth Gospel, p. 419.

49. Barrett, St. John, p. 34. John A. Bailey has also recently maintained that John knew Luke (as well as Mark), but he does not believe the amount of actual dependence was very great (The Traditions Common to the Gospels of Luke and John, NovTSup 7 [Leiden: Brill, 1963]).

Moreover, it is worth noting that although he might have thereby sustained his own view of John's purpose and method, E. C. Hoskyns in his commentary prudently refrained from claiming that John knew the synoptics in their present form.[50] Among those who deny that John used the synoptics there is substantial agreement that he drew his narratives from a tradition having some points of contact with the synoptic tradition. At this point, however, opinion diverges sharply. Although many would accept Bultmann's proposed passion source or something like it, his *semeia*-source (accounting for most of the narrative material in chaps. 1–12) has not been accorded wide acceptance. For example, Noack and Dodd believe instead that the tradition was entirely or largely oral, while Haenchen thinks that it came to the evangelist in the form of an *Urevangelium*.[51]

As for the discourses, Bultmann and Becker have apparently not succeeded in attracting others to their hypothesis of a source of Gnostic *Offenbarungsreden*, although Schnackenburg and Barrett have spoken of homilies later incorporated into the Gospel,[52] and many have thought that the prologue is based on a hymn or written source. Nevertheless, the special and kerygmatic character of the discourses—indeed of the whole Gospel—is widely acknowledged. In a variety of recent studies and interpretations the common factor is the conclusion or assumption that the discourses incorporate the Johannine preaching, whatever their relation to tradition and history may be.[53] Thus while Bultmann's discourse source may be

50. Hoskyns, *The Fourth Gospel,* ed. F. N. Davey, 2d ed. rev. (London: Faber & Faber, 1947), p. 82.

51. G. Ziener ("Johannesevangelium und urchristliche Passafeier," *BZ* 2 [1958]: 263–74) thinks the narrative source of John is a Jewish Passover haggada which also underlies Wis. 10:1–19:22, and R. H. Smith believes the Johannine narratives are a typological development of Exod. 2: 23–12: 51 ("Exodus Typology in the Fourth Gospel," *JBL* 81 [1962]: 329–42).

52. Schnackenburg, "Die 'situationsgelösten' Redestücke in Joh. 3," *ZNW* 49 (1958): 88–99; Barrett, *St. John,* p. 17.

53. Bultmann believes that the discourses are grounded upon—and even take as their texts—the segments of the *Offenbarungsreden*; thus the Gnostic source becomes the seedbed for the Christian proclamation of the gospel. Cullmann, quite in opposition to Bultmann, thinks that the Gospel is largely a cult-oriented exposition "which treats the two sacraments as expressions of the whole worship life of the early community and correspondingly sets forth the relation between

rejected in the form in which he proposed it, his (and Becker's) observations regarding the character and genre of the Johannine *Reden* are by no means to be set aside as worthless. Future studies of the nature and background of the Johannine preaching can scarcely afford to neglect them.

Finally, the discovery of the Qumran scrolls has led many scholars to see in them and the sectarian Judaism from which they emerged the proper milieu of the Fourth Gospel. This in turn has led to the recent widespread rejection of the once commonly held view that John is the gospel of the Hellenists. It should be remembered, however, that the scrolls by no means invalidate Bultmann's general

---

the Lord of the community *present especially in the two sacraments and the life of Jesus*" (*Early Christian Worship*, trans. A. S. Todd and J. B. Torrance; SBT 10 [London: S.C.M., 1953], p. 58). Bultmann has, of course, denied that the evangelist was interested in sacraments and has ascribed the references to them to the redactor. His former student, H. Köster, does not follow Bultmann exactly on this point, but maintains that the evangelist sometimes deliberately used sacramental language to emphasize the historicity of the Christ-event (cf. "Geschichte und Kultus im Johannesevangelium und bei Ignatius von Antiochen," *ZTK* 54 [1957]: 56–69). Wilkens, on the other hand, adopts Cullmann's sacramental interpretation, but also emphasizes in a more general way the kerygmatic nature of the Gospel. While maintaining the early and ultimately apostolic origin of the Gospel, he denies its historicity, claiming that it is rather preaching. The origin of this preaching is the spirit-inspired word of the authoritative witness speaking for the exalted Lord in the worshiping community (Wilkens, *Enstehungsgeschichte*, p. 169). Similarly, in a recent monograph on the Beloved Disciple, Alv Kragerud has argued that the Gospel originated in a circle of Christian charismatic prophets and is intented to assert the authority of the spirit-inspired prophet, represented by the Beloved Disciple, over against the growing power of the institutional ministry, represented by Peter (*Der Lieblingsjünger im Johannesevangelium, Ein exegetischer Versuch* [Oslo: Osloer Universitätsverlag, 1959]). Of late Käsemann has suggested that he also thinks the roots of the Johannine preaching are to be sought in early Christian prophecy ("Die Anfänge christlicher Theologie," *ZTK* 57 [1960]: 176). But A. Guilding in her ingenious and erudite book treats the whole Gospel as a kind of exposition of the Old Testament texts of an ancient Jewish lectionary system, especially the texts associated with the great feasts (*The Fourth Gospel and Jewish Worship, A Study of the Relation of St. John's Gospel to the Ancient Jewish Lectionary System* [Oxford: Clarendon Press, 1960]). For her the Gospel is a Christian recapitulation of the Jewish system of worship. Another much more modest effort to relate John to Jewish worship is B. Gärtner's *John 6 and the Jewish Passover*, ConNT 17 (Gleerup and Copenhagen: Munksgaard, 1959).

view of the origin of the Gospel of John. For while he views it as a Hellenistic document in the general sense in which all New Testament books are Hellenistic, he does full justice to its Semitic and even Jewish ancestry. The discourse source, while a product of Gnosticism, does not stem from Western, pagan Gnostic circles, but from a Semitic milieu, in which Jewish influences are quite strong— indeed, from the John the Baptist sect,[54] which is now often said to stand in close relation both to Qumran and to the Johannine tradition. Before the discovery of the scrolls and fifteen years before the publication of his commentary, Bultmann suggested a Semitic and even Palestinian origin of the Johannine material.[55] In the commentary he traces the *Offenbarungsreden*, which contain the basic Johannine theological conceptuality, to very much the kind of religious milieu and geographic locus which produced the Qumran scrolls.

So it is now possible to speak of a loose, but real, consensus regarding a Johannine tradition relatively independent of the synoptics, a typically Johannine preaching (found especially in the discourses of the Gospel and in the First Epistle), and the fundamentally Semitic and even Jewish character and background of this tradition and preaching. Whatever legitimate criticisms may be made of Bultmann's source theory, it is significant that in its own peculiar way it takes cognizance of all three of these factors. This is but one reason why his commentary remains a landmark in the history of Johannine study to which others will, or should, repeatedly turn for fresh stimulus, insight, and perspective on Johannine problems.[56]

54. *Johannes*, pp. 4–5, 14–15. cf. pp. 29, 76.

55. ZNW 24 (1925): 100–46. Note esp. pp. 142ff.

56. In dealing even with recent exegetical investigations, we have not been able to make a comprehensive presentation. Other scholars who have recently dealt with the source problem include S. Mendner, whose basic position is set forth in "Johanneische Literarkritik," *ThZ* 8 (1952): 418–34; S. Temple, "A Key to the Composition of the Fourth Gospel," *JBL* 80 (1961): 220–32, and "The Two Signs in the Fourth Gospel," *JBL* 81 (1962): 169–74; M. E. Boismard, "L'évolution du thème eschatologique dans les traditions johanniques," *RB* 68 (1961): 507–25; H. M., Teeple, "Methodology in Source Analysis of the Fourth Gospel," *JBL* 81 (1962): 279–86. In the last couple of years two more extensive treatments of the problem of the sources and composition of the Fourth Gospel have appeared in Germany: K. A. Eckhardt, *Der Tod des Johannes als Schlüssel zum Verständnis der johanneischen Schriften*, Studien zur Rechts- und Religionsgeschichte 3 (Ber-

lin: Walter de Gruyter, 1961); W. Hartke, *Vier urchristliche Partien und ihre Vereinigung zur apostolischen Kirche,* vol. 1: *Johannes und die Synoptiker,* Deutsche Akademie der Wissenschaften zu Berlin, Schriften der Sektion für Altertumswissenschaft 24 (Berlin: Akademie-Verlag, 1961). It is, of course, impossible to describe these books here. Both are impressive and erudite works which contain some valuable insights, but there is an element of what I can only call the fantastic in each of them. Suffice it to say that Eckhardt thinks that the original Gospel was written by John the son of Zebedee, the disciple whom Jesus loved and whom he raised from the dead ("Lazarus" is a later editorial fiction borrowed from Luke). His book was then revised by Ignatius of Antioch and translated from Aramaic to Greek by John the Elder at the turn of the century. Interpolations were later added by Papias! Hartke distinguishes first a *Grundschrift Z* (not unlike Bultmann's *semeia*-source!). The subsequent editing of this document by *V* produced a proto-John which was never published. Then came the final reworking by *H*, who published the Gospel in its present form. (The Johannine epistles are the work of only *V* and *H*, while *H* alone is responsible for the Apocalypse.) Hartke goes to great trouble to separate these three layers in John and to identify the persons responsible for each, concluding that *Z* is John the son of Zebedee, *V* is John Mark, and *H* is Judas Barsabbas!

Probably the best recent bibliography is to be found in Kümmel's revision of the Feine–Behm *Einleitung,* pp. 126–29.

The Milieu of the Johannine Miracle Source[*]

The scholarly career of W. D. Davies has evinced a distinct and primary focus. He has concerned himself with the religious and cultural milieu of the New Testament, especially within Judaism, as a necessity and presupposition for its interpretation. This essay touches upon his basic interest and attempts to relate it to another which has not been so much at the center of his attention, namely, the question of literary strata in, or behind, the documents of the New Testament. I propose to take up once again the question of the source of the miracles of the Fourth Gospel and to make a proposal concerning one stage of the tradition-history which preceded their incorporation into the present document. Although W. D. Davies has not made the Johannine literature the object of original research, his treatment of it in *Invitation to the New Testament* is a model of the careful and balanced judgment for which he is rightly well known. That discussion is also relevant to the theme of his volume. For in it he treats the problem of the background of John—Jewish or Hellenistic?—with nice discrimination, and, perhaps to the surprise of many familiar with his own research, declines to categorize it as predominantly Jewish at the expense of what he perceives to be genuinely Hellenistic features. In this essay I may, at least for purposes of argument, go further toward accepting a Jewish milieu as

*This article originally appeared in the Festschrift for Professor W. D. Davies (see Acknowledgments).

decisive for the historical placement of the Fourth Gospel and its underlying tradition than has my distinguished mentor and colleague.

THE *SEMEIA*-SOURCE AND ITS MILIEU

It is now rather widely agreed that the Fourth Evangelist drew upon a miracle tradition or written source(s) substantially independent of the synoptics, whether or not he had any knowledge of one or more of those gospels. Since the epoch-making commentary of Rudolf Bultmann, the hypothesis of a *semeia*- (or miracle) source has gained rather wide acceptance. A fruitful discussion of the narratives, and especially the miracles, of John can scarcely go forward without some consideration of Bultmann's proposal and the related source theories that it has spawned.

Whether such a miracle source can be precisely isolated and identified, as Bultmann and some who follow him think, is a question we need not decide here. The demonstration of the existence of a source (or sources) is not entirely dependent upon the possibility of isolating it with certainty and precision throughout the Gospel. The purpose of this essay is to sketch out some of the principal lines of development in research bearing upon the *semeia*-source and to ask what their meaning may be. Provisionally granting the existence of such a source or cycle, without defining it precisely, we shall attempt to make a positive contribution to the question of its possible *Sitz im Leben*.

Bultmann was notoriously laconic in describing the historical circumstances of the sources he so precisely identified in the Fourth Gospel. Most intriguing of all are his isolated and brief statements about the provenance and purpose of the *semeia*-source. We may infer from them that Bultmann thinks the *semeia*-source was composed among Christians converted from among followers of John the Baptist, and that it was used originally as a mission document to persuade members of that sect to follow Jesus.[1] Thus the evan-

1. R. Bultmann, *The Gospel of John: A Commentary,* trans. G. R. Beasley-Murray et al. (Philadelphia, 1971), states that the evangelist was probably converted from among the Baptists' following, as 1:35–51 may indicate (p. 108; cf. p. 18). That passage, in turn, is said to be based on a source which had formed a part of the propaganda developed by such disciples for promoting the Christian faith

gelist and his miracle source stem from the same Christian community; for, in Bultmann's view, the evangelist himself had once
been a disciple of John. The origin of the *semeia*-source and the
evangelist, not to mention the *Offenbarungsreden*,[2] in the Baptist
sect would itself say something important about the relationship of
the Fourth Gospel to Judaism, although Bultmann has only rarely
acknowledged the likelihood of the Gospel's Jewish provenance.[3]

For Bultmann the *semeia*-source represented a high view of the
evidential value of miracles to demonstrate the messiahship or sonship of Jesus. In using the source the evangelist clearly distanced
himself from the source's emphasis upon the miraculous per se as
validating or legitimating evidence of Jesus' role and dignity.[4] In
fact, it cannot be said with certainty that the evanglist assumed that
the miracles he reported had actually taken place.[5]

In this as well as other respects Käsemann's bold approach to the
interpretation of John stands Bultmann's on its head.[6] The objection

---

(p. 108 n. 6). This source is then said to be a part of the same source from which
2:1–12 was drawn, namely, the *semeia*-source (p. 113). The *semeia*-source, replete
with Semitisms, was probably written in Greek by a Greek-speaking Semite
(p. 98 n. 6). As to the source's having been used in a missionary effort of former
Baptist disciples to convert Baptist adherents to Jesus, this may be inferred from
the whole thrust of 1:35–51, which suggests that the Baptist must surrender his
disciples to Jesus (p. 99).

2. The prologue hymn and the *Offenbarungsreden* of which it is a part are traced
by Bultmann to the followers of John the Baptist, who celebrated him as the incarnate logos (ibid., pp. 17–18; cf. p. 169).

3. In *Theology of the New Testament*, trans. K. Grobel, 2 vols. (New York, 1952–
55), II, 5, 13, Bultmann grants that John's Gospel may emerge from a Jewish
context. Yet this consideration did not figure largely, except in a negative way, in
the commentary. There the *Ioudaioi* are said to represent the world's unbelief in
general (pp. 86–87). Interestingly enough, in light of 1:19 Bultmann thinks that
even the Baptist is set apart from "the Jews." Yet he also concedes that the evangelist's peculiar usage does not in itself allow us to infer one way or the other
whether he himself was of Jewish descent, for those who respond positively to
Jesus are immediately distinguished from "the Jews."

4. Bultmann, *John*, pp. 113–14, 206–7, 208–9; cf. pp. 217–18, 232–33, 452.
Bultmann says the source presents Jesus as a *theios anthropos* (p. 180).

5. Ibid., p. 119 n. 2.

6. E. Käsemann, *The Testament of Jesus: A Study of the Gospel of John in the
Light of Chapter 17*, trans. G. Krodel (Philadelphia, 1968), pp. 21–22, 52–53.
Käsemann specifically rejects Bultmann's view that the miracles are merely conces-
sions to human weakness.

that Käsemann has ascribed to the evangelist the view of miracles found in the source does not entirely dispose of his position. Aside from the fact that Käsemann was fully aware of, and accepted, the *semeia*-source proposal when he wrote,[7] there are substantial exegetical grounds for thinking that the evangelist regarded the historicity of the miracles as an important aspect of their reality.[8] Yet despite his disagreement with Bultmann, Käsemann apparently takes up and carries forward his teacher's view that the miracles per se embody what is now commonly called a *theios aner* Christology. God going about on earth, to use Käsemann's expression,[9] is the concept of *theios aner* taken to its logical extreme.

The existence of *theios aner* Christology in John is presently widely regarded as well established,[10] the only question being at what traditional or redactional level this Christology is to be found. Most certainly interest and assumptions represented in a shorthand way by the term *theios aner* are found in the Fourth Gospel. But the term itself and the assumption that it represents a fixed ideological system in antiquity have recently been subjected to criticism and qualification.[11] The odyssey of the ancient divine man through modern scholarship has been an intriguing one, and the ways in which that

7. Ibid., p. 37: "He the [evangelist] probably took over at least in part and without great modifications narratives from a source containing miracle stories, and the same is true with regard to the core of his passion and Easter accounts."

8. See 2:11, 23; 3:2; 9:13 ff.; 12:37 ff.; cf. 14:12.

9. Ibid., pp. 8–9, where he refers to F. C. Bauer, G. P. Wetter and E. Hirsch, and pp. 8–13 generally.

10. In addition to Bultmann and Käsemann, see, e.g. J. Becker, "Wunder und Christologie: zum literarkritischen und christologischen Problem der Wunder im Johannesevangelium," *NTS* 16 (1969–70): 141. Becker sees the *semeia*-source against the background of the Hellenistic *theios aner* figure and the aretalogical genre. Thus for him the lack of typical Hellenistic miracle terminology in the source is an unsolved problem (p. 137 n. 1). See also H. Köster and J. M. Robinson, *Trajectories Through Early Christianity* (Philadelphia, 1971), pp. 187–93. Also E. Haenchen, "Der Vater, der mich gesandt hat," *NTS* 9 (1962–63): 208–16, esp. 208-9. L. Schottroff, *Der Glaubende und die feindliche Welt: Beobachtungen zum gnostischen Dualismus und seiner Bedeutung für Paulus und das Johannesevangelium*, WMANT 37 (Neukirchen, 1970), p. 248, characterizes the Jesus of the *semeia*-source as a miracle worker legitimized through his miracles as a teacher come from God, a *theios aner* and thus no ordinary man. Yet she acknowledges that this figure answers also, and particularly, to Jewish demands for divine legitimation through signs (p. 245; p. 248 n. 3).

11. See below.

figure has been conceived are not without relevance for the interpretation of the Fourth Gospel.

The *theios aner*, as the Greek name implies, has been regarded as
principally an artifact of Hellenistic culture generally. M. Nilsson
expressly distinguishes the Greek *theioi andres* from the Palestinian
and Phoenician prophets mentioned by Celsus.[12] New Testament
scholars who make use of the concept usually have in mind the
Hellenistic divine man, a recognizable figure who may nevertheless
have taken on varied characteristics and coloration in the syncre-
tistic cultural and religious milieu of late antiquity.[13] Although some
such view of the divine man seems to have informed Bultmann's
understanding of the Christology of the *semeia*-source,[14] he nevertheless attributes the origin of this source to a Palestinian Jewish-
Christian sect which presumably used the document in a missionary
effort directed toward other Jews, specifically disciples of John the
Baptist.

Is Bultmann thus caught in a contradiction of his own making?
In defense of Bultmann one might regard his ascription of the *semeia*-source to Palestinian circles as a curious non sequitur stemming from his desire to honor the evidence which suggests some
connection between Johannine Christianity and the Baptist sect.
Alternatively, it may be claimed that the Hellenistic divine man ide-

12. Nilsson, *Geschichte der griechischen Religion*, HAW 5 (Munich, 1961), II,
527–28. The pivotal work on the subject is, of course, L. Bieler, ΘΕΙΟΣ ΑΝΗΡ,
Das Bild des "Göttlichen Menschen" in Spätantike und Frühchristentum (Vienna,
1935–36; reprint ed., Darmstadt, 1965).

13. For a good survey of research and statement of the present state of scholarly
opinion on the *theios aner* see P. J. Achtemeier, "Gospel Miracle Tradition and the
Divine Man," *Int* 26 (1972): 174–97; also Köster in *Trajectories*, pp. 187–93. Typical of the way in which Jewish evidence is not excluded but is regarded as chron-
ologically and conceptually secondary are the statements of Achtemeier: "Despite
such qualifications [differences from Hellenistic miracle stories] it is clear that the
miraculous accounts in the Gospels are more closely related to the Hellenistic than
to the rabbinic types" (p. 186). And again (p. 187): "The manner in which Hellenistic Judaism began to interpret its own religious history bears out the statement
that for a religion to be understood in that milieu, it had to make use of the
interpretative device of divine man." Cf. also L. E. Keck, "Mark 3:7–12 and Mark's
Christology," *JBL* 84 (1965): 341–58, who associates Marcan miracle tradition
portraying Jesus as a *theios aner* with Mark's interest in the Gentile mission
(esp. p. 349).

14. See n. 4 above.

ology was current also in Palestine. After all, there were many Hellenized Jews there. But one could scarcely expect it to find a warm reception among the disciples of John the Baptist, certainly not if it is a primarily Hellenistic, in the sense of non-Jewish, concept. To say that the *theios aner* is unthinkable in indigenous Palestinian Judaism may, however, be to accept an unnecessary and even false distinction or set of alternatives and thus to dismiss the possibly valid insight of Bultmann too quickly. Although there may indeed be an unresolved contradiction or antinomy in Bultmann's treatment of the provenance of the *semeia*-source as between Jewish (or Semitic) and non-Jewish (or non-Semitic) influences (an antinomy found elsewhere in Bultmann's work), recent research suggests that this antinomy may point to something more important than an inconsistency or self-contradiction in the work of a great scholar.

SEMEIA AND THE JEWISH EXPECTATIONS

It is beyond the scope of this essay to investigate fully, or even air, the complex network of problems pertaining to the question of Jewish versus Hellenistic origins of miracle stories. In noting some more recent work in this general area, particularly as it pertains to the *theios aner*, I wish to pose, or actually only to expose and restate succinctly, a question which suggests the proper direction for further and more intensive efforts to understand the miracle tradition of John and ultimately the Gospel itself: Are not the characteristics and functions associated with the *theios aner* in some sense native to Judaism?

The possibility that the *theios aner* figure or something like it could emerge within Hellenistic Judaism has been impressively argued by D. Georgi in his investigation of the opponents with whom Paul struggled in 2 Corinthians.[15] According to Georgi, the fact that Christ was understood by Paul's opponents as a divine man is grounded in and presupposes the prior application of this category to Moses in Hellenistic Judaism. That the Jewish Christians who understood Jesus as a *theios aner* themselves performed deeds worthy of a divine man is thoroughly commensurate with the ideology ascribed to them. Interestingly enough, Georgi accepts the possibil-

15. Georgi, *Die Gegner des Paulus im 2. Korintherbrief: Studien zur Religiösen Propaganda in der Spätantike*, WMANT 17 (Neukirchen, 1964), esp. pp. 145–67.

ity that the espousers of the *theios aner* Christology were of Palestinian origin.[16] Moreover, he reconstructs the concept of *theios aner* out of Jewish sources without undue reliance upon the earlier work of Ludwig Bieler.

Subsequently, D. L. Tiede's judicious and illuminating investigation of *theios aner* ideology in antiquity has contributed to the clarification of the subject and the terminology, the value of which had been questioned by those critical of Bieler's efforts to bring such a great variety and chronological range of evidence under one roof.[17] He, like Georgi, also finds religious types which can be designated *theioi andres* in the apologetic literature of Hellenistic Judaism. Moreover, the assumption of the prior existence of a uniform figure, and the ideologies associated with it, in Hellenism generally, as distinguished from Hellenistic Judaism, is carefully examined. Tiede judiciously and successfully avoids unnecessary and unwarranted hypotheses. Yet on balance I do not think it misleading or inaccurate to say that he often seems to grant the assumption that the sources of the divine man and accompanying ideology are to be sought in the wider world of late antiquity apart from Judaism. Within Judaism the *theios aner* is an assimilation or accommodation to a foreign form.[18]

From another quarter, however, Howard Kee, whose primary interest is the interpretation of the gospels, particularly Mark, has challenged the view that the literary genre of aretalogy and the figure of the divine man were fixed forms in antiquity which as such influenced the development and determined, positively or negatively, the purpose of the evangelists, particularly Mark and John.[19] (Kee be-

16. Ibid., pp. 51–60.

17. Tiede, *The Charismatic Figure as Miracle Worker*, SBLDS 1 (Missoula, 1972), a Harvard dissertation under the direction of Köster.

18. The organization of Tiede's work implies this. Yet he carefully avoids saying that Jewish portrayals of Moses as a *theios aner* were the result of wholesale borrowing of a foreign ideology (cf. p. 104): "It is probably not unfair to maintain that the unity that has been perceived in those depictions of Moses in Hellenistic Jewish literature arises as much from the Old Testament as from the consistency of the Hellenistic concept of the *theios aner*."

19. Kee, "Aretalogy and Gospel," *JBL* 92 (1973): 402–22. Cf. the presentation of M. Smith, "Prolegomena to a Discussion of Aretalogies, Divine Men, the Gospels and Jesus," *JBL* 90 (1971): 174-99, for an erudite survey of the relevant evidence and a very helpful summation of the literature.

lieves that Mark was more fundamentally determined by his association with and interest in apocalyptic thought and its implications
for a theological understanding of the history of Jesus.) Kee's reservations about the *theios aner* are based mainly on the scarcity of
evidence of persons specifically referred to by that term and of a
fixed literary form (aretalogy) governing the presentation of the lives
of such holy men. While Kee's questions about the appropriateness
of speaking of an ideology and literary form may be valid, the existence of miracle workers whose activity was understood as divine
empowerment is really not in question. Such figures existed, or were
though to exist, in Judaism as well as elsewhere. Moreover, Kee
willingly concedes the possibility that collections of miracle stories
existed in early Christianity (and elsewhere), but argues that the
meaning and function of such stories and collections must be understood from the total literary context in which they appear and cannot be taken as a given based upon a fixed literary form and ideology
associated with a divine man figure. Thus while advancing significant criticisms of certain trends in the investigation of miracle sources
and ideology, Kee does not foreclose the search for traditional collections of such stories in the Fourth Gospel or elsewhere.

Continuing interest in such a search is reflected in recent Johannine
investigations, particularly those of Fortna[20] and Nicol.[21] In view of
the recent tendency to find the *theios aner* in a (Hellenistic) Jewish
matrix, it is noteworthy that both these scholars think the Johannine *semeia*-collection is Jewish-Christian in origin. Although both
reflect the influence of recent opinion regarding the divine man and
aretalogies, neither is willing to say that the source portrays Jesus
as a divine man or to call it an aretalogy. Yet both understand the
miracles as answering to certain expectations and performing a recognized function.

Fortna places his Gospel of Signs, consisting of miracle and passion narratives and little else, in the setting of an early Christian
mission to Jews.[22] While avoiding the terms *theios aner* and aretalogy, he nevertheless ascribes to the source and its author a high,

20. R. T. Fortna, *The Gospel of Signs: A Reconstruction of the Narrative Source
Underlying the Fourth Gospel*, SNTSMS 11 (Cambridge, England, 1970).

21. W. Nicol, *The Semeia in the Fourth Gospel: Tradition and Redaction*, NovTSup
32 (Leiden, 1972).

22. Fortna, *Gospel of Signs*, pp. 223–25.

indeed naive, view of the legitimacy, function, and value of miracles, among which the resurrection is reckoned as the final and greatest sign of all. But Fortna does not regard the miracle tradition of his source as particularly primitive or of great historical value,[23] nor does he find in it an excess of specifically Jewish characteristics. Thus he agrees with E. Haenchen that the miracles of the Fourth Gospel represent a relatively developed and legendary form of the tradition.[24] His conclusions also seem to accord with the judgment that the miracles of the source are, following Dibelius' categorization, closest to the *Novellen* (tales) of the synoptic tradition.[25] Fortna thus presents us with a seeming anomaly, an early gospel consisting of a rather highly developed (and legendary) miracle tradition, which was used in a Christian mission to Hellenistic Jews but is not particularly distinguished by specifically Jewish motifs.[26] Moreover, J. Louis Martyn, whose views of the Fourth Gospel are closely allied with Fortna's, recognizes a difficulty in identifying a form of specifically messianic expectation in which miracles play a large role. At the same time, however, Martyn suggests that the solution to this problem may lie in the expectation of a prophetic deliverer, the prophet like Moses.[27]

Precisely this sort of expectation is said by Nicol to answer to a necessary aspect of the expectation of a miracle-working deliverer implicit in the Johannine source. Nicol endeavors to show that the miracle source or tradition upon which John drew contains important elements, including the use of *semeion* for miracle, that are

23. Ibid., pp. 227–28.

24. Haenchen, "Johanneische Probleme," *Gott und Mensch: Gesammelte Aufsätze* (Tübingen, 1965), p. 111: "Seine [John's] Tradition wie seine theologische Botschaft zeigen deutliche Spuren fortgeschrittener Entwicklung." Haenchen's article was originally published in ZTK 56 (1959): 19–54. Cf. Fortna, *Gospel of Signs*, p. 227: "On the whole the source shows a relatively developed form of the tradition."

25. *Gospel of Signs*, p. 227. The developed form of the tradition is said to be "evident both in its novelistic features and in the heightening of the miracle which it displays." Cf. Tiede, *Charismatic Figure*, pp. 280ff., who refers to unpublished papers of Georgi and James Brashler which make this point.

26. This seems to me to be a fair inference from Fortna, p. 223, where the Jewish-Christian milieu of the source is set forth.

27. Martyn, *History and Theology in the Fourth Gospel* (New York, 1968), pp. 84ff.

characteristically Jewish.[28] He, like Fortna, does not argue that the miracle source is primitive,[29] but he is able to explain some of its peculiarities by its putative Jewishness rather than as a result of a mainly inner-Christian development necessarily embracing a considerable period of time. Judaism and the Christian mission to Jews provide a sufficient and suitable context for the Johannine miracle tradition. Whether the Jewish background excludes Hellenistic traits, as Nicol appears to think, is however a pertinent question. In fact, there may be reason to think that the source in the form we have it is addressed to Jews who are already "Hellenistic."[30] Of course, Hellenistic Judaism was to be found within Palestine as well as without.[31]

A notable characteristic of the Hellenistic Judaism we know from such sources as Philo, Josephus, and the Wisdom of Solomon is its relative disinterest in apocalyptic eschatology. Precisely such disinterest is characteristic of the Johannine miracle tradition, in contrast to the synoptic, and of the Fourth Evangelist generally. But if in this important respect the source appears Hellenistic, what becomes of Bultmann's association of the *semeia*-source with the circle of Baptist disciples or the Christian mission to them? They were surely not Hellenists in any ordinary sense, and they like their founder prob-

28. See Nicol, *Semeia,* pp. 53–68. The evidence adduced by Nicol is summarized under the following heads (pp. 66–67): knowledge of Palestinian geography and customs; Aramaic words (Messiah, Cephas); Semitic sentence structure; LXX references to Elijah and Elisha; the presence of certain Jewish ideas: sin as the cause of illness (9:2); the expectation of an eschatological prophet (6:14); healing at a distance (4:46–54); the use of "Christ" as a Jewish title; the use of *semeion* rather than *dynamis* for miracle; the reaction to miracles of faith rather than astonishment.

29. Ibid., pp. 76–77. Yet Nicol thinks it is not without primitive and possibly historical features.

30. The language at least is Greek. In his review Fortna has correctly criticized Nicol's dichotomous distinction between Palestinian (or Jewish) and Hellenistic (*JBL* 93 [1974]: 120). On the basis of analogous use of the term *semeion* in John, the LXX and Hellenistic-Jewish sources, Formesyn opts for a Hellenistic-Jewish milieu as the basis for understanding the Johannine *semeia*. See Formesyn, *Le Sèmeion johannique et le Sèmeion hellénistique,* ALBO IV, 7 (Paris, 1962).

31. M. Hengel, *Judentum und Hellenismus: Studien zu ihre Begegnung unter besonderer Berücksichtigung Palästinas bis zur Mitte des 2. Jh. v. Chr.* WUNT 10 (Tübingen, 1969); note esp. pp. 191ff., "Das Judentum Palästinas als 'hellenistisches Judentum.' "

ably had a positive interest in apocalyptic. Does Bultmann's view again seem to be only an odd aberration? That a problem exists can scarcely be denied. But since the apocalyptic dimension of Jesus' own proclamation and activity is for the most part also missing from John's Gospel as a whole, its significance is not immediately clear. Whether this lack of apocalyptic perspective was characteristic of the Johannine tradition itself or only the result of the evangelist's editing is a fair question. Quite possibly it was already a feature of the miracle tradition in the form in which it was adopted by the evangelist. At any rate, the absence of apocalyptic motifs in the Gospel as a whole is the problem to be accounted for, and their absence from the miracle tradition only one aspect of it.

The association of the Fourth Gospel in some recent research with forms of Palestinian Judaism or Samaritanism in which miraculous deeds were expected from prophetic deliverers and quasi-messianic figures opens another avenue leading from the Gospel to the Baptist or his followers. In suggesting the expectation of a miracle-working Mosaic prophet as the solution to the problem posed by the lack of any very significant expectation that the Davidic Messiah would perform miracles, Martyn points to Wayne A. Meeks, *The Prophet-King*,[32] who has adduced impressive evidence suggesting a relation between Jewish speculation about Moses and Johannine Christology. Although earlier efforts to show that an elaborate and detailed Moses typology underlies the Johannine signs have not been convincing, the very term *semeion* evokes Moses' performance of signs—indeed, legitimating signs—before Pharaoh and the Egyptians. Other characteristics of the Johannine *semeia*, as of Johannine thought generally, are congenial with a milieu influenced by Jewish (or Samaritan) expectation of a prophet like Moses.[33] The fact that Moses appears in the Fourth Gospel as a foil for the presentation of Jesus is fully consonant with this view of the Johannine *semeia*. The later

32. Martyn, *History and Theology*, pp. 87ff. Cf. Meeks, *The Prophet-King: Moses Traditions and the Johannine Christology*, NovTSup 14 (Leiden, 1967), pp. 48–49, 162–64, 302ff. Nicol, *Semeia*, p. 80 n. 1, rejects E. Bammel's contention in *Miracles: Cambridge Studies in their Philosophy and History*, ed. C. F. D. Moule (London, 1965), pp. 188–89, that miracles were expected of the Messiah.

33. See Nicol, *Semeia*, pp. 79–87. Nicol also, in my opinion rightly, rejects efforts to show that John relates his seven *semeia* directly to the Exodus signs (p. 88 n. 4).

explicit Jesus-Moses dialectic might well then have its roots in the miracle tradition.

In discussions of Jewish expectations of a prophet or prophetic deliverer, Josephus' references to such figures as Theudas and the Egyptian, among others, are frequently cited.[34] These references are, of course, echoed in the New Testament (Acts 5:36–37; 21:38). Such personages worked, or promised to work, authenticating miracles. Their activity is of considerable interest for any consideration of prophetic ideology in the Fourth Gospel, and perhaps for the investigation of the historical Jesus. Most recently, Geza Vermes has set forth the evidence for such charismatic, miracle-working figures contemporary with Jesus. He also notes in this connection the expectation of the prophet like Moses, which is reflected in New Testament Christology.[35] Vermes regards those figures, who on the one hand raised hopes of God's deliverance of his people and on the other performed mighty deeds, as relevant to the historical understanding of Jesus. He also cites rabbinic evidence for the existence of other miracle-working charismatic figures such as Honi the Circle-drawer and Hanina ben Dosa.[36] In point of fact, over a quarter-century ago Franklin W. Young adduced some of the same evidence pertaining to the miracle-working prophets and drew similar conclusions about its importance for understanding Jesus.[37]

Vermes observes that the two key Old Testament figures associated with the expectation of an eschatological prophet were Moses and Elijah.[38] Moses, of course, looms large in the Fourth Gospel,

34. *Ant.* x x. 97–98 on Theudas; *Ant.* x x. 169ff. on the Egyptian; *Ant.* x x. 167–68 on the prevalence of such figures.

35. Vermes, *Jesus the Jew: A Historian's Reading of the Gospels* (London, 1973); see pp. 58–99 on charismatic and prophetic dimensions of Jesus and his Jewish milieu. On the figure of the prophet like Moses, see pp. 88, 94–99; cf. 66–67.

36. Ibid., pp. 67–82.

37. Young, "Jesus the Prophet: A Re-examination," *JBL* 58 (1949): 285–99. Young also draws attention to the dual role of such prophetic figures as miracle workers and deliverers of the people. There are recent and important discussions of the eschatological prophet in Ferdinand Hahn, *The Titles of Jesus in Christology: Their History in Early Christianity,* trans. H. Knight and G. Ogg (New York, 1969), pp. 352ff., and in R. H. Fuller, *The Foundations of New Testament Christology* (New York, 1965), pp. 46ff., 67ff., 125ff., 167ff. Both find the title and associated conceptuality to be quite primitive in the tradition, and Fuller at least thinks that Jesus himself may have consciously assumed the role, if not the title (pp. 127ff.).

38. *Jesus the Jew,* p. 94.

both as an alternative to Jesus (wrongly understood) and as one who points to him (rightly understood). Elijah seems to be less important, but not unimportant, in John. All the gospels reflect an early Christian or Christian-Jewish discussion about Elijah and the identity of Elijah *redivivus*, whether John or Jesus. Matthew (11:14; 17:10–13) and Mark (9:11–13), but not Luke, appear to accept the view that John is Elijah *redivivus*, while in the Fourth Gospel this is explicitly denied by the Baptist himself (1:19–21; cf. Luke 3:15ff.). This denial may have considerable significance.

JOHN THE BAPTIST AND THE QUESTION OF MIRACLE

Possibly John 1:19–21, or the tradition behind it, should be interpreted to mean that John is not *even* Elijah or the prophet, much less the Messiah. This is doubtless how Christians have usually read it. Probably the sense of the separate questions, as well as what is known about Jewish eschatological expectations, indicates three different figures are meant. Yet Bultmann is likely right in seeing in each title a form of the eschatological salvation-bearer, a messianic figure in the broader sense.[39] For John, along with the Christian tradition generally, Jesus is pre-eminently the Christ. Yet Elijah and the prophet, certainly closely related figures, were also important. The titles or roles of Elijah and the prophet are above and beyond the Baptist. Are they titles of Jesus? At least the eschatological roles assigned to Elijah and the prophet were fulfilled by Jesus in the view of the evangelist or his tradition source.[40] The expectation of the working of miracles, signs, associated with both these figures more than with the Messiah, is fulfilled by Jesus.

Interestingly enough, it is said of John the Baptist (who is, of course, never called that, but only John, in the Fourth Gospel) that he did no *semeion* (10:41). This statement may be held over against 1:19–21. Is it possible that both reflect a common viewpoint according to which Jesus is distinguished from John? John denies that he is the (miracle-working) prophet or Elijah as well as the Christ, and it is later said of him that he performed no sign.[41] The latter state-

39. *John*, pp. 88ff.
40. On the merging of Elijah and Moses motifs in the expected eschatological prophet, see Meeks, *Prophet-King*, p. 26. On Jesus as prophet in John, see Meeks, passim, but especially pp. 32–97 and 286–319.
41. Bultmann, *John*, p. 393 n. 2.

ment, which Bultmann with some hesitation assigned to the *semeia*-source, provides a link with Baptist circles which, if valid, would tend to support Bultmann's disposition of it and his original conjecture as to the origin of the source. John did not perform the miraculous signs of the eschatological salvation-bearer, whether Elijah or the prophet. Thus he is not Elijah, other Christian opinion to the contrary notwithstanding. In this connection it is worth noting that attention has been called to motifs linking Jesus' signs in John's Gospel with the Elijah-Elisha miracle cycles of the Old Testament.[42]

Although Bultmann assigns 1:19-21(ff.) to the evangelist, both Becker and Fortna ascribe it to the *semeia* collection.[43] E. Bammel hesitates to assign 1:19ff. to his sign-source ("Z"),[44] although he does not exclude the possibility of traditional materials here and at other points where John the Baptist unaccountably appears. It is tempting to conjecture that there is embedded in the Fourth Gospel a cycle of miracle stories which began with an account of the Baptist in which he explicitly denied that he was the miracle-working eschatological prophet (or Elijah, which amounts to about the same thing) and ended or reached an important culmination with the statement that John did no sign or miracle.[45] Such a miracle source

42. R. E. Brown, "Jesus and Elisha," *Perspective* 12 (1971): 85–104.

43. J. Becker, *NTS* 16 (1969–70), 135 and n. 2; Fortna, *Gospel of Signs*, pp. 167ff.

44. Bammel, *Miracles*, pp. 198–99.

45. R. E. Brown, *The Gospel According to John (i-xii)*, AB 29 (New York, 1966), p. 414, suggests "that at one time the Johannine sketch of the public ministry came to a conclusion with 10:40–42." Barnabas Lindars (*Behind the Fourth Gospel* [London, 1971], pp. 62, 70–71, 75–76), calls 1:19–10:42 the first division of the Gospel and suggests the original account of Jesus' ministry ended with the note about John in 10:41. Neither Brown nor Lindars accepts the *semeia*-source, of course. E. Bammel on the other hand thinks that 10:41 (as a part of the complex 10:40–42) "is the climax and summary of the report on the ministry of Jesus" in the *semeia*-source (*Miracles*, p. 201). Of the role of John in his own hypothetical reconstruction of the *semeia*-source ("Z"), Bammel says: "John was highly valued in Z, for his own actvity sets the course for Jesus' own way and his statements accompany the latter's activity. Indeed, Jesus' own direction evolves from the baptistic background. He is seen as the true disciple and successor of John, whose ministry is given special distinction by miracles, in a way like that of Elisha, in comparison with his former master." See Bammel, "The Baptist in Early Christian Tradition," *NTS* 18 (1971–2): 112.

would have presented Jesus as a performer of signs, and thus confirmed his prophetic role, over against John, who could not claim that role because he performed no sign. This is not to imply that elements of the *theios aner* figure and ideology are not present in the source. Something like that figure is to be found in the Gospel itself. Nor is it necessary to maintain that the traditional *semeia* are altogether free of Hellenistic influence. Yet such a proposal as we have just sketched locates the initial thrust for the development of the Johannine *semeia* within Judaism, where ample precedents are found, and even allows for the possibility that the portrayal of Jesus which we find in the Johannine miracle tradition may have ultimately descended from the historical Jesus himself.[46] Certainly Jesus was a miracle worker and apocalyptic preacher; he also accepted the title or description of prophet. That the miraculous and epiphanic elements are heightened beyond whatever historical basis the sign stories may have scarcely needs to be added.

The proposal of such a *semeia* collection is admittedly imprecise, for a comprehensive analysis of its content at this point is not my goal. Yet the credibility of the proposal, really an elaboration of Bultmann's suggestions in the light of more recent research, is further enhanced by an interesting consideration, which I believe has heretofore received little notice. John, like Jesus, was an apocalyptic preacher of God's judgment and deliverance. Like Jesus he was also martyred, if not crucified. Although we know of no direct claim by his disciples that John had been raised from the dead, the thought is said to have occurred to Herod and perhaps to others as well (Mark 6:14–16). In fact, Herod is said to have attributed the Baptist's (that is, Jesus') apparently newfound miraculous powers to his resurrection from the dead (Mark 6:14). But unlike Jesus, John had not been a miracle worker. Now, a *semeia*-source would not have convinced Jews generally that the crucified Jesus was the Messiah. For that, a passion narrative or the equivalent would have been necessary.[47] But a collection or cycle of miracle stories without a

46. Hahn emphasizes that Jesus' miracle-working answers to the expectations of the eschatological prophet rather than the Messiah (*Titles of Jesus*, p. 38; also nn. 199, 200).

47. See the following chapter in this book, "The Setting and Shape of a Johannine Narrative Source," originally published in *JBL* 95 (1976): 231–41.

passion narrative is entirely credible against the background of a general expectation of a miracle-working prophet, and specifically as a mission tract directed to members of the Baptist sect as a means of convincing them to shift their loyalty to Jesus. Jesus, not John, was the miracle-working prophet-messiah.

It may be granted that Jesus was probably also distinguished from John by virtue of his followers' belief in his resurrection, although some may have believed that John had been, or would be, raised from the dead. In any event, the argument that Jesus had been raised from the dead could not be based upon convincing public evidence or testimony. On the other hand, the miracles of Jesus could be presented as tangible public acts differentiating Jesus from John. Their public (that is, epiphanic) character is, in fact, emphasized in the Gospel, and presumably also in the source. Indeed, their public character is the presupposition of the discussions and debates which develop around them. If on other grounds a *semeia*-source with no accompanying sayings or discourses and passion suggests itself, the most plausible setting for it is the one adumbrated but not elaborated by Bultmann, namely the debate with and mission to followers of John the Baptist. In such a setting the absence of other features usually associated with a gospel, especially a passion narrative, becomes understandable. Moreover, the expectation of a miracle-working prophetic figure also helps explain the collection of Jesus' miraculous signs as a point of contrast with the Baptist.

A POSSIBLE OBJECTION

This suggestion needs further elaboration and testing. At least one problem or objection immediately presents itself, which we can here only mention and indicate why it does not militate decisively against the hypothesis just put forward.

The form of the Johannine miracle stories seems to resemble most closely the so-called *Novellen* (tales) of the synoptic tradition.[48] At least several of them function in their present setting as epiphany stories (e.g. 2:1–11; 2:12–22; 6:16–21). Not all the narratives with strong epiphanic traits are, however, clearly to be assigned to the *semeia*-source conceived strictly as a collection of miracle stories (e.g. 3:1–21; 4:1–25). Be that as it may, synoptic form criticism has

48. See n. 25 above.

tended to see stories with such novelistic and epiphanic characteristics as Hellenistic rather than Jewish.[49] While this classification of
the Johannine signs may be appropriate, it is not clear that it implies
a decisive objection. In the first place, the Johannine stories have
obviously been shaped by a strong christological, epiphanic interest, probably both in their formulation and in their collection. Certainly if their original purpose was to evangelize followers of John
the Baptist, this is what one would expect. Secondly, it is not clear
that the *Novelle* is exclusively a Hellenistic, rather than Jewish, form.[50]
Are not miracles and miracle stories as elaborate or novelistic as
anything in John to be found in the Jewish apocryphal and pseud-
epigraphal literature of the period, as well as in the Old Testament?[51] If Jewish characteristics appear in the Johannine *semeia*,
one is not obliged to regard them as secondary or peripheral. While
this specific question would profit from further investigation, there
is no need to acquiesce either in the view that so-called novelistic or
epiphanic stories or traits are Hellenistic or in the once-conven-
tional dichotomy of Hellenistic and Palestinian-Jewish, according
to which anything Hellenistic is considered *eo ipso* non-Jewish, or
at least non-Palestinian.

We began by calling attention to what seemed to be a curiosity,
if not an aberration, in Bultmann's opinion about the origin of the
semeia-source. But at length we have observed that in tracing the
hypothetical *semeia*-source to Christian converts from the John the
Baptist sect (who apparently used it as a missionary tract among
the Baptist's followers), Bultmann has pointed to a setting in which
the overall form (miracle collection without passion or sayings) and
the individual forms and content (novelistic, epiphanic stories) of
his source become intelligible and credible. Our development of this

49. Thus the position of Keck, *JBL* 84 (1965): 349ff., following Dibelius, is
typical. Against this widely held viewpoint see T. A. Burkill, "Mark 3:7–12 and
the Alleged Dualism in the Evangelist's Miracle Material," *JBL* 87 (1968): 409–17,
esp. 414–17.

50. See Burkill, *JBL* 87 (1968), 414–17; also Brown, *Perspective* 12 (1971): 96–
99, esp. 97. Brown protests against the tendency to classify longer, detailed miracle
stories (*Novellen*) as Hellenistic, when the Elijah and Elisha cycles of the Old
Testament offer ample specimens of the various miracle genres, with the Elisha
miracles generally closest to the more detailed stories of the gospels.

51. See e.g., 1 Kgs. 17:1–18:46, esp. 17:17–24; 2 Kgs. 4:18–37.

proposal does not immediately validate Bultmann's *semeia*-source hypothesis, for uncertainties and imponderables remain. Yet, if well-founded, it does constitute a significant contextual historical complement to the literary analysis.

3 | The Setting and Shape of a Johannine Narrative Source

T he purpose of this essay is to highlight certain directions of recent research on the character of Johannine narrative sources in order to inquire about their implications for determining the shape of any pregospel narrative.

THE EXISTENCE OF MIRACLE AND PASSION SOURCES

The search for the sources of the Fourth Gospel has a long history, but for much contemporary scholarship the issues have been most sharply delineated by the source-critical analysis of R. Bultmann, who found in the Gospel passion and miracle sources (*semeia*-source), as well as a revelation-discourse source and other lesser sources and traditions.[1] Although few scholars have accepted the discourse source, the evidence favoring the *semeia*- and passion sources has been widely acknowledged. The *semeia*-source has gained acceptance even among those who do not agree with Bultmann that, in adopting the source, the evangelist intended to correct or set aside its theology.[2]

1. *The Gospel of John: A Commentary* (Philadelphia: Westminster, 1971); cf. D. Moody Smith, *The Composition and Order of the Fourth Gospel: Bultmann's Literary Theory* (New Haven: Yale University Press, 1965), pp. 15–17.
2. E.g., E. Käsemann (*The Testament of Jesus: A Study of the Gospel of John in the Light of Chapter 17* [Philadelphia: Fortress, 1968]) takes the *semeia*-source for

The evidence for a *semeia*-source is partly circumstantial and partly exegetical (i.e., linguistic, contextual, and theological). Once it is granted that John's miracle tradition is not based upon the synoptics,[3] a miracle source (or a source that included miracles) becomes a reasonable hypothesis, and the attempt to identify it justifiable. Once such a task is undertaken, among the chief problems will be the limits and unity, or integrity, of the alleged source and the question of whether it lay before the evangelist in written form. These issues were already addressed by Bultmann in his exegetical analysis of the relevant texts. More recently R. T. Fortna has contributed substantially to the clarification of methodological questions and, through his own exegetical analysis, to the establishment of the written character of the miracle and related material.[4] If the very nature of the evidence may not permit a firm conclusion or a consensus on the question of the unity of any written source, there

---

granted (p. 37), but ascribes to the evangelist and the entire Gospel the positive view of miracles as manifestations of the glory of Jesus (pp. 21–22), which Bultmann assigns to the source.

3. Although the evidence is not entirely unambiguous and scholarly opinion is not unanimous, the trend of much recent work is against John's dependence upon the synoptics. J. Blinzler (*Johannes und die Synoptiker: Ein Forschungsbericht*, SBS 6 [Stuttgart: Katholisches Bibelwerk, 1965], 31–32) with some reason challenged my earlier statement ("The Sources of the Gospel of John: An Assessment of the Present State of the Problem," *NTS* 10 [1963–64]: 336–51, esp. p. 349) about an emerging consensus (e.g., P. Gardner-Smith, E. R. Goodenough, R. Bultmann, C. H. Dodd) on John's independence of the synoptics. Nevertheless, the positions taken by R. E. Brown (*The Gospel According to John (i-xii)*, AB-29 [Garden City, N.Y.: Doubleday, 1966], p. xlvii), R. Schnackenburg (*The Gospel According to St. John, Vol. 1: Introduction and Commentary on Chapters 1–4* [New York: Herder & Herder, 1968], pp. 41–43), J. N. Sanders (*A Commentary on the Gospel According to St. John*, ed. B. A. Mastin, HNTC [New York: Harper, 1968], pp. 8-12), L. Morris (*The Gospel According to John*, NICNT [Grand Rapids: Eerdmans, 1971], pp. 49–52), and R. T. Fortna (*The Gospel of Signs: A Reconstruction of the Narrative Source Underlying the Fourth Gospel*, SNTSMS 11 [Cambridge: Cambridge University, 1970], pp. 8–11, 226–28), all espousing Johannine independence of the synoptics, lead me to believe that I was pointing to the more significant direction of scholarship, whether or not that deserves to be called a consensus. C. K. Barrett (*The Gospel According to St. John* [London: S.P.C.K., 1956], p. 34), who believes that John knew at least Mark, carefully avoids claiming that he used any of the synoptics as sources in the sense that Matthew used Mark; cf. his article, "John and the Synoptic Gospels," *ExpT* 85 (1974): 228–33.

4. *The Gospel of Signs*, passim.

are nevertheless significant and widely acknowledge arguments and evidence on the side of a single (or major) collection of miracle stories.[5] These include: a degree of stylistic unity and distinctiveness among the miracle stories, which Fortna would extend also to the passion source;[6] the enumeration of (first and second) signs in 2:11 and 4:54 only, the latter somewhat incongruous in context; the inappropriateness of 20:30–31 as a summary of Jesus' ministry and of 12:37-38 as a summary of his public ministry, since only signs are mentioned (as would be appropriate for the conclusion of a *semeia*-source); the discovery, subsequent to Bultmann's proposal of a *semeia*-source, of evidence suggesting that Mark incorporated into his gospel written collections (or *catenae*) of miracle stories;[7] the fact that the redaction-critical analysis of the miracle complexes in John tends to isolate simpler miracle stories of similar type which seem in many cases to have been the basis for the development of distinctly Johannine discourses and dialogues.

The hypothesis that the aretalogy, or collection of miracle stories for propagandistic purposes, existed as a distinct and recognized literary form in Hellenism (or Judaism) is still a matter of discussion. If warranted, it would, of course, provide strong precedent for the Johannine source. The question of whether the theology of the source differed so decisively from the evangelist's as to afford a basis for source-critical judgments is a point debated among proponents of the *semeia*-source. Fortna was probably correct methodologically in assigning a secondary role to theological criteria in the separation of sources in John. Although such uncertainties commend

5. For a summation of the case for a Johannine miracle source, see J. M. Robinson, "The Miracles Source of John," *JAAR* 34 (1971): 339–48. Note also the survey and display of source-critical and related work on John 6 by R. Kysar, "The Source Analysis of the Fourth Gospel: A Growing Consensus," *NovT* 15 (1973): 134–52. While I cannot entirely share Kysar's high evaluation of consensus as the justification and basis for future work, I believe that his finding that "there is much greater agreement on the narrative portion of our chapter than the discourse passages" (p. 151) is typical of current scholarship, applicable to the whole Gospel, and, indeed, significant.

6. *The Gospel of Signs*, pp. 203–18, esp. 214–16.

7. L. E. Keck, "Mark 3:7–12 and Mark's Christology," *JBL* 84 (1965): 341–58; also P. J. Achtemeier, "Toward the Isolation of Pre-Markan Miracle Catenae," *JBL* 89 (1970): 265–91; "The Origin and Function of the Pre-Marcan Miracle Catenae," *JBL* 91 (1972): 198-221.

caution, the lines of evidence cited, when seen in conjunction with the probability that the Johannine miracle tradition is mainly independent of the synoptic and with the exegetical evidence of its written character, understandably persuade many of the existence of a *semeia* or miracle source of considerable size and scope.

If the passion source, also proposed by Bultmann, has not been so much in the center of discussion as the miracle source, it is perhaps only because many scholars would agree that John must have employed some such independent source (or tradition), if, as seems likely, he did not rely upon the synoptics.[8] Whereas the question of the unity of the miracle or *semeia*-source remains a matter for discussion, the very character of the passion suggests, or indeed requires, that a passion source should have had some elemental unity or continuity. The existence of such a source may be regarded as probable; that it was written rather than oral somewhat less so.

Thus among scholars presently working on the problem of narrative sources in John some points of agreement have emerged, which

8. For the isolation of the passion source, see Fortna, *Gospel of Signs*, pp. 113–58, and the works cited on p. 113 n.2, pp. 113–15, and passim. In more recent literature, note also R. E. Brown, *The Gospel According to John (xii-xxi)*, AB29A: Garden City, N.Y.: Doubleday, 1970), pp.787–91, esp. 789–91, in whose view John used a passion tradition (or source) independent of the synoptics. A. Dauer (*Die Passionsgeschichte im Johannesevangelium: Eine traditionsgeschichtliche und theologische Untersuchung zu Joh. 18, 1–19, 30*, StANT 30 [Munich: Kösel, 1972]) isolates a pre-Johannine passion tradition (influenced at points by the synoptics, although not dependent upon them) which, he very tentatively suggests, may have lain before the evangelist in written form (p. 227). Even less than Dauer is E. Haenchen ("Historie und Geschichte in den johanneischen Passionsberichten," *Die Bible und Wir: Gesammelte Aufsätze* [Tübingen: Mohr (Siebeck), 1968], II, 182–207) willing to hypothesize a written passion source. He remarks, "Der Evangelist schreibt nicht (umarbeitend) eine Quelle aus, sondern erzählt eine ihm—vielleicht nur vom Hören bekannte—Geschichte neu auf seine Weise" (p. 192 n. 25). Yet Haenchen also thinks that John's passion tradition is independent of the synoptics. Earlier, C. H. Dodd (*Historical Tradition in the Fourth Gospel* [Cambridge: Cambridge University Press, 1964]) had thought primarily in terms of an independent oral tradition (p. 150), but explicitly conceded that written sources may have intervened between the oral stage and the present gospel (p. 424). Cf. also F. Hahn, "Der Prozess Jesu nach dem Johannesevangelium: Eine redaktionsgeschichtliche Untersuchung," in EKKNT (Vorarbeiten Heft 2; Neukirchen: Neukirchener Verlag, 1970), pp. 23–96, who speaks of a "vorjohanneische Überlieferungskomplex" which consisted of certain material in chaps. 11–17 as well as 18:1–3.

may be stated in a decreasing order of probability as follows: (1) John used a passion narrative and (2) a tradition of miracle stories independent of the synoptics; (3) the passion narrative was in written form; (4) the miracle stories had already been written down (5) in a single (or major) source document. (Points 1 and 2, as well as 3 and 4, may be regarded as interchangeable.) Without going so far as to claim the existence of a consensus, the significance of which would in any case be subject to question, I wish now to entertain the hypothesis, already comprehensively argued by others, that the Fourth Gospel is dependent on a written source for its miracle stories and a written source for its passion narrative, and to ask about the possible literary relations of those two source narratives prior to the composition of the Gospel in its present form. In doing so, the question of the milieu of the *semeia* or miracle source becomes significant.

THE MILIEU OF THE MIRACLE SOURCE

Bultmann's understanding of the milieu of his *semeia*-source was somewhat ambiguous. On the one hand, he states that the term σημεῖον is the equivalent of miracle in Hellenism[9] and that the *semeia*-source portrays Jesus as a θεῖος ἄνθρωπος.[10] Yet the same source is apparently to be traced to Christian circles stemming from the Palestinian-Jewish sect of John the Baptist.[11] If these positions are not necessarily contradictory, Bultmann does not clarify how they stand in relation to one another. But J. Becker, taking up and refining Bultmann's proposal in opposition to E. Käsemann's view of the theology of John, probably represents a widely held estimate of Bultmann's own view when he writes: "Alle theologischen Wesenzüge der Wundergeschichten in der Quelle gehören in diese

9. *Gospel of John*, p. 114 n. 1.

10. Ibid., p. 180.

11. Bultmann states that the evangelist was probably converted from among the Baptist's followers, as 1:35-51 may indicate (ibid., p. 108; cf. p. 18). That text is in turn said to be based on a source which had formed a part of the propaganda disseminated by such disciples for the Christian faith (p. 108 n. 6). This source is then a part of the same source from which 2:1-12 was drawn, viz., the *semeia*-source (p. 113). The *semeia*-source, replete with Semitisms, was probably written in Greek by a Greek-speaking Semite (p. 98 n. 6). On this set of problems see the immediately preceding chapter of this book.

θεῖος-ἀνήρ-Vorstellung des Hellenismus."[12] At about the time this verdict was announced, however, R. Fortna published a monograph on the narrative source of John, which he conceived to include both signs and passion, and suggested that it originated and served a missionary purpose in the Christian mission to the synagogue.[13] That viewpoint was developed in connection with the overall theory of J. L. Martyn regarding the origin of the Fourth Gospel in the synagogue controversy over the messianic claims advanced for Jesus.[14] The Gospel of Signs reconstructed by Fortna single-mindedly pressed home these messianic or christological claims.

Subsequent to the appearance of Fortna's work W. Nicol published a monograph in which he sought to make meaningful progress on several fronts in the investigation of the signs material.[15] Not only did he subject it to form-critical analysis in an effort to establish its traditional character, *Sitz im Leben*, type, and affinities with synoptic miracle stories.[16] He also compared it with other narrative material in the Fourth Gospel and established that it can be distinguished stylistically and linguistically from that narrative material which can be ascribed more directly to the evangelist.[17] Perhaps most important for our purposes, he proposed a *Sitz im Leben* for the miracle material within the Johannine community by showing its predominantly Jewish character and, as he thinks, the absence of Hellenistic traits.[18] He understands its milieu to be a Christian community in conflict with the synagogue but still conducting a mission

12. "Wunder und Christologie: Zum literarkritischen und christologischen Problem der Wunder im Johannesevangelium," *NTS* 16 (1969–70): 130–48, esp. 141.

13. *Gospel of Signs*, pp. 223, 225, 228–30. Cf. "From Christology to Soteriology: A Redaction-Critical Study of Salvation in the Fourth Gospel," *Int* 27 (1973): 31–37.

14. *History and Theology in the Fourth Gospel* (New York: Harper, 1968).

15. *The Semeia in the Fourth Gospel: Tradition and Redaction*, NovTSup 32: (Leiden: Brill, 1972), He cites Fortna, but his work is principally independent.

16. Ibid., pp. 41–43.

17. Ibid., pp. 16–18.

18. Ibid., pp. 48–68. Cf. R. Formesyn, *Le sèmeion johannique et le sèmeion hellénistique*, ALBO IV (Paris: Desclée de Brouwer, 1962), who agrees that the *semeia* tradition is indeed Jewish in character, but argues for a Hellenistic-Jewish (Christian) provenance. Note also Fortna's criticism of the attempt to exclude Hellenistic influence in his review of W. Nicol, *JBL* 93 (1974): 120.

among Jews. For this mission the *semeia*-source was composed; it was a missionary tract. Nicol's view of the function and milieu of the miracle material thus also comports well with Martyn's (and Fortna's) developing understanding of the setting from which the Fourth Gospel arose.

Although I find Nicol's arguments for Jewish and Old Testament parallels, allusions, and characteristics in the source impressive, my purpose is not to evaluate his work. I wish principally to point out that, in arguing for such a provenance and purpose of the signs material, Nicol has, in effect, and apparently unwittingly, suggested a rationale for Fortna's position that the narrative source lying behind the Fourth Gospel was a primitive gospel, i.e., a document containing both miracles and a passion narrative. For in developing a case for the Jewish milieu of the *semeia*, Nicol raises a question about the viability of his own delineation of the source, which he limits to signs-narratives.[19] Would a collection of miracle stories alone have sufficed as a missionary document for use among Jews? The simple and obvious answer to such a question is that it could not have. Of course, such a simple and obvious answer may prove misleading and obscure genuine complexities. Yet it is hard to see how any narrative source which failed to take account of and in some way explain the execution of the messianic claimant could have long proved useful as a missionary tract for Jews. The reasons for this are clear enough. The purpose of the sign source was to demonstrate that Jesus was the expected Messiah by displaying his miraculous power. Such miraculous power may have carried considerable probative force, despite its tenuous correspondence with conventional Jewish messianic expectations. Yet the weight of such demonstrations could scarcely set aside the objections or questions raised by the fact of Jesus' crucifixion. The observation that the *kerygma* of the cross (and resurrection) was not necessarily central to all early Christian preaching, while possibly true, would not be relevant to refute this line of argument, for it is not a matter of the

19. Nicol actually leaves open the questions of whether his source may have contained other narratives (*Semeia*, p. 6) and whether it was copied verbatim (p. 5). Yet, as his work unfolds, he seems to envision a written source consisting principally of miracles. Had an accompanying passion narrative been contemplated, other considerations (e.g., its relation to the Jewish-mission milieu) would have demanded attention.

unity or diversity of the *kerygma*. The death of Jesus as a criminal seems to have been the one historical fact about him known to both Jew and Greek.[20] It is hardly conceivable that for years on end a mission to Jews could have been prosecuted on the basis of such a document alone, without the problem of the crucifixion having reared its head.

There are, of course, a number of conceivable settings and functions in which a miracle collection might have a long and useful life. For example, L. E. Keck points to the lack of distinctively Jewish characteristics in the miracle stories of Mark 4:35–5:43, as distinguished from Mark 2:1–3:6, and suggests that they constitute a pre-Marcan miracle cycle in which Jesus is portrayed as a θεῖος ἀνήρ.[21] P. J. Achtemeier, in proposing a double miracle *catena* in Mark, similar to but more elaborate than Keck's proposed cycle, postulates a eucharistic setting for it in early Christianity.[22] He also thinks that a divine man Christology inspired and informed the substance and shape of the collection and suggests a plausible setting in Christian worship. Both Keck and Achtemeier understand the *theios aner* Christology expressed in their hypothetical sources as Hellenistic and not Jewish, a view which comports well with the widely held view of the Gentile Christian provenance of Mark's Gospel. In such a religious thought-world a miracle *catena* could even have served a missionary purpose. There the crucifixion of a Jewish messianic claimant need not have presented a crucial problem, since he was now proclaimed as raised from the dead. But the use of such a source as a missionary tract in a setting in which Jewish opposition would surely have raised questions about the crucifixion is more difficult to imagine. In that case, the "scandal" of the crucifixion of the Messiah would in all probability have led to a questioning of the claims made for him, i.e., both of the messianic claims and of the claim of resurrection itself. Thus, for apologetic reasons

20. See the Jewish and pagan evidence conveniently collected by M. Goguel, *The Life of Jesus* (New York: Macmillan, 1933), pp. 70–104. Especially noteworthy are the references in the Baraita of *b. Sanh.* 43a to the hanging of Jesus on the eve of Passover and in Tacitus' *Annals,* 15.44 to his being executed by Pontius Pilate during the reign of Tiberius.

21. See n. 7 above.

22. See n. 7 above.

a miracle source intended to convert Jews would have required a passion narrative designed to forestall such hostile questioning.

The passion narratives of the gospels are not without traces of such Christian apologetic interests, and John's Gospel is no exception. The tendency to shift the blame from the Romans to the Jews is already present in Mark, becomes stronger in Matthew and Luke, and is perhaps strongest of all in John. In all probability the statements of Jesus and Pilate in John which make this shift most explicit are compositions of the evangelist, perhaps reflecting Jewish-Christian polemic. Yet, the passion account of Fortna's Gospel of Signs also manifests this interest.[23] On the face of it, such a shift does not appear to be a missionary tactic, and it may also be understood as an effort to placate the Roman authorities. Yet it might well have appeared in a Christian community whose efforts to convert the synagogue had been rebuffed and whose claims about Jesus had been rejected by those in authority there. Doubtless the tendency to shift the blame to the Jews grew stronger with the passage of time and as it became ever more apparent to the earliest Christians that the Jewish authorities, and Jews in general, were not going to follow them in their belief that the crucified Jesus was the Messiah of Israel. The polemic actually has some potential as a missionary device, for through it the sin of the Jewish nation (and ultimately of the individual, on the one hand, and of mankind, on the other) in rejecting the messianic claims of Jesus is exposed and the basis is laid for the preaching of repentance and forgiveness of sins through Jesus Christ.

There is also another line of apologetic, viz., the passion apologetic[24] based upon Old Testament testimonia. It presupposes a Jewish audience and probably arose out of the necessity to preach and defend the gospel by showing that the death of Jesus took place according to God's will. In John, as in the other gospels, Old Testament testimonia form an important part of the passion narrative and are probably also a primitive element. All of the Johannine fulfillment-formula quotations fall within the broader scope of the passion

23. See 18:38–40 in Fortna's reconstruction, *Gospel of Signs,* 243.

24. The term is B. Lindars's. See his stimulating study, *New Testament Apologetic: The Doctrinal Significance of the Old Testament Quotations* (Philadelphia: Westminster, 1961), pp. 75–137, and esp. pp. 265–67.

narrative.[25] These quotations are largely derived from or related to a traditional stock of testimonia used by the earliest Christians to interpret Jesus' death.[26] They are probably more primitive in interest, outlook, and form than the references and allusions to scripture which appear so frequently elsewhere in the Gospel.[27] C. H. Dodd regards them as a part of the early (oral) passion tradition, upon which John built his narrative.[28] B. Lindars argues that John stands closer to the interests and circumstances of their original use than does Matthew.[29] Moreover, Fortna finds all of the Old Testament quotations in the Gospel of Signs in the passion narrative.[30]

The interests reflected in the Johannine passion narrative comport well with the view that John used a primitive passion source not

25. See 12:38; 13:18; 15:25; 17:12; 19:24; 19:28; 19:36, all of which have to do with the rejection, betrayal, and death of Jesus. The notion of fulfillment is also present in 12:13–16 and in 2:17, 22, as Lindars (*New Testament Apologetic*, p. 267) has pointed out. Since in each case the text "gives scriptural warrant to one essential element of the story," they are all testimonies in the strict (and primary) sense. The temple cleansing (2:13–22), although not a part of the passion in the present form of the Gospel, is closely related to it and may have stood within the passion narrative at an earlier stage of the tradition or composition history behind the Gospel.

26. Lindars, *New Testament Apologetic*, p. 269; C. H. Dodd, *Historical Tradition*, pp. 46–47.

27. Cf. Günter Reim, *Studien zum alttestamentlichen Hintergrund des Johannesevangelium*, SNTSMS 22 (Cambridge: Cambridge University Press, 1974), who finds that the quotations are mostly traditional in origin and appear in traditional contexts (pp. 93–94). The knowledge of the Old Testament displayed in the references and allusions of the discourses, although derived mainly from Christian or Jewish tradition (rather than from a written text), is, however, employed by the evangelist in the development of his own creative and distinctive theological perspective. Commenting on 19:28b, A. Dauer (*Passionsgeschichte*, p. 204) writes: "[John's] Schriftgebrauch unterscheidet sich wesentlich von der 'simple testimony method,' die keine enge Verbindung 'with the specifically Johannine theology' zu haben scheint." His quotations are from C. K. Barrett, "The Old Testament in the Fourth Gospel," *JTS* 48 (1947): 155–69, who long ago saw this distinction between John's own use of scripture and his adoption of the traditional testimonies and testimony method.

28. *Historical Tradition*, pp. 44–49. Dodd writes (p. 49): "Where the narrative is ultimately related to testimonies from the Old Testament . . . there we may be fairly sure that we are in touch with the common tradition of the Church, and not with the theological construction of some individual."

29. *New Testament Apologetic*, pp. 271–72.

30. *The Gospel of Signs*, p. 229.

identical with the synoptics. Moreover, they embrace such apologetic and theological concerns as would have arisen in a Christian community under the necessity of explaining or defending the gospel when confronted by accusations stemming from the crucifixion of Jesus. While a good deal of the material expressing these interests is on most accountings the work of the evangelist himself, it is not best perceived as an imposition upon a neutral source, but as a development of interests already clearly present in the basic source or tradition. Thus the Old Testament citations in the Johannine passion are of traditional origin and are found in traditional contexts.

It should now be amply clear why Nicol's plausible case for the use of the *semeia*-source as missionary tract for Jews, when set in the broader contexts of the question of Johannine narrative sources generally and of the kinds of issues such a use of a miracle source designed to prove the messiahship of Jesus would have actually raised, really implies rather strong support for Fortna's proposal of a Gospel of Signs as at least an intermediary stage between the formation of the two types of narrative material and the present highly articulated Gospel with its rather sophisticated theological perspectives and insights.

THE REDACTION-CRITICAL DISPOSITION OF 12:37–40 (41)

Bultmann, followed by Becker, assigned 12:37–38 (but not vv. 39-41) to the *semeia*-source, mainly on the basis of its suitability (with 20:30–31) as the conclusion of that source and its theological and contextual inappropriateness as a description of Jesus' total public ministry.[31] One is then left, however, with a source which simply ends on the note of Jewish rejection of Jesus together with a statement about Jesus having done other signs (20:30–31). That this has seemed to some an improbable ending is not surprising. Fortna, followed by Nicol, assigns 12:37–38 to the evangelist rather than to the source.[32] Yet against the latter solution one may object

31. Bultmann, *The Gospel of John*, p. 453. Cf. Becker, "Wunder und Christologie," pp. 133, 135.

32. Fortna, *The Gospel of Signs*, p. 199: "The possibility of not believing in signs is one which only John (not SQ) conceives." Cf. W. Nicol, *The Semeia in the Fourth Gospel*, p. 30. But if our disposition of 12:37–38 is correct (below), the introduction of the possibility of not believing in signs at this point is explained.

that for the evangelist to sum up Jesus' public ministry in terms of "signs" is strange in the present context, particularly when Jesus has just been speaking with the crowd rather than working miracles. It is true that in other instances Jesus' ministry is described in terms of signs or miracles, as Fortna (followed by Nicol) points out. Yet these instances occur at points where someone, or a group, refers to the signs that Jesus has done as a basis for an estimation of him, and such characterizations uniformly convey the point of view of outsiders, or of those who have not yet come to a truly adequate understanding and knowledge of Jesus. 12:37–38, on the other hand, is an overall statement, presumably made from an adequate faith perspective (whether it stems from the evangelist or the source), according to which faith is the intended or proper result of Jesus' ministry of signs. Thus neither disposition of 12:37–38 is without objection.

Without attempting to refute either or both of them, however, I wish to suggest a third view of these verses (together with vv. 39–41) which presents an intriguing possibility. May not 12:37 be regarded as a primitive transition from sign source to the passion, whereby the seemingly contradictory narratives of the Messiah's mighty works, already understood as *semeia*, and his suffering and death are brought together and the latter are made understandable in the light of the former? "Though he had done so many signs before them, they did not believe in him" writes John, or his source, and in support of this statement an Old Testament testimonium is cited: Isaiah 53:1, quoted also by Paul in Romans 10:16, and in the context of a general effort to explain Jewish unbelief. If Fortna's proposal of a primitive Jewish-Christian gospel is justified, and there are grounds to think that it is, such a gospel would seem to require such a transitional statement. Where it might best fit in his reconstruction I hesitate to say, although before or among the narratives of Jesus' entry into Jerusalem and his deeds there (chap. 12) would be an obvious place.

The traditional ring of this passage with its Old Testament testimonium, and therefore its place in the source, would be reinforced if one could also regard vv. 39–41 as an original part of it rather than a later addition by the evangelist. Certainly Isaiah 6:9–10 was also a traditional early Christian testimonium; like Isaiah 53:1, it appears elsewhere in the New Testament (Mark 4:12, and par.; Acts

28:26–27) to explain Jewish unbelief. Bultmann's argument that 12:38 and 40, which represent different text types, "can hardly have been written by one hand" applies only to the points at which they were adopted into the Christian apologetic tradition and is not necessarily relevant to the question of whether they belonged to the *semeia*-source. The *semeia*-source (or whatever tradition one posits) may have incorporated the quotations from different Old Testament apologetic traditions. That Isaiah 6:10 in John 12:40 is not cited according to the LXX or the Hebrew bespeaks its traditional Christian origin, rather than its incorporation by the evangelist. Bultmann, probably rightly, identifies the introductory formula (*dia touto . . . hoti*) as typical of the evangelist, but this does not necessarily mean that the evangelist did not derive the quotation from the same source as the Isaiah 53:1 quotation in v. 38. The parenthetical comment of v. 41 may also be from the evangelist, as Bultmann thinks, but again this says nothing about the origin of the citation of v. 40, whose fundamental sense and purpose accord with that of v. 38. Moreover, the fact that John's rendering of Isaiah 6:10 omits all reference to hearing but speaks only of seeing (and understanding) is surely significant. This omission is in accord with the character of the hypothetical source—one only sees miracles—rather than the viewpoint of the evangelist. Since a reference to "believing a report" stands in the immediately preceding testimonium, the evangelist would likely have left intact the original reference to hearing in Isaiah 6:10 had he introduced the testimonium. For this reason too one may be justified in regarding 12:37–40(41) in toto as a part of John's larger source, or at least in seeing in the second testimonium (v. 40) a vestige of the same source or literary stratum found in vv. 37–38.[33] The character and probably the traditional function of both testimonia correspond well with the proposal that they are the keystone of a primitive transition from signs to passion. Their use fits exactly the Jewish *Sitz im Leben* which Martyn, Fortna, and Nicol ascribe to the sign material, as well as the evident interests of the Johannine passion.

In conclusion, we ask whether one may not see here, at this nexus (12:37–40), a primitive nucleus of the gospel genre, and thereby

33. G. Reim (*Studien zum alttestamentlichen Hintergrund*, pp. 36, 39, 209, 217, 272) assigns 12:37–41 to the *semeia*-source.

gain some insight into the forces which brought the genre itself into being? A primitive gospel appears once a written miracle tradition is combined with a traditional passion story.[34] Perhaps in some instances (e.g. Mark) this combination occurred for inner-Christian, theological reasons. But in others it may have been occasioned by apologetic considerations, i.e., considerations forced upon the church by its adversaries or by those who were objects of its missionary endeavor. This may well have been the case in the Johannine community. There miracle tradition and passion tradition quite possibly grew side by side, but were brought into juxtaposition when questions and objections made the one useless without the other. In the Johannine community, and perhaps elsewhere, the passion may not have originally occupied the central role in preaching which it held, for example, in Paul. But its inclusion among the basic elements of Christian proclamation and thought need not have, and probably did not, come about for theological reasons arising within a Christian community only, but as a result of questions posed to that community by those outside to whom the community addressed itself in mission.

To summarize: If the miracle narratives were directed to a Jewish audience with the missionary purpose of proving that Jesus was the Messiah, the questions of that audience would in all probability have necessitated the early addition of a passion narrative, if it had not been a part of the narrative source in the first instance. It is also arguable that the Johannine passion source reflects such an audience. If passion and miracle sources were drawn together in view of such a purpose, John 12:37–40 with its two testimonia, both of which are used elsewhere in the New Testament to explain Jewish rejection of Jesus or the gospel, becomes intelligible as an early transition between them.

34. I leave aside for the moment the question (raised by R. E. Brown in his critique of R. T. Fortna at the 1969 meeting of the SBL in Toronto), whether a "gospel" without a sayings tradition is a gospel, or whether a document of such sort ever actually existed. It is not necessarily a problem for the proposal suggested, which is not bound to a rigorous separation of discourse from narrative. Nevertheless, it is well worth observing that the discourses of the Fourth Gospel, particularly in chaps. 2–12, seem to presuppose and devolve from earlier traditional stories, usually from miracle stories.

Part 2	John and the Synoptics

4 | John 12:12ff. and the Question of John's Use of the Synoptics

Nothing better indicates the uncertain state of our knowledge of the origins of the books of the New Testament than the question of the relation of the Gospel of John to the synoptics. After it had become apparent to most scholars that John was not the work of the son of Zebedee, and probably not the work of an eyewitness at all, it was generally regarded as a later product of the Hellenistic church, written after all the other gospels had been completed and were in circulation. It was widely supposed and frequently asserted that John (I use the term because it is convenient as well as traditional) had at his disposal one or more of the synoptic gospels.[1] Those who held this view could even cite in support of their position the testimony of the Muratorian Canon and Clement of Alexandria (cf. Eusebius, *HE* 6. 14. 7), for both ancient sources imply that John wrote his gospel in full cognizance of the others.[2]

The last twenty-five years, however, have seen a perceptible shift in the tide of critical opinion, and not without reason. It must be conceded that the value of the patristic evidence is negligible, since the early Christian writers were naturally concerned to explain why the Fourth Gospel differed so markedly from the other three. In

1. B. H. Streeter, *The Four Gospels: A Study in Origins* (rev. ed., 1930), pp. 395–426.
2. Cf. C. K. Barrett, *The Gospel According to St. John*, pp. 96–97.

order to do so it was necessary to assume that John himself was familiar with the other gospels and purposefully set down a different one in order to supplement them. Critical scholarship, of course, has no apologetic interest in John's knowledge of or dependence upon the other gospels, although many scholars have thought that there were ample grounds for affirming it. It is obvious enough that John and the synoptics share some of the same tradition, e. g., the passion, the feeding of the multitude, the anointing of Jesus, and the entry of Jesus into Jerusalem. But many of the narratives and most of the discourses in John are just as obviously quite different from anything in Matthew, Mark, and Luke, and the narratives that are parallel differ in inaccountable ways. It goes without saying that much of the tradition contained in the other gospels does not recur in any shape or form in John. Therefore, efforts to understand John over against the synoptics are subject to question, whether it is maintained that John sought to displace,[3] correct,[4] or interpret[5] those gospels. In 1938 P. Gardner-Smith published a significant monograph emphasizing the necessity of taking proper account of the dissimilarities and differences, as well as the parallels and similarities, in dealing with the problem of John and the synoptics.[6] He argued that the parallels and similarities have been greatly overemphasized, and that a careful assessment of both factors leads to the conclusion that there is no compelling reason for believing that John used the synoptics in composing his work. This conclusion has received impressive support in the subsequent investigations of Goodenough, Bultmann, Noack, Haenchen, and Dodd.[7] While it

3. H. Windisch, *Johannes und die Synoptiker.*

4. E. C. Colwell, *John Defends the Gospel,* esp. pp. 7–14.

5. E. C. Hoskyns, *The Fourth Gospel,* ed. F. N. Davey (1947), pp. 58–85. Hoskyns maintains that the Fourth Evangelist exercised an interpretative function in relation to a tradition like that of the synoptic gospels. He wisely avoids the claim that John used the synoptics in their present form: "That the author of the Fourth Gospel had the three synoptic gospels before him when he composed his gospel is most improbable, for his relation to them is not that of an editor. But that he was familiar with the synoptic material, and even with its form, is certain" (p. 82). The form in which Hoskyns sets forth the thesis is most suggestive and productive for exegesis.

6. *St. John and the Synoptic Gospels.*

7. E. R. Goodenough, "John a Primitive Gospel," *JBL* 64 (1945): 145–82, esp. 150–60, 169–70; R. Bultmann, *Das Evangelium des Johannes* (1957 ed.) passim;

cannot be claimed that the question is settled and the subject closed, there is a growing consensus that John's reliance upon, or use of, the synoptics is to be minimized, if not denied.[8] Certainly it can no longer be assumed that the burden of proof lies solely on whoever questions or denies the relationship. Nor can one who affirms this relationship assume it and merely bring forth evidence to illustrate and support it. It is precisely the question of the relationship itself which is at issue.

In a recent and instructive article[9] Edwin D. Freed maintains that a study of the Old Testament quotations in John's account of the entry into Jerusalem (i. e., Ps. 118:25-26 and 12:13 and Isa. 40:9 [?] with Zech. 9:9 in 12:15) "reveals some interesting insights into John's method when using Synoptic material." Freed proposes to show that "in the composition of the account of Jesus' entry into Jerusalem John was indebted to the Synoptics, even for the quotations, and that he used elements from their account to strengthen his theme of Jesus' kingship."[10] Now, if one can assume that John knew and used the synoptics at all, Freed's article must be considered an admirable illumination of the way in which the evangelist employed his sources. But if — as I believe — this cannot be assumed, it is necessary to ask whether Freed is able to make a con-

---

B. Noack, *Zur johanneischen Tradition* (1954), pp.89–109, 111ff.; E. Haenchen, "Johanneische Probleme," *ZTK* 56 (1959): 19–54; C. H. Dodd, *The Interpretation of the Fourth Gospel*, pp. 448–49. Several recent monographs on the origin of the Fourth Gospel make no attempt to show a dependence upon the synoptics. Cf. W. Wilkens, *Die Entstehungsgeschichte des vierten Evangeliums* (1958), esp. p. 174; A. Guilding, *The Fourth Gospel and Jewish Worship: A Study of the Relation of St. John's Gospel to the Ancient Jewish Lectionary System* (1960).

8. Although Barrett seems to adhere to the view that John knew and used the synoptics, he carefully qualifies and restricts it: "It may be laid down at once that John did not use any of the synoptic gospels as, for example, Matthew used Mark. The most that may be claimed (and it will be claimed in the present discussion) is that John had read Mark, and was influenced both positively and negatively by its contents . . . and that a few of John's statements may be most satisfactorily explained if he was familiar with matter peculiar to Luke" (p.34). In a footnote (p. 34 n. 1) Barrett says that "the literary problem urgently calls for further examination."

9. Edwin D. Freed, "The Entry into Jerusalem in the Gospel of John," *JBL* 80 (1961): 329–38.

10. Ibid., p. 329.

vincing case for John's use of the synoptics with the evidence he cites. This question is all the more pressing in view of the growing skepticism of this once commonly held position.

A comprehensive examination of Freed's presentation would result in an article longer than his. I wish only to examine what seem to me to be his important arguments in the light of one decisive question: can the similarities and differences in the Johannine account be explained — or even best be explained — only by the hypothesis that John used the synoptics as sources?

In any comparison of the parallel pericopes in all four gospels, two things are at once clear: (1) the Johannnine account deals with the same events as the others; (2) the Johannine account is not a variant of any or all of the synoptic accounts in the way in which for example, Matthew's account is a variant of Mark's. In both John and the synoptic versions, tree branches of some sort play a role. In both, the event is viewed as the fulfillment of Old Testament prophecy; the quotation from Psalm 118:25 (LXX Ps. 117:25) appears in all the synoptics and John, and Zechariah 9:9 in Matthew and John. In contrast to the synoptics, however, John places the whole incident immediately after the anointing of Jesus, while Matthew and Mark put the anointing after the entry and Luke places the anointing in an entirely different context. John says nothing about the preparation for the entry. Neither does he report that the crowd cast garments upon the animal Jesus was to ride and strewed them, together with branches, in his path. (Unlike the synoptics, however, John specifies that the crowd took palm branches.) John alone portrays the crowd of festival pilgrims as coming out from Jerusalem to meet Jesus rather than joining him on the way in, and he alone omits reference to the procession. Only John reports the disciples' later recollection and understanding of the scripture and the event, mentions the connection with Lazarus, and reports the reactions of the Pharisees — all typically Johannine motifs. John's wording is so different from the synoptics' that except for the Old Testament quotations comparison is almost impossible. Neither are the similarities so striking nor most of the differences so typically Johannine that one is immediately constrained to see in John a reworking of the synoptic accounts. But since Freed makes a close, detailed investigation of the texts, we must examine his salient arguments before passing more definitive judgment.

He claims that the direct source for the quotation in John 12:13 (Ps. 118:25) is the synoptics rather than the Old Testament, but his arguments are not altogether convincing to me. I cannot see, for example, that "the context [i. e., the position of the saying in the narrative] differs from that of the synoptics in a way that indicates John knew the synoptic account of Jesus' entry into Jerusalem and used it in his own way to suit his purpose."[11] It is quite true that the kingship of Jesus is here and throughout the Gospel of John a more important theme than in the synoptics, and it is possible, as Freed contends, that John places this quotation at the beginning to emphasize Jesus' kingly role. But even if he is responsible for the position of the quotation, this in itself does not indicate that he was using the synoptics as his source. It is very possible that John's order of quotations is based upon a nonsynoptic tradition concerning the entry. The theme of the kingship, the attraction of Jesus' sign(s) for the crowd, the recurring mention of Lazarus — all of these are indicative of common Johannine interests or literary methods. They may have been imposed by John upon a traditional source, but is one compelled to believe that this source was one or all of the synoptic accounts? It is true, as Freed points out, that the quotation of Psalm 118:25, like the synoptic parallels and unlike any other extensive quotation in John, has no accompanying formula (e. g., 12:15, "As it is written . . . "). But the use of a formula here would have been extremely awkward. As a rule Matthew also supplies the formula with Old Testament quotations, but he omits it here. Although it may be claimed that John follows Matthew, it is not unthinkable that all the gospels omit the formula — including Matthew, who like John prefers it — because of its awkwardness in the context. The similarity is not even too striking to be attributed to sheer coincidence. That εὐλογέω does not occur in John outside the scripture quotation of 12:13 is not evidence of John's use of the synoptics, since εὐλογημένος not only is natural for translating the Hebrew בָּרוּךְ, but is also the word employed at this point by the translators of the LXX. Neither did John need the suggestion of Luke 19:38 to add his καὶ ὁ βασιλεὺς τοῦ 'Ισραήλ, since the kingship of Jesus is already an important theme of his gospel. Jesus is called βασιλεὺς τοῦ 'Ισραήλ, in 1:49, and the theme recurs elsewhere, as Freed points

11. Ibid., p. 331.

out. To say that John "omits Matthew's words 'to the Son of David' because they do not fit his unique view of Jesus as king"[12] only assumes what must be decisively shown, namely, that John was working with Matthew's text before him. The "other changes in his account characteristic of his method when using the Synoptics,"[13] seem to me to have no purpose or pattern about them. Indeed, they are largely the kind of relatively insignificant differences that prove nothing about John's use of the synoptics, except perhaps that he was not using them at all! Thus John's ὀνάριον (12:15) where the synoptics have πῶλος and ὄνος, since it is a *hapax legomenon* in the whole New Testament as well as this gospel, can be construed as a bit of evidence indicating John's use of a nonsynoptic source or tradition at this point. It is not impossible that the τὰ βαΐα τῶν φοινίκων, specified only in John, are intended to emphasize the royal character of the reception. This phrase could, however, stem from a separate tradition, or it could have been introduced by the evangelist into a separate tradition. If the rest of the sentence bore any noteworthy resemblance to the synoptics, Freed's suggestion that the Johannine variation is the result of the author's alteration of his synoptic source would be more convincing. But in point of fact John's whole description is just different, and the differences do not need to be explained as purposeful departures from a synoptic source.

Freed also concludes that "the quotation in John 12:15 is a free artistic composition on the basis of Matthew to give added strength to the writer's theme of Jesus as king."[14] A possible objection, the fact that John has καθήμενος where Matthew (following LXX) has ἐπιβεβηκώς, is turned to advantage by the claim that John uses κάθημαι because he "clearly thinks that Jesus' merely sitting on the ass fulfills the prophecy of his kingship." But why should John have thought that the "mere sitting" instead of "being mounted" — the difference is in itself negligible and its meaning unclear — upon the ass fulfilled the prophecy unless he found, or thought he remembered, the καθήμενος in his version of the Old Testament prophecy? Moreover, John wishes to emphasize that Jesus rode on the ass, not

12. Ibid., pp. 332-33.
13. Ibid., p. 333.
14. Ibid., p. 337.

merely that he sat on it. (For what other purpose would one sit on an ass?) "Behold your king is coming." It is this line which, as Freed says, forms "the whole basis for John's use of the quotation in the first place." Neither the similarities nor the differences between John's quotation in 12:15 (Zech. 9:9 and possibly Isa. 40:9 or Zeph. 3:14–17) and Matthew 21:5 (Isa. 62:11; Zech. 9:9) are such as to compel one to conclude that John must have been using Matthew as his source. If it is "clear that for the quotation from Zechariah, John has more in common with Matthew than with the Hebrew or Greek Old Testament," it is equally clear that his version varies widely and inexplicably from each of these other three. If John uses πῶλος and ὄνος together, can it be convincingly maintained that these words must have come from Matthew, where they do occur (in contrast to LXX, which does not have ὄνος), but not in the same combination?[15] The kind of variation from both the LXX and the synoptics, as well as the MT, which John displays here is exactly in keeping with his use of the Old Testament elsewhere. His quotations are consistent only in their inconsistency with any known text.[16]

If we suppose that John did not use the synoptics, how then can we account for the similarities to be found in the account of the entry into Jerusalem — not to mention other parallels? This question is not as troublesome as might at first appear. The similarities are very general except in the case of the Old Testament quotations. (In fact, the various lists of verbatim or nearly verbatim parallels between John and the synoptics never turn out to be very long.[17]) There the similarities, as well as the differences, can be accounted for about as well assuming a Septuagintal rather than a synoptic *Vorlage*. But these are not the only alternatives, and very likely not even the best ones. That Matthew and John quote the same passages does not, of course, prove a direct literary dependence. It has long

15. It is possible that John's version is an abbreviated form of the Hebrew. πῶλος translates עַיִר in the LXX, and ὄνος often translates אָתוֹן (ibid., p. 336 n. 6).

16. Noack, pp. 71–89; C. Goodwin, "How Did John Treat His Sources," *JBL* 73 (1954): 61–75. Noack and Goodwin attribute John's aberrant quotations to his reliance on memory or oral tradition.

17. E.g., Barrett, pp. 35–36; Streeter, pp. 397–98. Neither scholar pretends that his list is exhaustive, but each doubtless selects the most impressive parallels he can find.

been suspected that the Old Testament testimonies in the New Testament are based on certain very early collections of quotations which predate the New Testament books, and which in one form or another were drawn upon by the New Testament and other early Christian writers.[18] The choice of the same texts as well as the similarities and differences may very well stem from the use of variant forms of a collection or tradition of Old Testament testimonies, and the collection in turn from early Christian circles or schools of Old Testament interpretation.[19] Again, it is not impossible that the Fourth Evangelist drew the quotations from the oral tradition stored up in his own memory, and even the conjecture of an aberrant and now extinct Old Testament text is not incredible. The various possibilities are not mutually exclusive.

As to the Johannine narrative of the entry as a whole, need we presuppose dependence upon the synoptics to account for it? Apart from the Old Testament quotations the parallels are too vague, and the differences too diffuse and inexplicable. The hypothesis that John drew upon traditional material parallel to, but not identical with, the synoptics is too near at hand to be overlooked. That such parallel tradition existed is almost beyond doubt. Its existence is probably attested by the evidence of the apocryphal Gospel of Thomas and is supported by the evidence of the early patristic writers.[20] Form criticism has, of course, shown that the traditional sayings and stories circulated independently before they were incorporated in written documents, and W. L. Knox has contended that they were written down and circulated as "tractates" incorporating one or more narratives, sayings, or parables during the period between the oral and the gospel stages of the tradition.[21] Furthermore, whether

18. R. Harris, with the assistance of V. Burch, *Testimonies*, esp. II, 71–76. C. H. Dodd, *According to the Scriptures*, does not accept Harris' theory of an elaborate testimony book (pp. 26–27), but sets forth the modified and more modest proposal of a common tradition of Old Testament testimonia (pp. 28–60). Regarding the quotation of Zech. 9:9 in Matt. 21:5 and John 12:15, Dodd concludes, "We seem to have a true case of independent citation, surely on the basis of a common tradition of testimonia rather than of any written source" (p. 49). Dodd also declares that "citations common to the Synoptics on the one hand and the Fourth Gospel on the other are *prima facie* independent" (p. 30).

19. K. Stendahl, *The School of St. Matthew*.

20. H. Köster, *Synoptische Überlieferung bei den apostolischen Vätern*.

21. *The Sources of the Synoptic Gospels*, ed. H. Chadwick.

one accepts the complex source analysis which Bultmann carries out in his *Das Evangelium des Johannes,* one must admit that in this commentary he has brought forth impressive internal evidence for John's use of independent narrative traditions parallel to the synoptic. It is more than probable that John had access to the tradition at a presynoptic stage or, more likely, that he knew and employed variant strands of the tradition.

While we can never exclude the possibility that John knew the synoptic gospels (as long as we assume that John is actually later than the synoptics[22]), the evidence that he did not use them as a principal source, if he knew them at all, has been mounting in recent years. It has now reached such a point that the burden of proof may be said to lie upon the scholar who wishes to maintain that John knew and used them. It does not appear to me that the extent of this burden has been satisfactorily perceived in the article under consideration, nor, in my opinion has it been successfully borne.

22. Before the discovery of the Qumran scrolls, E. R. Goodenough, *JBL* 64 (1945): 145–82, argued against the generally held assumption that the Fourth Gospel is necessarily a relatively late book. In recent years the affinity of some of the Qumran documents with some aspects of Johannine thought has encouraged scholars to propose a Palestinian origin and early date for the Gospel of John, or at least the Johannine tradition (e. g., W. F. Albright, "Recent Discoveries in Palestine and the Gospel of St. John," *The Background of the New Testament and its Eschatology, In Honour of Charles Harold Dodd,* pp. 153–71). Interestingly enough, the early Palestinian origin of the Johannine tradition was once suggested by Bultmann, who, however, never developed his proposal ("Die bedeutung der neuerschlossenen mandäischen und manichäischen Quellen für das Verständnis des Johannesevangeliums," *ZNW* 24 [1925]: 142–43). R. Gyllenberg refers to Bultmann's proposal and seeks to revive it in the light of the scrolls ("Die Anfänge der johanneischen Tradition," *Neutestamentliche Studien für Rudolf Bultmann* [1954], pp. 144–48). O. Cullmann has also drawn heavily upon the evidence of the scrolls for his understanding of the historical position of John (e. g., "L'opposition contre le temple de Jérusalem, motif commun de la théologie Johannique et du monde ambiant," *NTS* 5 [1959]: 157–74). For a vigorous dissenting opinion on the importance of Qumran for Johannine studies see the article by H. M. Teeple, "Qumran and the Origin of the Fourth Gospel," *NovT* 4 (1960): 6-25.

5 | B. W. Bacon on John and Mark[*]

We celebrate this year not only the centennial of the Society of Biblical Literature, but the ninety-second anniversary of Benjamin Wisner Bacon's membership in it and the seventy-eighth anniversary of his presidential year. He served the Society as secretary, editor of *JBL*, and member of Council, as well as president. In his last year he wrote: "It is still among the chief enjoyments of my life to attend the annual meetings of the Society, greet and consult with the few that still remain of my contemporaries, and wish Godspeed to the younger men, so much better qualified than I was then for the tasks on which I ventured."[1] Bacon never earned a Ph.D. In an excess of modesty he wrote, "I could not even today pass a Yale Ph.D. examination in the required subjects."[2] This is surely nonsense. Never-

*A paper delivered before the seminar on John and Mark at the 1980 Annual Meeting of the Society of Biblical Literature, Dallas, Texas, November, 1980.

1. Bacon, "Enter the Higher Criticism," *Contemporary American Theology: Theological Autobiographies*, ed. Vergilius Ferm (New York: Round Table, 1932), 1, 24. This essay is an extraordinarily interesting self-portrait, extremely useful in understanding how Bacon perceived and assessed his life, work and contributions to scholarship. For a concise and, for different purposes, equally valuable treatment of Bacon's scholarly life, see Roy A. Harrisville, *Benjamin Wisner Bacon: Pioneer in American Biblical Criticism*, Studies in American Biblical Scholarship 2, Schools and Scholars 2 (Missoula, Mont.: Scholars Press, 1976), in which Bacon's positions on various significant New Testament issues are surveyed and summarized.

2. Bacon, "Higher Criticism," p. 34.

theless, after receiving his B.D. degree from Yale, Bacon did not pursue further formal study but successively served two parishes, returning to his alma mater in 1896. In 1897 he was appointed Buckingham Professor of New Testament Criticism and Interpretation, a position he held until his retirement in 1928. Bacon was born on January 15, 1860 and died February 1, 1932. His life began before the Civil War and ended in the midst of the Great Depression. His academic career spanned the American presidencies from McKinley to Coolidge. He was born before the election of Abraham Lincoln and died just before the election of Franklin Roosevelt. There is a splendid photograph of Bacon in the front of *Studies in Early Christianity*, the *Festschrift* in honor of him and F. C. Porter,[3] edited by their student, Shirley Jackson Case. He seems a large and expansive man, in some contrast to Porter, who, at least in his photograph, appears somewhat wan and bookish by comparison.

Bacon's first scholarly article in New Testament was "The Displacement of John XIV," *JBL* 13 (1894): 64–76. It ends with his taking note of the problem of the relationship of John to the synoptic gospels. Our interest in John and Mark finds a deep kinship with his own. In his last work, *The Gospel of the Hellenists*, published posthumously in 1933,[4] Bacon is still involved in one way or another with the question of John and the synoptic gospels.

I have been asked to prepare a paper on "B. W. Bacon and the Sources of and Relationships Between Mark and John." Long distance telephone communication has enabled us to recreate the situation in which oral tradition flourished. I have little doubt this was the subject proposed all along, but I have no written record of it. Probably because of my selective hearing, "sources of" dropped out of the picture, only to reemerge in the printed program. But because my interest, not to mention my preparation, has been focused that way, I shall stay away from the question of sources except as it is raised by the other question, the question of relationships between John and Mark. It will become evident, however, that the source question cannot be ignored in any such consideration of relationships.

3. New York: Century, 1928.
4. Ed. C. H. Kraeling (New York: Henry Holt).

Before moving on to the principal matter, Bacon's position on John and Mark, and any implications it may have for our own situation, a word should be said about the shape of Bacon's interest in the Fourth Gospel and the direction his own work took. He obviously regarded his attack upon the traditional, churchly view of the origin and authorship of the Gospel and Epistles of John and the part he played in the successful overthrow of the defenders of that tradition as one of his major contributions to the scientific study of New Testament.

In his early, exhaustive work on John, *The Fourth Gospel in Research and Debate,*[5] Bacon spells out and insists upon the inevitable historical alternative first posed by D. F. Strauss: "Either Synoptics, or John. Either the former are right in their complete silence regarding pre-existence and incarnation, and their subordination of the doctrine of Jesus' person, in presenting his work and teaching concerned with the Kingdom of God ...; or else John is right in making Jesus' work and message supremely a manifestation of his own glory as the incarnate Logos effecting an atonement for the world which has otherwise no access to God. Both views cannot be true, and to a very large extent it is the science of literary and historical criticism which must decide between them."[6] Well said, and at the time it was important to say it. But such statements nevertheless put us in mind of the era of criticism Bacon represents, an era in which the axioms and assumptions of an earlier age were being overthrown, particularly in the English language and in North America. Yet Bacon did not find it necessary to attack all the assumptions of the earlier and more conservative scholarship championed by the defenders of the Fourth Gospel.

Several of these assumptions he let stand, and in some cases employed in a positive way. For example, he simply continued to assume, with most scholars in his own day and through most of Christian history, that John knew the synoptic gospels and wrote in cognizance of them.

> Anyone who will take the pains to verify the evidence (as presented in the footnotes we here subjoin), can see for

5. New York: Moffatt, Yard, 1910, pp 1–2.
6. Ibid., p. 3.

himself the general method of the fourth evangelist in dealing with Synoptic material: (1) Matthew is practically ignored; (2) Mark is made the basis; (3) supplements and changes are made with large use of Luke both as to motive and material. The formative principle determining the entire construction is, as we have already made clear and now reiterate, the "spiritual" gospel of Paul. It is this which forbids any such mere transcription as that which characterizes our first and third evangelists in their combination of Mark and Q.[7]

With the dependence of John on the synoptics goes the evangelist's knowledge and appropriation of Paul as the explanation of why his use of Mark was so different from the other later evangelists'. Both directions of dependence could be assumed, asserted, or regarded as obvious when Bacon wrote, although neither seems quite so clear today. In *The Fourth Gospel in Research and Debate* Bacon stated: "In its general structure the outline of the Fourth Gospel is simple and clear, and reproduces that of Mark *as modified by Luke*."[8] Thus it is not surprising that in assessing the use of Mark 6:14–9:50 in John, Bacon came to this conclusion: "Nothing accordingly of Markan material remains unaccounted for. The fourth evangelist really employs every available shred of Mark in his own way; nor has he even added, except from Luke."[9]

When, twenty-three years after the appearance of *The Fourth Gospel in Research and Debate*, Bacon's last major work, *The Gospel of the Hellenists*, appeared, published posthumously, his positions had shifted perceptibly. By now Bacon had read Windisch[10] and was deeply impressed by the cogency of his arguments. He was prepared to grant that John wished to displace the synoptics in the way Matthew or Luke wished to displace Mark, but not with the hostility which Windisch attributes to him.[11] On the other

7. Ibid., p. 368.
8. Ibid.
9. Ibid., p. 381.
10. *Johannes und die Synoptiker: Wollte der vierte Evangelist die älteren Evangelien Ergänzen oder Ersetzen?* Untersuchungen zum Neuen Testament, 12 (Leipzig: Hinrichs, 1926), still a work of fundamental importance to the discussion.
11. *Hellenists*, pp. 117–18.

hand, Windisch's arguments that John knew the synoptics were accepted as an entirely convincing demonstration of the generally held position:

> So far as the extent and character of John's dependence on Mark, Luke and Matthew are concerned there will be little dissent from the conclusions of Windisch, supported as they are by detailed comparison of texts, and adopted rather as admissions to opposing views than in support of his own. He considers John's use of Mark certain, his use of Luke highly probable, and his use of Matthew not improbable.[12]

One cannot fail to note the similarity between this, essentially correct, assessment of Windisch's views and the statement of Bacon's own position of nearly a quarter of a century earlier which we quoted above.[13] It is, however, correct to say that Bacon has now backed off somewhat from his earlier assumption that John was entirely, or in the main, derivative from the synoptics. In *The Gospel of the Hellenists* he writes:

> John is more than a midrashic commentary on accepted tradition. He "sets out to interpret the Christian story and the Christian experience to the new world of Hellenism by translating the gospel into a form intelligible to Greek modes of thought."And "the gospel" interpreted is not merely the Synoptic tradition. It is a masterful selection of material chosen from a wide variety of sources with special references to the purpose in mind.[14]

That John wrote with the synoptics in view, however, provides a clear line of continuity through Bacon's work. He is far from abandoning that position in *The Gospel of the Hellenists*. But Bacon now emphasizes his view that John was the gospel of a specific

12. Ibid., p. 113.
13. *Fourth Gospel*, p. 368.
14. *Hellenists*, p. 112. (Quotations are from MacGregor's then recent commentary in the Moffatt series.) Even in *Fourth Gospel* Bacon had recognized the existence of some independent tradition in John (p. 279).

community or territory of early Christianity, namely Western Asia.[15]
"The Elder goes his own way, selecting from the huge mass of
current material, oral and written, such signs and discourses as
suit his purpose."[16] He draws them presumably from the tradition
of Asian Christianity which was "utterly independent of the Petrine
tradition and only secondarily influenced by Pauline theology." Bacon continues:

> It owed its origin and peculiar character to the movement
> begun by the Hellenists of Jerusalem. If, then, the Elder
> boldly presented in his Gospel a Jesus who is independent
> of and radically different from the Synoptic firgure, it is
> because he regarded himself as a member of a long succes-
> sion of believers with views like his own, and because he
> aimed fundamentally to write *their* gospel, the Gospel of
> the Hellenists. Had this aim not been recognized and
> approved, the work could not have survived.[17]

Bacon thus calls his own book *The Gospel of the Hellenists*. His
general view of its origins and milieu is strikingly similar to several
enjoying wide currency today. He has combined the rooting of the
Johannine community in Palestine and Syria with the emergence
of the published Gospel in western Asia Minor.

Yet Bacon maintains intact, while modifying in degree and detail,
his view of the relation of John to the synoptics. At the same time
he abandons his earlier position that John was a "Paulinist," that
Pauline theology influenced his gospel at the very heart. Rather, he
now thinks that both Paul and John are products of that Hellenistic
Christianity which had its roots among the Jerusalem Hellenists
who fled to Antioch under persecution (cf. Acts 11:19) and later
undertook the sponsorship of missionary preaching to the broader
Greco-Roman world. While there are Pauline traces in both the
Epistles and Gospel, "the total effect is not what we might expect
of the Elder were he consciously a disciple of Paul, speaking to
churches of Pauline origin."[18]

15. Hellenists, p. 118.
16. Ibid., p. 117.
17. Ibid., pp. 118–19.
18. Ibid., p. 58.

The recession of Pauline influence in Bacon's assessment of John goes hand in hand with his developed view that the Gospel of John is the product of a distinct strain of early Christianity. It does not imply, or even suggest to him, that John is independent of the synoptic gospels. Yet it is fair to say that the role and importance of the synoptics decline if one is to judge by the difference between *The Fourth Gospel in Recent Research and Debate* and *The Gospel of the Hellenists*.

In the remainder of this paper I shall concentrate primarily on John's relationship to Mark as Bacon conceived of it in his later work, giving specific examples, and at some points comparing his later with his earlier views.[19] In conclusion there will be some critical discussion and a few general observations.

Before I underake such a presentation, it is relevant to note that Bacon had definite and well-developed views on the composition history of the Fourth Gospel. It consists of three stages.[20] The first stage was the composition of a series of festal discourses: that is, discourses appropriate to the Jewish annual feasts. The discourses were not, like the Sermon on the Mount, composed on the basis of "a theme suggested by Jesus' teaching." Presumably the elder/ evangelist was the author of these discourses. The second stage was the expansion of the these discourses into a narrative of Jesus' ministry (composed between 90 and 120 in Asia). These discourses were then placed in the period of obscurity, "which begins, in Synoptic narrative, at the end of the Galilean ministry." This re-cension included the passion and resurrection narrative and the prologue. It did not, however, include the appendix (chap. 21) or contain other narrative elements (e.g., 2:12–22, the temple clean-sing; 2:23–3:21, Nicodemus) which were composed by the redactor or added by him out of the elder's literary remains. The final re-dactor has conformed the Gospel to the synoptic model or has introduced Pauline elements.[21] This redaction is, of course, the third

19. See ibid., p. xi, for Kraeling's statement of the difficulty of presenting Bacon's views in *Hellenists*.

20. Ibid., pp. 138–40.

21. B. W. Bacon, "Pauline Elements in the Fourth Gospel," *ATR* 11 (1929): 199–233, 305–20.

and final stage of the composition of the Fourth Gospel, dated ca. 150 at Rome.[22]

For Bacon sign and discourse were already united in the initial stage of composition. Each of the festal discourses was attached to a sign of Jesus. Already at this stage there was influence from the synoptics in that several of the signs were adapted from the synoptic accounts. This influence continued as these were combined into a narrative, concluding with an account of Jesus' passion and resurrection. Thus at every stage the Fourth Gospel was composed under the influence of the synoptics, especially Mark.

JOHN'S RELATIONSHIP TO MARK

The Gospel of the Hellenists reveals that even at the end of his career, after all the qualifications of his earlier position (*Fourth Gospel in Research and Debate*), Bacon still regarded the bulk of the Johannine narrative as dependent upon, or somehow related to, the synoptic. Yet (p. 114)[23] he acknowledges the "high-handed" way in which John has treated the synoptics, prefering elements "taken from the mass of legendary material referred to in 20:30." Synoptic material may be related to the Johannine in negative rather than positive ways. Thus, for example, John cancels "the institution of the Eucharist and . . . [substitutes] the Footwashing for it" (p. 222).

If one surveys *The Gospel of the Hellenists* with a view to whether or how in Bacon's view John's account is related, positively or negatively, to the Marcan; he makes some interesting discoveries. Almost all the public ministry (chap. 1–12) is thought to be directly related to the Marcan account. Obviously some narratives like the feeding of the multitude or the annointing of Jesus are closer to Mark than others. In such cases it can reasonably be supposed that John draws upon the Marcan, or synoptic, narrative. But where the relationship is not obvious Bacon may move in one of two ways. On the one hand, he may acknowledge, as in the case of the wine miracle or the raising of Lazarus, that John has employed an independent story. Yet he speaks of John as *substituting* the Cana

22. *Hellenists*, pp. 231–40, 417–29.

23. In this section references to *The Gospel of the Hellenists* are given in parentheses in the text.

miracle for the synoptic (Marcan) story of an exorcism in the synagogue at Capernaum (p. 332). He thinks its theme of the displacement of the law by Jesus is suggested by the discussion of fasting, with the saying about new wine, in Mark 2:18-22 (pp. 167–68). In the case of the raising of Lazarus, Bacon concedes that "for the last and greatest of his symbolical 'signs' the Elder, as in the case of the first (2:1-11), departs entirely from the synoptic tradition" (p. 208). Yet he can refer to it as being substituted for the story of Jairus' daughter (p. 403; cf. Mark 5:21-43).

On the other hand, in some instances Bacon regards a Johannine narrative whose relationship to the synoptics is not obvious as having been derived from Mark, and perhaps also from the other synoptics or Q. For example, the healing of the lame man in John 5:1-8 Bacon regards as John's recasting of Mark 2:1-12. We shall return to this text to show in detail Bacon's conception of how John works with a synoptic source. Other similar instances may be cited. John presents what Bacon describes as "a complete recasting of Mark's account of the call of the first disciples and the beginning of [the] miracles" (p. 156). "Recasting" is a favorite word of Bacon, for it aptly describes what in his view the Fourth Evangelist has done with the Marcan or synoptic, narrative. The recasting is often said to be obvious. For example, as far as Bacon is concerned, John 1:19-51 is so clearly a rewriting of the Marcan accounts as to leave no question in any critical mind" (p. 188). Similarly, the story of Jesus' encounter and dialogue with his brothers followed by the clandestine departure for Jerusalem is said by Bacon to be derived from Mark's mention of Jesus' unbelieving brothers (3:20-21, 31-35) and the secrecy of Jesus' departure from Galilee (9:30) for Jerusalem (p. 198).

Not only the narrative content, i.e., the pericopes of Mark, are taken up by the Fourth Evangelist, but also the basic structure of his gospel. Bacon does not repeat his earlier statement (above) that John's outline is clearly that of Mark as modified by Luke. Nevertheless, the evangelist conceives of the structure of his gospel in relation to the synoptics (p. 139), although, as Bacon himself puts it, "No competent scholar will today contend that the Fourth Gospel was composed merely as a supplement to the other three" (p. 112).

The structure of John, even as it left the evangelist's hands, reflects the synoptic, i.e., Marcan, outline. The prologue (1:1-18) is, of course, entirely distinctive. There is then a pre-Galilean ministry (1:19–4:42) which begins with a "complete recasting' of the call and the beginning of the miracles (p. 156). Originally this concluded with 2:11, but it has been augmented by the later redactor, who inserted 2:12–3:21, 31-36, in part out of material bequeathed him by the evangelist (pp. 169–71; 248–51). To the total redactional design that led to this insertion belongs also the placing of the present chapter 5 before chapter 6 (pp. 187–89). Prior to that rearrangement, a brief pre-Galilean ministry (without synoptic parallel) was followed by a somewhat longer continuous Galilean ministry (4:43-54; 6:1-71), preceded by the scene in Samaria (4:1-42). The latter John deliberately substitutes for Mark 7:24-37, the Syrophoenician woman and the healing of a deaf man in the region of the Decapolis (pp. 413; 177-82), as he simultaneously works in themes derived from other synoptic and Pauline sources. With 5:1 following upon chapter 6 the post-Galilean ministry of the original Gospel begins. It spans a year and substitutes a series of festal visits (5; 7–12) of Jesus to Jerusalem for "the indefinite wanderings which the Synoptic Gospels assign to this period." Interestingly enough, Bacon thinks the redactor moved 5:1-47 forward to its present position because he saw its fundamental thematic agreement with Mark 2:1-12, 23-28; 3:1-6 (p. 188). Thus he sandwiched it into the Galilean ministry, where it makes better sense thematically than geographically. After the final festal journey to Passover (11:55–12:50) there follows the passion and resurrection narrative (13:1–20: 31). The appendix (chap. 21) is the composition of the redactor. Bacon notes that the original form of the Gospel, prior to redaction, was closer to the synoptics in outline. The pre-Galilean ministry was shorter and the Galilean ministry longer. The post-Galilean ministry was John's original contribution, although even it contained many allusions and references to the synoptics.

Obviously, the passion narrative of John is related to the synoptic. Interestingly enough, Bacon speaks of John's following the Lucan form of the synoptic tradition (p. 226). John's resurrection narrative (chap. 20) is also Lucan (p. 230). Basically, the synoptic narration together with the evangelist's own theological interests and narrative style suffice to explain the Johannine passion-resurrection narrative. In *The Gospel of the Hellenists* Bacon seems more interested in the dating of the last supper and the crucifixion, and in the Johannine roots of quartodecimanism, than in displaying what he regards as an obvious relationship to the synoptic gospels.

Not just the narrative portions of John are viewed by Bacon as in some sense derivative from the synoptics. Also the discourses, although obviously in large measure sui generis, draw upon the synoptics, Q as well as Mark, for their inspiration. Thus the Nicodemus of John 3 is more than the Naq Dimon Ben Gorion of rabbinic tradition. He is also the rich inquirer of Mark 10:17–22 and in part the scribe "not far from the kingdom of God" of Mark 12:28–34. Like Gamaliel of Acts 5:34 he stands up in the Sanhedrin on behalf of giving the accused a fair hearing (p. 413). More importantly, the discourse and debate of Jesus with his Jewish opponents that follows the healing narrative in chapter 5 is a development of motifs found in Mark 2:1–3:6 (pp. 187–91); the authority of Jesus as Son of man is contrasted with that of Moses (p. 407). Interestingly enough, aside from chapter 13, which parallels the synoptic traditions about the last supper, Bacon does not view the farewell discourses and high priestly prayer of Jesus as having been derived directly from the synoptics. (By common consent chaps. 14–17 are the most distinctively Johannine part of the Fourth Gospel.)

Taken as a whole, the Gospel of John is nevertheless indebted to the synoptics, although Bacon is no longer willing, as he was in *The Fourth Gospel in Research and Debate*, to regard it as a kind of midrash upon Mark in particular or the synoptics in general.

JOHN'S MANNER OF EMPLOYING A MARCAN NARRATIVE

In his 1926 article "Sources and Method of the Fourth Evangelist"[24] Bacon sets forth in detail his understanding of how John made use of the Marcan narrative. Eschewing the task of demonstrating anything so obvious as John's use of the Marcan account of the multiplication of the loaves, Bacon deliberately chooses a passage,

24. *HibJ* 25 (1926): 115–30. In-text page references are to this article. Bacon still endorses this article in *The Gospel of the Hellenists*, pp. 169–70 n. 9. He maintains there the same basic position set forth in the article, developing it somewhat.

chapter 5, whose relationship to the synoptics (i.e., Mark) is not so clear. According to Bacon, John 5:1–8 has "features irresistibly recalling Mark's story of the lame man bidden to 'take up his bed and walk.' " Moreover, Bacon believes he can show that John 4:46–54; 5:1–47 (of which 7:15–24 seems to be the continuation) is "best regarded as a blend of Mark's section on the Growth of Opposition (Mark ii. 1–iii.6) with the Q material on the Stumbling of Israel, adapting this material to the nature and purpose of the dialogue form" (p. 119). This Q material, consisting of Matthew 11:2–12:45/Luke 7:18–50, begins with the account of John the Baptist's sending emissaries to question Jesus. Bacon regards it as "hardly probable" (p. 117) that the Fourth Evangelist did not have direct as well as indirect (through Matthew and/or Luke) knowledge of Q. At least John knew the Lucan form of Q, if not the original S (p. 121). (S is a source peculiar to Bacon.)

According to Bacon; "the *subject* of the great discourse of v. 19–47 is undeniably a defense of the Authority of 'the Son of Man' as higher than that of Moses. It naturally follows the dialogue with the Samaritan Woman (iv. 1–45), whose subject is the Spiritual Temple for all Humanity (iv. 21–26). Temple and Law are the two prerogatives of Israel opposed in the speech of Stephen" (p. 120). And, of course, Stephen was a Hellenist as is the Fourth Evangelist. The problem, according to Bacon, is to determine "what we can of Johannine method by observing how he has employed both the narrative arrangement of Mark and the Q method of diatribe—that is, a discourse introduced by a brief narrative setting" (pp. 121–22).

John takes over Mark's opening anecdote (5:1–8 is derived from 2:1–12). He does not take up the material intervening Mark 2:1–12 and 3:1–6, but appends the basic elements of the latter story "in the paragraph beginning 'Now it was the Sabbath on that day'" (p. 122). "The whole narrative introduction (Mark 2:1–3:6) to the discourse on the Authority of the Son of Man (John 5:1–47) is thus reduced to a single illustrative incident containing all the elements required for the purpose in view" (p. 122). The scene is changed to Jerusalem at the feast; Jesus' opponents become, typically, "the Jews," and the conflict takes place in the temple (v. 14), the center of their authority. The "demonstrative power" of the healing is heightened by the statement that the man has lain helpless for thirty-eight years (p. 122).

Following upon the miracle, John 5:10–18 goes directly to the grounds upon which, according to Mark 3:1–6, the Pharisees and Herodians conspire to put Jesus out of the way, skipping over the "minor occasions of conflicts" of Mark 2:1–20. John 5:17 "introduces the principal subject by combining the Sabbath theme of Mark ii.23–iii.6 with the Mighty Works theme of the Q discourse, much as Matthew has done in Matt. xi.1–xii.14, but with greater skill" (p. 123). The true imitation of God is not to desist from labor on the sabbath but to do such "divine works of beneficence," e.g., making the lame walk, as are named in Isaiah, the *Shemoneh Esreh* and the message of John to Jesus (Matt. 11:5 = Luke 7:22; cf. Isa. 61:1). The supreme manifestation of God's gracious presence is, however, the raising of the dead (John 5:21–29). That theme is admittedly barely touched upon in Mark (3:4), although in Q it plays a larger role (in Luke 7:22 and Matt. 11:5). "Thus the claims of Mark and the Q section on behalf of Jesus as Lord of the Sabbath and bringer of Life from God are skillfully blended" (p. 123), and "the Johannine vindication of the Authority of the Son of Man in John v. 17–29 can best be explained as a blend of the Markan in Mark ii.10 and 28 with that of the Q section Matt. xi.2–19 = Luke vii.18–35" (p. 124). The witness of John (5:33–35) is said to correspond with Mark 9:2–10 and Q, presumably Matt.11:7–19 and Luke 7:24–35 (p. 124). That is, Elijah and Moses in the transfiguration scene of Mark underlie the witness of the Baptist (John 5:33–35) and of scripture and Moses (John 5:39ff.), albeit John is denied the role of Elijah in the Fourth Gospel. In this final section of the discourse, however, Jesus says he relies on the witness of scripture and that of his own "mighty works" (*sic*; 5:36), not that of the Baptist. The appeal to mighty works harks back both to Mark (2:1–3:6) and to Q (centurion's servant; Luke 7:22/Matt. 11:5). "The Jews' failure to be convinced by the law and the prophets [John 5] proves as in the Lucan parable [16:19–31], that 'they would not be persuaded though one rose from the dead' " (pp. 124–25).

The discourse of John 5:17–47 continues in 7:15–24, as if there were no break, and in the original form of the Gospel there was not. The themes of keeping or breaking the law and the opponents' desire to kill Jesus tie 7:10 (cf. v. 23) to Mark 3:1–6 (p. 125). In fact, Jesus' argument that healing on the sabbath is lawful (John 7:18–29) has a certain affinity with Mark 3:4. Bacon concludes his discussion of John's use of Mark and Q with a caveat: "The absence from the great Johannine discourse on the Paramount Authority of the Son of Man of certain elements present in the corresponding section of the two Synoptic sources should not blind us to the larger parallelism" (p. 125). He points out that we should not expect to find reference to Jesus' friendship for publicans and sinners in John. "Publicans and sinners are total strangers to the Ephesian Gospel. We should expect the composer of the Johannine Discourse to utilize for it just those elements of narrative from Mark, and of discourse from S (or Q) which are appropriate to his purpose, *and no more*. The surprising thing is not that so much is passed over of the material of Mark and Q that had no direct bearing on the special issue he wished to treat, but that he could find room for so much of what we find in the two Synoptic sections in support of his principal theme."

Bacon sums up (p. 126):

> The Markan story of the Lame Man made to Walk is both relocated and rewritten, as we have seen, to adapt it to the purpose of the dialogue. But its essential feature remains in the command. "Rise, take up thy bed (*krabaton*) and walk," with its sequel (verses 8f.). The conspiracy against Jesus' life (verses 16, 18) is occasioned by his healing on the Sabbath, as in Mark iii.1–6.

> Again the Markan motive of the Son of Man as Lord of the Sabbath is utilized, in combination with the Q motive of the Mighty Works done as the agent of the God that raiseth the dead and quickeneth them [presumably Luke 7:33 and Matt. 11:5].

Inasmuch as he regards the synoptic origin of 5:1–47 as now established, Bacon proceeds on that basis to instance other Johannine relationships to synoptic tradition which might otherwise be disputed. For example, the healing of the blind man in John 9:1–34 is related to that of Mark 8:22–26 in a way reminiscent of the relation of John 5:1–8 to Mark 2:1–12 (pp. 128–29). Bacon concludes by conceding that in the case of some Johannine narratives, e.g., the wine miracle at Cana or the raising of Lazarus, John obviously adopts narratives unknown from the synoptics. But he then asks (p. 129): "Must we, because of a few instances suggestive of independent lines of report postulate a Johannine tradition, or even a 'Johannine' document, in addition to the festal discourses?" The question obviously expects a negative answer, and Bacon's final statements imply that he believes even those discourses may be shown to have been derived from "the free handling of known synoptic themes" (p. 129).

EVALUATION AND CRITIQUE OF BACON

One learns increasingly and impressively in the course of academic life and a scholarly career how patently sane and well-informed people, in possession of the same or similar data, can draw from them vastly different or obviously contradictory inferences or conclusions. I hope I do not flatter myself unduly if I instance myself with Bacon as illustrating this point!

I wish now to make a few critical observations about Bacon's efforts to see John 5 as a combination of Mark 2:1–3:6 and what he calls "the great Q [really on his terms S] discourse on the Stumbling of Israel." At the level of general criticism, one may ask whether Bacon ever proves more than he assumes. He assumes, because it is a given of the gospel criticism of his day, that John knew and to some extent used Mark and the other synoptics. Bacon affords a classic example of Gardner-Smith's point that scholarship had heretofore concentrated on explaining the similarities between John and the synoptics while ignoring, or playing down, the differences.

Yet it does not necessarily follow that Bacon is wrong. Nevertheless, we must ask in relation to his specific argument whether his assumption is really borne out and whether there is reason to think he ignores evidence pointing in another direction. One wonders, for example, whether if John derived his healing of a lame man (5:1–8) from Mark it was necessary to move it to Jerusalem, particularly in view of the redactor's sensing the need to bring it back into a Galilean context. Perhaps so, in order to hold the dispute in the temple. But why set it at a pool (Bethzatha) instead of in a house? The thirty-eight years of illness, like the blindness from birth (chap. 9), accentuates the power of Jesus' healing, as Bacon suggests, but really says nothing about the origin of the story. None of the narrative details actually agree except Jesus' command to the healed man to arise, take up his bed, and walk. It embodies only indirectly the central, common motif of the stories or complexes. On the other hand, the theme of forgiveness of sins, so prominent in the Marcan story, is missing from the Johannine, except that Jesus later tells the man healed to sin no more (5:14). It is true that Jesus is set at odds with his fellow Jews and Jewish authorities in Mark 2:1–3:6, as increasingly in John 5:9–47, but in Mark it is over specific points of the law, in John over his claims for himself. It can be argued that the latter are latent in the authoritative posture of Jesus in the Marcan controversy stories, but Bacon makes little effort to show in any detail or with specificity how from those controversy stories, even when taken in conjunction with the Q complex (Luke 7:1[18]–50/Matt. 11:2–12:45), John derives the controversy found in chapter 5. It is true that both have in view the question of the authority of the Son of man and Jesus' opponents' plotting against him. By the same token, it is true that the theme of sabbath-breaking is predominant in Mark 2:23–3:6 (the stories of the disciples' plucking grain and the healing of the man with a withered hand) and that the fact that Jesus has healed on the sabbath sets in motion the controversy of John 5:10–47. Yet there is no more specific correspondence. Once again the literary relationship is unclear, unless it is assumed.

The question of authority is a major issue that arises in many forms both in John and in the synoptics. Similarly, the accusation of sabbath-breaking is common in the synoptics and part of the general polemic of Jesus' opponents against him. Moreover, the question of authority is cast in terms of eschatology in John 5:19-29, which is at most in the background in Mark 2:1–3:6 and does not come forward as an explicit theme. There are eschatological dimensions of the putative Q source (e.g., Matt. 11:2–14, 20–24; 12:38–42 and pars.), but they are of a rather different sort. How they might be related to John's somewhat programmatic statements about Jesus' raising the dead and giving life is not made clear. Admittedly, Bacon points to the mention of saving life in Mark 3:4

and of raising the dead in Matthew 11:5/Luke 7:22. But the theme
of resurrection and life is pervasive in John. Is there any compelling
reason why the evangelist should have derived it from these synoptic texts?

From John 5:30 onward the question of authority is cast in terms
of the witness to Jesus, in which the Baptist shares. This has little
to do with Mark 2:1–3:6, although the Baptist does figure prominently in the Q discourse (Matt. 11:2–19 = Luke 7:18–35). Bacon
here has recourse to the Marcan transfiguration narrative (9:2–10).
Undoubtedly many themes and motifs in John are reminiscent of
the synoptics. If one is seeking a synoptic parallel, or origin, for
some element of John it usually can be found, especially if the rules
of the game are more or less flexible. That the Marcan motif of the
Son of man as Lord of the sabbath suggested to John the discourse
on Jesus' authority in chapter 5 cannot be disproved. Nor can the
claim that Jesus' word (taken from Isaiah) in Q about the dead
being raised gave rise to Jesus' eschatological discourse in John
5:19–29 be disproved. Neither is impossible. But in the face of
methodological, and genuine, doubt that John knew or used Mark
or Q, Bacon's arguments are far less than a demonstration to the
contrary. The same might be said of almost every instance in which
he invokes Mark, or the synoptics, to explain John, whether in the
case of an individual pericope or with respect to overall content
or structure.

PERSPECTIVE IN ASSESSING THE EVIDENCE

Bacon asserts that John's use, and disuse, of Mark or the synoptics can be understood as a function of his distinctive purpose
and perspective. Yet because John's knowledge of them is assumed,
points of similarity are chalked up to it, points of difference which
can reasonably be accounted for (e.g., Jesus' carrying his own cross)
are laid to the evangelist's purpose, but other differences are, as we
have seen, ignored. Methodological controls, or criteria, by which
to determine whether John *must* have used Mark, in distinction
from whether he *might* have, are lacking.

When, as in John 5, a common title (e.g., Son of man), an ab-
straction, or general theme such as Jesus' authority is said to be
taken over by John from Mark or the synoptics, such a proposal

seems reasonable or even obvious, on the uncontested assumption that John knew Mark. But otherwise there is nothing compelling about it. Likewise, a similarity of structure derived by John from Mark is credible on those terms, particularly if the order of chapters 5 and 6 is reversed in order to restore the original order (obscured by the redactor), resulting in a somewhat longer Galilean ministry, as in the synoptics. Yet in this as in other cases, no real system or rationale for John's use of Marcan material is proposed; but none is needed, for John's knowledge of Mark is a given.

Bacon, in *The Gospel of the Hellenists* (in some contrast to *The Fourth Gospel in Research and Debate*), acknowledges John's use of material independent of the synoptics, although as late as 1926 he had minimized that possibility.[25] Bacon does not, however, give intensive or systematic consideration to the possibility that John drew upon a relatively independent strain of oral tradition or upon written sources of an analogous sort. There was, in fact, no reason to launch or pursue such an investigation as long as John's narrative and structure could be regarded as basically derivative from the synoptics and his discourses as basically the composition of the evangelist. Bacon is truly pre–Gardner-Smith in that he has not seriously considered the possibility that it might be easier to explain the similarities of John with the synoptics on the view that John was independent of Mark than to explain the differences on the assumption that the Fourth Evangelist knew and used Mark.[26]

As far as I can see, no useful purpose would be served by a concluding discussion of "lessons we may learn from Benjamin W. Bacon." We might find it useful, however, to reflect further on how it happens that Bacon's view of the evidence relating John and Mark (or the synoptics) differs so radically from that of many scholars who have worked on the problem more recently, especially since Gardner-Smith.

In his book *The Structure of Scientific Revolutions* Thomas Kuhn points out that scientists characteristically employ an established paradigm or model for the explanation or resolution of problems in their field as long as it seems possible to explain the empirical

25. *Hellenists*, pp. 112–17. Cf. "Sources and Methods," p. 129.

26. Cf. P. Gardner–Smith, *St. John and the Synoptic Gospels* (Cambridge: Cambridge University Press, 1938), pp. x–xii.

data on the basis of it.[27] Thus in astronomy the Ptolemaic view of the universe went unchallenged as long as it appeared to correspond to the known data and to offer solutions to problems people were then interested in solving. But when data were discovered and problems were posed which could not be solved on the basis of the Ptolemaic view, there occurred a crisis in the scientific community. In Kuhn's view such a crisis is the necessary presupposition for the development of a new paradigm. In view of the crisis of the Ptolemaic paradigm Copernicus put forward a totally new view, a new paradigm, according to which the sun rather than the earth was the center of the universe. Gradually the scientific community went over to the Copernican view as offering a better paradigm, and therefore a better possibility for explaining the data and solving pressing problems. Thus there were "conversions" of individual scientists and a "scientific revolution."

Kuhn cautions against transferring his interpretation of scientific revolutions to other disciplines. As a rank amateur in the philosophy of science, I do not wish to rush in where angels fear to tread. But what he is describing seems to me not unrelated to our procedures. For we also work with established paradigms which are more or less adequate to explain the data. Thus, for example, in biblical research one accepted, by tradition and schooling (also the determiners of scientific opinion), the view that the Fourth Evangelist knew Mark or the synoptics. The problem then became one of explaining how, if he knew them, he wrote such an enormously different gospel. Traditionally, the answer has been that he intended to supplement, correct, or interpret them. Perhaps principally one of these; perhaps all three. In the face of what he regarded as the irreconcilable differences and contradictions between John and the synoptics, and seeing no valid way to explain John as supplementary, Windisch made the radical proposal that John intended to displace the synoptics. This proposal amounted to a new paradigm to solve the John-synoptic problem. But it did not take hold, for scholars felt that it, like its rivals, lacked adequate explicit warrant in the text.

27. *Foundations of the Unity of Science*, 2nd ed. (Chicago: University of Chicago Press, 1970), pp. 43–51.

Thus Windisch only continued and exacerbated the crisis. But this crisis became fruitful for further research in that it prepared scholars who were working independently of one another to reconsider the generally held premise of the whole discussion. When Gardner-Smith proposed a new paradigm by arguing that John did not know the synoptics in the first place, his proposal fell upon fertile ground, prepared among other things by Windisch and the acknowledged difficulties of the traditional view. Scholars working on the Fourth Gospel needed to test the new hypothesis or paradigm to see whether it would explain the data and solve relevant problems. Certainly it seemed to explain the profuse data relating to John's differences from the synoptics. It left the similarities as a problem to be explained, but the advocates of the new view felt that these could be handled much more easily under the new paradigm than could the differences and contradictions under the old.

Thus, since Bacon a scientific revolution of sorts has been set in motion in the study of the relationship between John and the synoptics. That is not to say it is complete; nor can one be certain that it will become so. There are still defenders of the view that John knew and used at least Mark among the synoptics; and new arguments are now advanced, particularly from the standpoint of redaction criticism, in support of that position.

Kuhn notes that "once it has achieved the status of a paradigm, a scientific theory is declared invalid only if an alternative candidate is available to take its place. . . . The decision to reject one paradigm is always simultaneously the decision to accept another, and the judgment leading to that decision involves the comparison of both paradigms with nature *and* with each other."[28] The paradigm of John's knowledge and use of the synoptics (and of Mark) will be rejected only if the Johannine text can be more adequately explained on the basis of the opposite paradigm, John's ignorance and disuse of them.

We are not yet in a position to state that a "scientific revolution" in the resolution of this problem has occurred. But we are, so to speak, between paradigms, and that may be where we shall stay, given the state of our knowledge and the nature of our field of inquiry:

28. Ibid., p. 77.

> Confronted with anomaly or with crisis, scientists take a
> different attitude toward existing paradigms, and the na-
> ture of their research changes accordingly. The prolifera-
> tion of competing articulations, the willingness to try
> anything, the expression of discontent, the recourse to
> philosophy and to debate over fundamentals, all these
> are symptoms of a transition from normal to extraordi-
> nary research.[29]

One is tempted to say that extraordinary research is precisely "normal" in the biblical field! Thus the analogy with natural scientific inquiry would break down. In fact, one major point at which a well-established paradigm had been thought to exist, the Marcan hypothesis, now seems to have been brought into serious question. If that goes, what else could possibly stand? I now would like to risk a tangential but not unrelated judgment. It seems to me the Marcan hypothesis has not yet fallen, and for two reasons. First, no alternative paradigm capable of gaining remotely comparable consensus has appeared or even seems to be on the horizon. Second, in the judgment of most "scientists" in the field, the Marcan hypothesis continues to offer the best possibility for solving the relevant problems, namely, of understanding and explaining the texts on both sides (i.e., Marcan, on the one hand, and Matthean and Lucan, on the other). For the task of exegesis, the hypothesis or paradigm that Mark was used by Matthew and Luke still seems the most satisfying, especially in comparison with the view that Mark conflated Matthew and Luke.

Similarly the best evidence that there has been a shift in paradigms on the question of John's use of Mark or the synoptics is the number of recent commentators who have found the old paradigm of John's use of them unnecessary in explaining the text of John. Here again the test of how a paradigm works in exegesis is significant. True, the paradigm shift is not complete, and may never be. But a good test of whether you may think some significant shifting of paradigms has occurred already is to read Benjamin Bacon on this issue. If his assumptions, perspective, and exegetical proposals seem initially as foreign to you as they did to me, and

29. Ibid., pp. 90–91.

if after reading his exegetical arguments you are similarly less than satisfied, that should be sufficient indication that since he wrote, something really has happened in our field of inquiry.

6 | John and the Synoptics: de Solages and Neirynck

The year 1979 saw the publication of two interesting and important books, each entitled *Jean et les Synoptiques*, the one by Monsignor de Solages and the other by Professor Frans Neirynck[1]. Although very different in method and approach, together or individually they represent a substantial and significant demurral from the still widely held view that John wrote without knowledge of the synoptic gospels. Both Neirynck and Solages are strongly of the opinion that the Fourth Evangelist knew the synoptics or, in the case of Solages, at least Mark. But on the question of whether he employed them in the composition of his gospel they differ widely. Neirynck believes that he did and that a great deal remains to be said on the subject of the redactional use of the synoptics by the Fourth Evangelist. Solages, on the other hand, sees John's disuse of the synoptics, despite the fact that he knew at least Mark, as a problem to be explained.

Solages's work is a wonderful combination of complexity and simplicity. The complexity of the book consists in his effort to marshal and measure the actual extent of the agreement between John and the synoptics, both over the extent of the gospels and in indi-

1. Mgr. de Solages, *Jean et les synoptiques* (Leiden: Brill, 1979); Frans Neirynck, with the collaboration of Joël Delobel, Thierry Snoy, Gilbert Van Belle, Frans Van Segbroeck, *Jean et les synoptiques: Examen critique de l'exégèse de M.-É. Boismard*, BETL 49 (Louvain: University Press, 1979).

vidual pericopes; the simplicity in his explanation of why, if John knew the other gospels, he did not use them as sources.

Part One, entitled "Jean n'utilise pas les Synoptiques comme source," begins with an effort simply to identify those verses of John which may reasonably be said to be paralleled in the synoptics. These are displayed in a table of columns (pp. 4–20) in which every verse of John is given down the left-hand side and every synoptic verse that could be considered a parallel is noted under the respective gospel and across from the Johannine verse. Many of the corresponding verses of the synoptics are bracketed or framed to indicate they are not in the same wording or not in the same order as their synoptic counterparts. Not surprisingly, most pages are largely blank. Solages observes (p. 21) that one cannot fail to be struck by the relative paucity of such correspondences as compared with those among the synoptic gospels. Moreover, such correspondences as exist are usually isolated rather than continuous. Totaling the corresponding verses, Solages concludes that of the 868 verses of John, 153, or 17.6 percent, have synoptic counterparts. He might have noted that this would compare with upward of 90 percent of Marcan verses having Matthean counterparts. (Allan Barr, *A Diagram of Synoptic Relationships* [Edinburgh, 1938], p. 3, indicates 609 of Mark's 662 verses have Matthean counterparts). Even such a figure as Solages proposes for John and the synoptics is really not comparable to the figures for Mark and Matthew, however, for the incidence of verbatim agreement or near agreement is much greater in the latter case than in the former. Nevertheless, Solages performs a useful service in quantifying Johannine-synoptic relationships in this way. He dramatizes the obvious but significant fact that most of what John contains is simply not found in the synoptics and vice versa. Perhaps the extent of agreement in the passion and resurrection narratives lessens the impact of this fact, even on the sophisticated reader.

After this useful inventory of Johannine and synoptic content, Solages turns to a comparison of the order of verses in passages which correspond (pp. 23–27). For good reason the passion is examined in greatest detail. A table (p. 24) compares the order of corresponding verses in the passion narratives of John and Mark. Mark and John frequently have the same verse sequence in the passion where they correspond, but this sequence is sometimes broken or interrupted by omissions or dislocations on one side or the other. There are, of course, significant parallels outside the passion narrative, especially in John 6, where Jesus first feeds a multitude then walks on the sea.

Particularly useful is Solages's effort to quantify, i.e., set a percentage value on, the verbal agreements between John and the synoptics in the passion, John 6, and certain common logia (pp. 27–66). To spread the linguistic net as wide as possible, Solages uses three categories of agreement: verbatim agreement (abbreviated I); equivalent words (i.e., same root but different inflexion; abbreviated E); and synonyms (abbreviated Σ). He finds, for example, that through John's entire passion narrative (chaps. 18–19) there is a 15.5 percent agreement with Mark (i.e., the total agreement comprising categories I, E, and Σ). That percentage of agreement rises to 33.3 percent if only the corresponding verses are considered (p. 27). This compares with Luke's percentages of 65.2 in relation to Mark for the entire passion and 66.6 for the corresponding passages or verses. With Matthew/Mark those percentages are 65.2 for the passion as a whole and 70.0 for the corresponding verses. In the case of traditions within the synoptics known to be independent (i.e., the Beelzebul accusation of Luke 11:14–15, 17–23, from Q, and Mark 3:21–30) the percentages of agreement are, on the same terms, somewhat higher than those between the passion narratives of Mark and John. Solages can think of no better proof of the independence of their passion traditions.

As a kind of test case, Solages conducts an extensive comparison of the wording of John 6:1–21 (feeding and walking on the water) and the corresponding synoptic passages (pp. 30–49), which constitute the longest continuous parallels outside the passion. The result is a maximal 27.2 percent agreement (bear in mind this passage corresponds to the synoptics throughout), somewhat lower than in the corresponding parts of the passion. The percentage of identical agreement (I) is only 13.9 percent. The identical agreement is only a little more than one-half of the broader agreement, and both are relatively low. This is exactly what one would expect to find in independent but parallel traditions. Moreover, the verbatim relationship of Matthew or Luke to Mark is generally more than twice as strong as the verbatim relationship of either Matthew or Luke to

John, again a token of the independence of the Johannine traditions (p. 50).

The comparison of a series of logia (John 4:44; 5:23*b*,29; 6:51; 8:51[52], 12:23*b*,25,26; 13:16,20; 14:25–26,31; 15:19*b*,20*a*,20*b*–21,26,27; 16:23) yields similar results (pp. 50–66). None of these logia occur in the same context in John and Mark, an indication that John does not follow Mark. In those cases in which the verbal correspondence seems quite high (e.g. John 13:20 and Mark 9:37), the logia are relatively brief and the correspondences might easily result from memory, and in any event are not sufficient to prove literary dependence.

Solages begins the second part of his work ("Jean connaît la tradition synoptique," pp. 67–185) with the confident assertion that although John does not use the synoptics as sources, he nevertheless knows the synoptic tradition. Because the percentage of resemblance is usually stronger between John and Mark than between John and the other synoptics, and because Mark as the most ancient gospel could scarcely have been ignored by John, Solages first studies the relation between John and Mark. Despite the fact that the overall percentages of verbal agreement between John and Mark are not great, there are some pericopes in which they are sufficiently high to be difficult to explain apart from John's knowledge of Mark. Already the higher percentage of agreement in the corresponding passages of the passion has been noted. In several episodes of the passion the degree of agreement rises even higher: the mocking of Jesus (John 19:2–3 = Mark 15:16–19); the crucifixion (John 19:16–19 = Mark 15:33–39); the cleansing of the temple (John 2:13,15,16,18[19] = Mark 11:15,17,28; 14:58); the anointing at Bethany (John 12:1–8 = Mark 14:1–9). The percentage of total agreement (I + E + Σ) between John and Mark in these passages ranges between the upper 40s and the lower 60s, i.e. closer to the percentages between Mark and Matthew or Luke in corresponding passages of the synoptics than to the much lower percentages of the independent traditions as represented by the Beelzebul accusation in Mark 3:21–30 and Luke 11:14–15,17–23 (Q). Solages concludes that such passages as these reflect John's direct knowledge of Mark. Looking again at the feeding stories of Mark and John (pp. 98–99), which on grounds of wording did not seem to require a literary relationship, Solages observes that they contain exactly the same numbers: two hundred denarii, five loaves and two fish, five thousand men, twelve baskets. He concludes that this agreement indicates John's knowledge of Mark.

Comparisons of data held in common between Matthew and John (pp. 99–113) and Luke and John (pp. 113–58) lead Solages to the conclusion that John did not write with the text of either before him, although the affinities with Luke are acknowledged to be more numerous than those with Matthew. The story of the official's son (John 4:46–53 = Luke 7:1–10/Matt. 8:5–10,13) is, however, taken to be an adequate indication that John knew Q, a conclusion that the few logia held in common would not suffice to demonstrate.

What then is John's attitude toward the synoptic tradition (pp. 170–85)? Although John knew at least Mark (p. 170), unless he had specific reason for taking up synoptic episodes he avoided repeating them. Thus he omits some essential episode like the baptism of Jesus. He repeats others when necessary, e.g., the temple cleansing—his moving it forward is sufficient reason to repeat it. His use of the synoptic material indicates he affirmed its validity (pp. 172–73). He completes the synoptic tradition, adding episodes of Jesus' ministry in Judea and giving the circumstances of Jesus' word about the destruction of the temple reported at the Marcan trial (14:53–59). At points he corrects the synoptics (pp. 182–85), particularly with regard to the general temporal and geographic framework of Jesus' ministry, but also in such relatively minor details as Jesus' carrying his own cross to the place of crucifixion.

Finally, the crucial question: Why does the Fourth Evangelist, who knows such an important source as Mark, which was used by Matthew and Luke, largely ignore it? Because, thinks Solages, he was himself the Beloved Disciple, an eyewitness, as 21:24 (written by a later hand) avers. Solages takes chapter 21 to be substantially authentic, that is, from the same author who composed the rest of the Gospel, and he devotes a long chapter to demonstrating this, showing that it is stylistically almost as close to chapters 1–20 as chapter 20 to chapters 1–19, and much closer to those chapters of John than to Luke chapters 1–24.

The claim that the author was an eyewitness is said to be supported by the Gospel's precision about geographical locations and dates. Moreover, it gives the impression of "things seen" (details such as six water pots, the whip of cords, Jesus' fatigue at the well, etc.). But what of the discourses (pp. 248–57)? Solages faces this problem head-on, acknowledging in view of the synoptics the difficulty of taking them as verbatim reports of what Jesus said on the occasions reported. Yet their nuclear historical basis is supported by elements within them familiar from the synoptics (e.g. 5:29 = Matt. 25:46) and by the way they are bound to traditional, and presumably historical, narratives. Who was the author? The ancient tradition that the Beloved Disciple was the son of Zebedee is embraced. After Peter, John is mentioned more often than any disciple, and in the list of Acts 1:13 he has moved up to second place among the Twelve from fourth, where he is found in Luke 6:13–16. The almost total silence of the Gospel about the son of Zebedee is taken to support the traditional view. John was not, however, written much earlier than the end of the first century, if then. The son of Zebedee lived, as one tradition (or legend!) has it, until the time of Trajan.

If the evangelist was the son of Zebedee, an original disciple and an apostle, a number of characteristics of the Fourth Gospel are thus explained: the precision with which facts are reported; the independence toward the synoptics, which he sometimes neglects and sometimes corrects; the relative paucity of traces of Luke and Matthew, whose authors were not eyewitnesses; acquaintanceship with Q (probably the logia of Matthew). The unique connections with Luke are to be explained by the latter's having inquired of eyewitnesses (such as John) in composing his gospel.

The diligence of Solages and the complexity of his linguistic-statistical work are matched by the simplicity of the solution which he proposes. It is perhaps not difficult to find points with which to take issue with Solages. Yet he has, it seems to me, made a significant contribution in his effort to quantify the degree of similarity and differences of language and content between John and the synoptics. Two sets of facts, the sheer divergence of content between John and the synoptics and the much lower level of verbatim agreement where they correspond, have impressed Solages, and he has performed a useful service in setting forth these differences in forms that can be measured.

Solages's view that John knows the synoptics, or at least Mark, but does not use them as sources makes a certain sense of the data. The explanation that this state of affairs results from the author's having been not only eyewitness to the events he describes but one of the Twelve has a wondrous simplicity and attractiveness. But Solages hardly meets the objections that have been mounted against this view. Indeed, his references to scholarly discussions of the problems with which he deals are at best minimal. Moreover, the "supplementation theory" (Windisch) which Solages represents as basically explaining John's treatment, or omission, of the greater part of the synoptic material is more satisfactory as a general theory of their relationship when one does not examine individual cases or pericopes in order to assess how well they may actually be interpreted on this basis. Nevertheless, Solages's simple solution is at least as plausible as many a more complicated and sophisticated treatment of the perplexing data of the Johannine and synoptic texts.

Neirynck's work shares with Solages's a subject, John and the synoptics, and the belief that the author of the Fourth Gospel knew the others, or at least (in the case of Solages) Mark and Q. Beyond that they are vastly different works. While Solages scarcely cites the work of other scholars, and never builds upon it or criticizes it in any systematic or fundamental way, Neirynck's awareness of contemporary scholarly literature and his willingness to enter into detailed discussion with colleagues is scarcely equaled in contemporary scholarship. To read his *Jean et les Synoptiques* is to stand in awe of the erudition and precision of Neirynck and his colleagues at Louvain. There is apparently little they have not digested and do not stand ready, if necessary, to refute, criticize, or at points accept.

The book of Neirynck and his colleagues is, in effect, an extensive review of Boismard's and Lamouille's *Commentaire* on John (*L'évangile de Jean* [Paris, 1977]). As is well known, that commentary is the third volume of a series in which Boismard develops his rather complex position on gospel origins: *Synopse des quatre évangiles en francais: Tome I. Textes* (Paris 1965, 2d ed. 1973); *Tome II. Commentaire* (Paris, 1972). (As Neirynck points out, Boismard's own views have changed somewhat in the course of his work.) There is something faintly absurd about reviewing a review. Perhaps the most useful course will be to characterize the positions of Boismard and Neirynck and then to dwell upon certain more important aspects which distinquish their positions and are characteristic of Neirynck's critique.

Neirynck's basic position is that John, the Fourth Evangelist, knows all the synoptic gospels. In that respect he does not differ from Boismard, who also believes that the author or editor who gave this Gospel its basic form knew all three synoptic gospels. What then is the area of disagreement? It concerns the point in the composition of the Fourth Gospel at which the synoptics became an important influence.

For Neirynck, who refuses to allow a complex system of sources to replace the complexity of the evangelist's redaction (p. 390), the synoptics are the sources of the Fourth Evangelist. Apparently, he wishes to insist that the differences of John from the synoptics can be explained as the work of the evangelist without recourse to theories of independent sources or traditions.

For Boismard the influence of the synoptics on John arrives on the scene rather late. First, there was an independent, primitive gospel narrative called by Boismard Document C (or John I); it was composed by an unknown author about *A.D.* 50 in Palestine. This document was taken up, within the "Johannine" school, by the evangelist who composed the first recension of his gospel in Palestine in the sixties (John II-A). He revised it extensively thirty-odd years later at Ephesus (II-B). Only at the stage of the second revision was he influenced by the synoptics. But at that point he knew and used all three, and their influence upon him was significant. At the level of II-B the discourse material, added in II-A, was augmented and the Gospel received what is essentially its present shape. Finally, a later redactor (John III) worked the finished Gospel over, making some changes and additions, sometimes laying material from older level II-A alongside II-B material intended to displace it.

Neirynck observes (p. 15) that Boismard's position differs from that of a number of recent commentators, in that he takes the evangelist himself (II-B) rather than the later, final redaction to have been influenced by the synoptic gospels. In his second volume he had seen the direct influence of the synoptics upon John occurring only at the level of the final "post-Johannine" redaction, but now it is moved, so to speak, back one stage. Moreover, in Boismard's revised position the so-called sign-source falls out of the picture. Instead, the miracle stories are assigned to Documents C or A (Proto-Matthew). Proto-Luke becomes superfluous as a source of John, inasmuch as the final recension of the evangelist (II-B) is influenced by the synoptic gospels themselves. Neirynck can only applaud Boismard's recognition that the evangelist himself knows and uses the synoptics. In his view the commentary has the great merit of placing that whole problem at the center of the discussion. Neirynck's question is whether, given that knowledge, it is necessary to suppose that John based his narrative on a more primitive gospel (Document C = John I) and composed an earlier version of his gospel without knowledge of the synoptics (cf. p. 21).

Neirynck raises some questions about Boismard's choice of readings in examining the text-critical principles which underlie his work (pp. 23–29; cf. 205–26). Neirynck's judgments, while often at odds with Boismard, do not, it seems to me, play a fundamental role in his critique of the latter's work. He also closely examines, and refines, the list of more than four hundred stylistic characteristics which Boismard has assembled. Neirynck affirms the contribution Boismard has made in assembling and classifying of Johannine characteristics. Although Boismard himself is relatively cautious in the use of these for purposes of source criticism, Neirynck is dubious even of their limited value for that purpose: e.g., circularity is difficult to avoid; the classification of a characteristic as "non-Johannine" because it is "synoptic," when the Fourth Evangelist (II-B) was influenced by the synoptics, creates difficulties.

Neirynck's reservations about the fruitfulness of stylistic characteristics in source criticism take very specific form in his arguments against the proposal that the evangelist used a hypothetical Document C in the composition of the initial recension of his gospel (pp. 71-91). Four passages in which Boismard detected that source are examined (20:1–10; 18:15–16; 2:13–22; 12:1–11). While Neirynck's criticisms are as detailed as Boismard's own analysis, his fundamental objections can be simply stated. In every case the two agree that the synoptic gospels have influenced the Johannine narrative at some point. The question is always at what point. By attacking the stylistic, linguistic, and contextual grounds on which Boismard separates Document C, II-A, or II-B, Neirynck calls into question the existence of these hypothetical sources or literary strata. He then suggests that the explanation of the existing text of John on the basis of his use of Mark or the synoptics is equally possible and, in view of the fact that these are extant rather than hypothetical documents, to be preferred. In the case of the healing of the royal official's son, Neirynck's attack follows a similar line (pp. 93–120).

Neirynck questions the necessity of supposing that there was a nonsynoptic traditional account at the basis of this Johannine narrative, regarding as preferable his own view that the Johannine account is based directly on that of Matt. 8:5–13 and Luke 7:1–10. Considerations of style and vocabulary do not suffice to demonstrate the existence of a primitive, nonsynoptic source.

In Boismard's view the numbered signs (2:1–11; 4:46–54; as well as 21:1–14) formed a section of Galilean miracles at the beginning of the account of Jesus' ministry in Document C. (Thus there is no longer any need for a miracle source per se.) Boismard thinks that John II-B removed the miracle of the catch of fish in 21:1–14 from the Galilean ministry to its present position at the end of the Gospel. In doing so, he combined it with a primitive appearance scene by the lake in Galilee, which in Document C and II-A had followed the appearance to Mary Magdalene. In an amazingly complex and subtle analysis Boismard has derived this appearance scene not only from parts of John 21:1–14, but from elements of Luke 24:26–43 (albeit in Jerusalem!) and the synoptic account of Jesus' walking on the sea, for which it was a source. Moreover, elements of this primitive narrative can be detected in John 6:19bd,20a. Not surprisingly, in the measure that this analysis is subtle and complex it is also unconvincing to Neirynck, who fails to see the need or the legitimacy of positing John's dependence on one of Luke's sources as well as on the final version of that gospel. (Boismard thinks that in general Luke and John depend on a common source, C, through the mediation of Proto-Luke and John II-A; but John II-B also knows Luke.) The "pure fish story" of John 21:2,3,4a,6 is the common source of John 21:1–14 (where II-B has combined it with the appearance story) and Luke 5:1–11. Yet even in Boismard's view the redactor of John 21 (II-B) knows the Gospel of Luke. Again, is it really necessary or helpful to suppose that he also knew a source which he shares with Luke? Neirynck is not convinced by the several stylistic traits identified by Boismard as uncharacteristic of John and indicative of a primitive source.

While Neirynck obviously regards Boismard's effort to distill a third Galilean sign from 21:1–14 as most dubious and vulnerable, he is not convinced that the first and second Cana miracles of 2:1–11 and 4:46–54 can safely be ascribed to a more primitive source, Document C, from which these miracles were derived by the evangelist at the level of John II-A. "The point of departure of all *sēmeia*-source theories, that is to say, the grouping of the two narratives at the level of pre-Johannine tradition, remains an undemonstrable hypothesis" (p. 174). But Neirynck does not, as far as I can see, attempt to derive these two miracles from the synoptics.

Nor is Neirynck persuaded by Boismard's arguments that along with Document C, John used the ultimate source of Matthew (Document A) from which he took the stories of the healing of the blind man and the feeding of the multitude. Also the motifs of sin and the Son of man which appear in John 5:1ff. are, like the healing story of 5:5–9a, derived from Document A, and not from Mark. These stories were incorporated at the level of II-A, before the evangelist knew the synoptics. Yet later on (II-B), he did know and was influenced by the synoptic accounts. Neirynck's basic argument against Boismard's proposal at this point is that once Mark's influence upon John is granted, it is unnecessary to deduce from the Johannine text on stylistic and other grounds a primitive form of the story that does not show Mark's influence. The same principle applies to Boismard's attempt to show that the multiplication of the loaves in John is based on an originally independent account which only secondarily (level II-B) was influenced by Mark. Boismard attributes the latter narrative to a primitive source, in part because of its affinities with the Elisha narrative of 2 Kings 4:42ff. But inasmuch as the influence of that narrative is already conceded at the level of John II-B, which was influenced by Mark, it scarcely speaks decisively on the side of a primitive source.

Neither is Neirynck convinced of the influence of John II-A upon the Gospel of Matthew, a relationship which Boismard proposes to account for such affinities as exist between John 1:41–42 and Matthew 16:16,18 (the naming of Peter). After all, on Boismard's terms, the evangelist ultimately (II-B) knew and was influenced by the Gospel of Matthew itself. Neirynck sees no compelling reason to ascribe 1:37–42,43*b*,45–49 to II-A (and ultimately Document C), as Boismard does, rather than to II-B. The factors which Boismard thinks distinguish II-A (prior to synoptic influence) from II-B (under synoptic influence) are at best ambiguous, and if the affinities are between Matthew and II-B, the dependence must lie on the Johannine side rather than the Matthean.

Neirynck's examination of Boismard's classification of the Johannine use of οὖν and his use of it as a criterion of literary criticism reaches an almost unbelievable level in the mastery and refinement of detail (pp. 227–83). Neirynck has concentrated on this particle because Boismard's use of it is illustrative of his way of working throughout the commentary. Boismard has argued that οὖν is characteristic of the II-B level of redaction, where John tends to add it to his source immediately after an insertion, but some instances are attributed to II-A. Also, οὖν is used by the later redactor (John III) to tie in elements from earlier levels that he himself has transposed. Neirynck remains, with some reason, unconvinced; more likely, οὖν reflects a homogeneous style throughout the Gospel and affords no reliable grounds for distinguishing redactional levels.

In sum, Neirynck believes Boismard's chief contribution lies in his inventory of the characteristics of the language and style of John. But he cannot agree with the way Boismard attempts to make such data profitable for source analysis of which also on other grounds Neirynck remains skeptical. While agreeing with Boismard generally that the synoptics have influenced John, Neirynck believes that influence lies at a more fundamental level and can satisfactorily explain much of the data that lead Boismard to propose primitive sources or redactional levels which are no longer extant.

There are several appendixes, consisting of related articles, most of which have been published previously. In a final brief postscript (pp. 389–90), Neirynck makes some insightful generalizations about the analogies between Boismard's view of John's development and his proposals about the synoptics (e.g., all went through intermediate stages). Neirynck is gratified that "Boismard has made a great step forward by accepting the dependence of John upon the Synoptic Gospels in their actual form" (p. 389). Nevertheless, "he ought to ask himself whether the knowledge of the same Synoptics does not explain equally the elements of the Johannine text which he still attributes to a level of pre-Synoptic redaction (John II-A) or to a primitive Gospel (Document C)." In conclusion, Neirynck notes that Boismard is fond of saying that the solution to the problem of the development of the gospels can only be complex. Neirynck avers that no diametrically opposed taste for simplicity has guided his colleagues and himself. Yet it would be wrong, he thinks, "to replace the complexity of the gospel redaction by one of multiple sources which the evangelist simply composed and fused" (p. 390). Perhaps after diagramming Boismard's theory of gospel origins (which indeed "looks like a twelve-man football team with a lot of motion in the backfield," as Raymond Brown suggested), Neirynck could not resist diagramming his own, which is simplicity itself, a quadrilateral with one gospel at each corner and one line bisecting it in order to connect John to Mark, as well as to Matthew and Luke!

The book ends with a splendid set of indexes, including authors cited, Greek words, and scripture references.

Obviously, the issues dividing Boismard and Neirynck can scarcely be adjudicated in any detail in this review. As we have seen, they are really in agreement that John in the form in which it was published—indeed, as it left the hand of the evangelist (for Boismard, level II-B)—was importantly influenced by all the synoptics in the form in which we know them. The only question is, At what stage did this influence occur?

Boismard's theory of Johannine origins, one aspect of a complete theory of gospel origins, is so detailed and complex as to suggest that in its totality it could never attract an appreciable consensus of scholarly opinion. Is there adequate reason to think, as Boismard seems to believe, that given the Johannine text, along with the synoptic texts which bear some relation to it, we can coax from them the secrets of their origins, development, and relationships? At many, if not most of the points at which Neirynck undertakes a critical analysis of Boismard, he is able to make telling points, in no small part because Boismard in attempting so detailed a reconstruction has given many hostages to fortune.

Raymond Brown, who demurs from accepting Boismard's theory (*CBQ* 40 [1978]:624–28), nevertheless points out that this theory, insofar as it touches the Fourth Gospel, moves in the same direction as, or reflects, a broad spectrum of opinion in Johannine studies. Quite remarkable, for example, are the affinities between Boismard's Document C and Fortna's Gospel of Signs. (Of course, Boismard has been able to read Fortna, but his viewpoint is not derivative from Fortna's work.) Boismard has, of course, gone much further in the direction of separating literary strata and assigning them to the developmental history of the Fourth Gospel than most scholars would be willing to do. Nevertheless, in objecting to Boismard's procedure Neirynck is calling into question the direction of much current Johannine scholarship.

While Neirynck's objections to Boismard's criteria and results are at many points impressive, his contribution is so far mostly on the negatively critical side. His own view of Johannine origins is yet to be developed, although the way he would go is clear enough. John not only reflects knowledge of the synoptics; the evangelist himself knew them; he not only knew them; they apparently lie at the basis of his narrative. Unless I badly misunderstand, Neirynck believes John can be explained mainly in terms of this relationship to the synoptics. It seems to me that the exegetical task which Neirynck faces on the positive or constructive side is, however, a considerable one. But there is no doubt that Neirynck and his Louvain colleagues have the industry and ingenuity to carry it through. Whether they will be able to rally a sizable consensus of scholarly opinion to their perspective only time will tell.

A few concluding observations by way of comparing the works and positions of de Solages and Neirynck may be useful. Perhaps it says something that I found not a single reference to the one man in the work of the other. They apparently inhabit different worlds of scholarship.

There are other senses in which these two works, on the same subject and with the same title, do not touch. They agree that John knew the synoptic gospels. They obviously disagree on whether he made much positive use of them. Neirynck believes that it can be shown that he did. Solages is impressed with what seems to him (and to me) the very great difference in sheer content between John and the synoptics. If Solages gives a figure of 17.6 percent agreement between John and Mark, that is certainly maximal, for he is counting correspondences which do not share anything like the level of verbatim agreement that can be found between Mark and Matthew, or even Luke. For Solages to account both for this divergence and at the same time for John's knowledge of the synoptics is a major problem, as it will be for anyone who is convinced John knew the synoptics. Solages seems to sense the acuteness of this problem more than does Neirynck.

Why does one think John knew and used the synoptics in the first place? There is ample reason to doubt that he did, as the very different works of Bultmann, Goodenough, Gardner-Smith, Dodd, and Brown have shown. Moreover, as Solages clearly demonstrates, it is possible to believe John knew them without using them as sources. If it be granted that in all probability oral tradition circulated and narratives or sayings were written down in the forty-odd years between the death of Jesus and the composition of Mark, not to mention the half-century following, it is intrinsically likely that what survives to us in the New Testament is only a part of the evangelical traditions about Jesus. The extent of the tradition may have been much broader than the gospels. This does not, of course, mean that John could not have known the synoptics, but it renders it possible that he might not have, or that he need not have been confined to them. In that event the situation of John and the synoptics becomes uncontrollable, or uncontrolled, in two senses, as I shall attempt to indicate.

First, scholarship may not be able to control the relationships among the gospels. Those relationships can only be controlled if one can, on good grounds, predicate direct literary relationships among the gospels. Only after generations of effort was a consensus about the existence of such relations among the synoptics attained, despite the extensive verbatim agreements and similarities of order and content generally. In that case hypotheses which attempted to account for the agreements on the basis of oral tradition or common sources seemed superfluous, although it cannot be said that they have completely died out (witness Boismard!). The grounds for predicating direct, literary dependence between John and the synoptics are much less obvious, of course, and there is all the more reason to doubt that the former was determined by the latter, even in the sense of writing with them in view. To the degree that one seriously countenances the possibility, or the likelihood, of other narrative (or saying) sources than are comprehended by the synoptics, the viability of any effort to control the relationship between John and, let us say, Mark, as one controls that between Mark and Matthew, is diminished, particularly in view of the wide divergence of content. Whether or how this fact may be relevant to their present works, I hesitate to say, but it is interesting that both Solages and Neirynck made significant contributions to synoptic scholarship, basically on the side of the Marcan hypothesis, before turning to the question of John and the synoptics.

At this point another kind of control, or concept of control, may bear upon the issue. Was the evangelical tradition under some canonical or quasi-canonical control from the beginning or from a very early time as, for example, Birger Gerhardsson's view of its transmission implies? On the side of such control are perhaps the synoptic relationships, especially the fact that both Matthew and Luke, probably independently, used Mark. There is not, however, prima facie grounds for extending the kind of control, if that is what it is, that may have existed behind or among the synoptics to the Fourth Gospel. The fact that all four ultimately compose the gospel canon does not necessarily mean they were intended to complement one another, or specifically that John was intended to complement the other three. Käsemann's argument that John became a part of the canon because it was misunderstood cannot be lightly dismissed. In other words, the canon may represent the convergence of originally disparate trajectories, rather than parallel and originally related trajectories.

I do not wish to appear to brand Solages and Neirynck as "orthodox" or "catholic" in their approach to this problem, although I do not consider those at all derogatory terms. Nevertheless, it seems to me that they, and even Boismard, tend to think of gospels, and by implication of evangelical traditions, that grow within specific boundaries, which are not breached even in the case of John and the synoptics. Thus in a certain sense they stand in the tradition of Clement of Alexandria, who believed that John, realizing that the others had recorded the bodily facts (or whatever), wrote a "spiritual gospel." It is not a bad tradition to stand in, I recognize, while at the same time wishing I could be more confident of it.

I do not think it possible to prove that John did not know the synoptics in the form we have them, as real as are the grounds for doubting that he did, much less that he wrote primarily with them in view. It does seem to me, however, that John presupposes more than he narrates, whether that "more" is one or the other of the synoptics, the synoptic tradition, a related tradition, or a more primitive gospel narrative. John's view is retrospective. This becomes clear, for example, in the account of John the Baptist and Jesus in 1:19ff., where the Baptist is looking back upon and narrating elements of what would appear to be a scene like that described in Mark. We read the Fourth Gospel on the assumption that Jesus was baptized by John and scarcely realize that the event itself is not recounted. Mark tells what one might call a primary, straightforward account. That account is augmented, but left to stand, by Matthew and Luke. John does not take up that account as Matthew and Luke do. His narrative is not so straightforward but, notwithstanding the author's literary skill (cf. chap. 4 or 9), moves in fits and starts. (Thus rearrangements of the extant text are frequently proposed in order to restore the putative original John, but such scholarly tampering with Mark's narrative is almost unthinkable.) The mystery of John's relation to the synoptic tradition may always divide scholarship, but two things are certain: there is a relationship and it is mysterious. The contributions of Solages and Neirynck are in very different ways significant attempts to explore that relationship and clarify the mystery.

7 | John and the Synoptics: Some Dimensions of the Problem*

The relationship of John to the synoptic gospels has been a recurring problem, not only for two centuries of modern critical scholarship, but for Christian theology and exegesis over a much longer period. To my knowledge a full history of this problem is yet to be written,[1] although it might well be helpful in arriving at a solution, as well as illuminating the present situation. The purpose of this paper is not to treat the history or to resolve the problem, but to sketch out and assess its dimensions.

The dominant view until World War II was that John knew and used the synoptic gospels. That is, he wrote in light of them. Even Hans Windisch, who sharply dissented from the prevailing view that John approved of the synoptics, was convinced that he knew

---

*Paper read at the Annual Meeting of Society for New Testament Studies in Durham, England, 20-24 August, 1979. It is here presented in almost exactly the form in which it was delivered. I have, however, in the conclusion elaborated somewhat upon my statement concerning the possible independence of the Fourth Gospel.

1. Brief but helpful is the review of scholarship by Josef Blinzler, *Johannes und die Synoptiker: Ein Forschungsbericht*, SBS 5 (Stuttgart: Katholisches Bibelwerk, 1965), which is not, however, intended to be a thorough history of the problem. Earlier scholarship, through the first quarter of the present century, is treated by Hans Windisch, *Johannes und die Synoptiker: Wollte der vierte Evangelist die älteren Evangelien ergänzen oder ersetzen,* Untersuchungen zum Neuen Testament 12 (Leipzig: J. C. Hinrichs, 1926), pp. 1-40.

145

them.[2] It was not until after the war that the consensus on this point, which had already in 1938 been sharply challenged by Percival Gardner-Smith,[3] began to crumble. Gardner-Smith's challenge, which so many of his colleagues found persuasive, was based mainly on two considerations, one a new development in biblical research, the other a simple but basic observation. The new development was, apparently, the appearance of form criticism, which brought with it much greater allowance for, and attention to, oral tradition as a factor in the composition of the gospels. Gardner-Smith argued that similarities between John and the synoptics which had previously been ascribed to literary dependence might just as well or better be the result of common, or related, oral tradition.[4] He also observed that in comparing John and the synoptics attention had been focused almost exclusively upon the similarities between them, with the result that the substantial differences had not been adequately taken into account. Furthermore, Gardner-Smith called attention to the difficulty of explaining all of them, as many and varied as they are, on the basis of John's distinctive character and purpose.[5] In the aftermath of Gardner-Smith's work, whether or not under his influence, critical opinion began to shift. A generation later one could speak of a growing consensus in favor of John's independence of the synoptics and cite on that side of the issue Bultmann, Goodenough, Dodd, Raymond E. Brown and Schnackenburg, among many others.[6]

2. Windisch, *Johannes und die Synoptiker*, pp. 42-54. Indeed, as Bultmann pointed out, the contention that John was intended to supplant the other gospels presupposes the evangelist's knowledge of them. See his review of Windisch in *TLZ* 52 (1927):198: "Hat er sie nicht gekannt, so hat er sie auch nicht verdrängen wollen." Bultmann at that time clearly expressed his reservations about both Windisch's position and its presupposition.

3. *St. John and the Synoptic Gospels* (Cambridge: Cambridge University Press, 1938).

4. *Ibid.* p. 93; cf. pp. x-xi. Gardner-Smith mentions form criticism only on p. 93, but he frequently refers to oral tradition as the explanation of existing agreements.

5. This is in a real sense the recurring theme and thesis of his work. But see esp. pp. x-xii and p. 88.

6. See my articles, "The Sources of the Gospel of John: An Assessment of the Present State of the Problem," *NTS* 10 (1963-64): 349; and "Johannine Christianity: Some reflections on its Character and Delineation," *NTS* 21 (1974-75): 229. Both articles are included in this present volume.

The consensus did not, however, rest long. The present state of scholarship is well epitomized by Frans Neirynck in his important article on John and the synoptics in the 1975 Louvain Conference volume.[7] Much to my satisfaction, at the beginning of his article Neirynck sided with me against Josef Blinzler in agreeing to the existence of a consensus on John's independence of the synoptics. He then went on, however, to devote the entire article to a sharp attack upon the grounds for such a consensus. And Neirynck is not alone. Recent developments in North America have once again raised this question, as scholars working on Mark, especially its redaction history, have espoused the view that the points of contact between John and Mark, particularly in the passion narratives, bespeak John's knowledge and use of that gospel.[8]

We have begun by speaking of the problem of the relationship of John and the synoptic gospels. It may not be superfluous to unpack that somewhat laconic description or label just a bit. What exactly is meant or implied by it? It is first of all the question of whether John knew and used any or all of the synoptic gospels, and not vice versa. It is unlikely, if not impossible, that John in its present form was a source for any other canonical gospel, although it is certainly not inconceivable that sources or traditions used by John were known also to the other evangelists.[9] There is no disputing that John knew

7. "John and the Synoptics," in *L'evangile de Jean: Sources, rédaction, théologie,* ed. M. de Jonge, BETL 44 (Louvain: University Press, 1977), pp. 73-106.

8. See Norman Perrin, *The New Testament: An Introduction* (New York: Harcourt Brace Jovanovich, 1974), pp. 228-29. Representative of the Perrin school is the collection of essays, *The Passion in Mark: Studies on Mark 14-16,* ed. W. H. Kelber (Philadelphia: Fortress, 1976). Of course, the consensus on John's independence has at no point included every significant voice. C. K. Barrett, *The Gospel According to St John: An Introduction with Commentary and Notes on the Greek Text,* 2d ed. (Philadelphia: Westminster, 1978), pp. 42-54, espouses John's knowledge of Mark and probably Luke, as does Kümmel, *Introduction to the New Testament,* rev. ed. trans. H. C. Kee (Nashville: Abingdon, 1975), pp. 200-17, esp. 200-4. (The most recent editions of their works reflect long-standing positions.)

9. For nearly a decade and through a number of publications, F. Lamar Cribbs has pursued the possibility that Luke knew either John or, more likely, traditions or sources used by John. In his article "St. Luke and the Johannine Tradition," *JBL* 90 (1971):422-50, he first called attention to the remarkable fact that Luke often differs from Mark (and usually also from Matthew) precisely at points where John is at odds with Mark. Subsequent articles developing this line of evidence have appeared in the *Society of Biblical Literature 1973 Seminar Papers,* ed. George MacRae, pp. 1-93, and in *Perspectives on Luke-Acts,* ed. C. H. Talbert, Perspectives

at least some traditions closely paralleling the other canonical gospels. The question at issue is then whether John had access to one or more of the synoptic gospels in the form in which we now have them, or something very closely approximating it, and if so which. That John knew one of the synoptics does not, of course, mean he knew all, or even another, of them. Nor may it be assumed on the basis of the Marcan hypothesis alone that if he knew any of them he must have known Mark. Also, we should ask what is meant by "knew." There is a tendency, to which I also find myself succumbing, to speak of John's knowledge and use of the synoptics as if one necessarily meant the same as, or followed from, the other. Only a moment's reflection will reveal that this is not the case. John may have known the synoptic gospels without having used them as sources. Few, if any, scholars would argue that John used the synoptics as Matthew, for example, used Mark (or if you will, Mark used Matthew) or even that he always had them in mind as he wrote. Apparently John either stood at some remove from the synoptics, even if he knew them, or for some important reason made no greater or more obvious use of them.[10] In any event, if he knew them, the question of why he made no greater use of them requires a convincing answer.

In the history of exegesis there have emerged several ways of explaining why John seems to know or use the synoptics at some points but over vast stretches ignores them. Hans Windisch offers a suitable typology of them.[11] The classical, traditional explanation

---

in Religious Studies: Special Studies Series 5 (Danville, Va.: Association of Baptist Professors of Religion, 1978), pp. 40-61.

10. Even scholars who believe John knew the synoptics do not, as a rule, regard them as his only, or even principal, sources. See Barrett, "John and the Synoptic Gospels," *ExpT* 85 (1974):31: "It seems clear that John did not use Mark (or Luke or Matthew) in the way in which most students of the synoptic problem suppose that Matthew and Luke used Mark....For this there simply is not enough parallel material. The greater part of John has no parallel in the synoptic gospels and the evangelist must have drawn it either from non-synoptic tradition, or out of his own head. This nonsynoptic material is very extensive, and undoubtedly gives to the Fourth Gospel not only its main substance but its familiar characteristics." In the recent, revised edition of his commentary Barrett makes clear that in his judgment the nonsynoptic material is not sheer fabrication, but owes much to other sources (*St. John*. p. 17). Cf. Windisch, *Johannes und die Synoptiker*, pp. 54-58, esp. 54-55.

11. *Johannes und die Synoptiker*, pp. 1-40.

is, of course, that John wrote in order to *supplement,* or perhaps in some small way correct, the other accounts. But, in Windisch's view, the overall structure and content of the Fourth Gospel do not encourage and support this theory. Often John simply overlaps the others. Where he does not he gives no clear or adequate indication as to how his gospel should be supplemented from the synoptics or should supplement them. (This is as true of individual narratives or accounts as it is of the Gospel as a whole.) The view that John wrote *independently* of the others had always been a minority opinion, frequently associated with conservative scholars. Having once held this view himself, Windisch ultimately felt compelled to abandon it. In his view, the position that John wrote in order to *interpret* the synoptics is a variant of the supplementation theory and suffers from the same deficiencies. So it comes about that the only satisfactory resolution of the conundrum posed by John's wide divergence from the synoptics is the one Windisch adopts, namely, that John wrote to *displace* the other gospels, because he found them inadequate vehicles for the Christian proclamation as he understood it.[12] Writing authoritatively and with his own ends in view, he largely and intentionally ignored them. Windisch's position presents its own problems, however, not the least of which is that John, except perhaps in the colophons, never recognizes the existence of other gospels, much less explicitly polemicizes against them. Yet his position is a logical culmination of his reading of the history of research on the problem of Johannine-synoptic relationships. If it is impossible adequately to explain John's gospel on the assumptions that he knew and approved the synoptics, but was somehow attempting to supplement, enlarge upon, correct, or interpret them, the only alternative would seem to be to question one or the other of the prior assumptions. Windisch thus challenged the assumption that John approved of the synoptics; twelve years later Gardner-Smith revived the challenge to the other assumption, that he knew them at all.[13]

12. Ibid., p. 134. Interestingly enough, Windisch differentiates his own position from the conservative independence theory on two points: (1) in his thinking that John knew and rejected the synoptics, and (2) in finding John significantly less worthwhile historically than the synoptics. Of course, what Windisch rejects in the latter point is not germane to the independence theory.

13. Interestingly enough, Gardner-Smith appears to be unaware of his German predecessors, who are cited by Windisch (*Johannes und die Synoptiker,* pp. 12-

One is tempted to accept the alternatives posed by Gardner-Smith and Windisch, independence or displacement, and attempt to adjudicate between them. Either position has the apparent advantage and attractiveness of sweeping aside the complexities and perplexities of Johannine-synoptic relationships by in effect denying that there is a relationship at all, or in the case of Windisch at least denying that the maintenance of such a positive relationship is in any sense a goal of the Fourth Evangelist. To begin at that point would, however, be tantamount to begging a number of questions which are important and debatable. It will be more profitable to pursue another course and to air some of those questions as we attempt to take stock of the evidence and the dimensions of this problem.

The evidence bearing upon the problem of John and the synoptics can in a general way be described very simply. There is first of all the matter of some common content, pericopes, sayings, and stories. Next there is the order of those materials in the gospels. With only a few exceptions John has those pericopes which he shares with Mark in the same order as Mark.[14] This striking feature does

---

20), as, indeed, of Windisch himself, whom he does not cite. Nor does he entertain the possibility that John wrote to displace the other gospels. (My colleague W. D. Davies reminds me, however, that C. H. Dodd, whose theory of realized eschatology is generally taken to be a response to Albert Schweitzer's thoroughgoing futuristic eschatology, does not characteristically mention Schweitzer by name or direct his arguments against him.)

14. Morton Smith has expanded and helpfully refined the evidence of similarity of order between John and Mark in his article, "Mark 6:32–15: 47 and John 6: 1–19: 42," *Society of Biblical Literature 1978 Seminar Papers* (Missoula, Mont.: Scholars Press, 1978), II, 281-87. He finds in the latter part of each gospel twelve common reports (counting the passion, in which the order is mainly the same, as only one) of which seven are in the same order. Of the five that are not, three (the cleansing of the temple and the accompanying prophecy of its destruction, as well as the question about Jesus' authority) are found in the single cleansing pericope, which John has placed at the beginning of his Gospel. The other two, the plot against Jesus and the anointing in Bethany, are in John placed before the triumphal entry, whereas in Mark they come after. Smith believes this difference is related to the omission of the Lazarus cycle, with which in John they are associated, in canonical Mark (but not, in Smith's view, in the early second-century Carpocratian longer text of Mark). Moreover, Smith identifies eight brief geographical notices which occur in much the same order and relationship to parallel stories in canonical Mark and John (Mark 6:32/John 6:1; Mark 6:45/John 6: 16-17a; Mark 6:46/ John 6:15; Mark 6:54-5a/John 6:24-5a; Mark 9:30-31/John 7:1; Mark 10:1a/

not, however, extend to those few pericopes John has in common with Matthew and/or Luke only. Then there is the evidence of verbatim agreement, mostly within the common materials or material of common content. After this we move into a grey and less easily definable area in which points of contact nevertheless exist; for example: Johannine allusions to matters narrated in the synoptics (baptism of Jesus; 3:24); Johannine sayings that seem to have synoptic counterparts (12:25-26); assumptions about the character of course of Jesus' ministry shared by John and the synoptics.

But in discussing the evidence the differences must also be kept constantly in mind. They are, in fact, well known. Apart from the passion narratives, the accounts of the discovery of the empty tomb, and the Johannine-Lucan appearance scenes, contact between the Johannine and synoptic narratives is not extensive. The itinerary of Jesus' public ministry is different, and such other parallels as exist cluster around the Baptist and the central events of the public ministry in John 6 and Mark 6 and 8 (i.e. the feeding, walking on the water, etc.). Not only does John employ no exorcism, but all his healing stories are without clear parallel in Mark; and the one healing narrative he shares with the synoptics is an anomaly, a Q miracle story. A similar situation pertains in the case of the sayings material, which is by and large quite different, although there there other issues are involved.

John 7:10; Mark 10:1b/John 10:40-41a; Mark 10:32/John 11:7-8). Cf. Smith, *Clement of Alexandria and a Secret Gospel of Mark* (Cambridge, Mass.: Harvard University Press, 1973), pp. 158-63. To explain these phenomena Smith conjectures that a common source (an *Urevangelium*) in different Greek recensions underlies the greater part of Mark and John. In his later article Smith suggests (p. 281), I think quite accurately, that in the discussion of other issues raised by his book his contribution to the question of Johannine-Marcan relations was overlooked. The similar ordering of the common reports is more readily explained by common tradition than is the paralleling of geographical notices. (Cf. Edward F. Glusman, "Criteria for a Study of the Outlines of Mark and John," *Society of Biblical Literature 1978 Seminar Papers*, II, 239-49, for a vigorous reformulation of that viewpoint, rooted, as Glusman readily acknowledges, in the work of Dodd and Bultmann. Also, idem, "The shape of Mark and John: A Primitive Gospel Outline," Ph.D. thesis, Duke University, 1977). The question of whether there was a common tradition or common written source would then depend largely on one's assessment of the parallels in these notices, which it seems to me are clearer in some cases than in others.

Considerable work might well be devoted to examining, analyzing, and classifying the evidence bearing upon the relationship between John and the synoptics. Some such quantification of the differences and similarities between John and the synoptics as is available for synoptic relationships would be most useful.[15] But even estimates of, for example, the number of common verses and the extent of verbatim agreement, which is scattered and diffuse, seem to be hard to come by. Be that as it may, we cannot here pursue the potentially fruitful course of refining the evidence as a whole. Rather, I want now to ask what the evidence with which we are all familiar may amount to, how it looks, and where it may lead, by approaching the problem from the standpoint of several interrelated tasks, disciplines, or, if you will, dimensions of New Testament scholarship.

TEXTUAL CRITICISM

As is well known, the number of verbatim agreements between John and the synoptics, especially John and Mark, is not insignificant, although the agreements are more impressive when isolated and collected than when put over against extensive stretches of material in which such agreement is lacking. Nevertheless, verbatim agreements seem on the face of it to be strong evidence for John's having used Mark or another synoptic.

The precise extent of such verbatim agreement is, however, in some part a problem of textual criticism. The most striking example of this state of affairs appears in the comparison of the scenes of the encounter of the risen Jesus with his disciples in John 20 and Luke 24. Luke 24:12, which corresponds to John 20:3-10 in that it presents *in nuce* what is described at much greater length there, is

15. For example, Allan Barr, *A Diagram of Synoptic Relationships* (Edinburgh: T. & T. Clark, 1938), which allows one to see the relationships at a glance. The relationships among the synoptics are so clear and obvious that such a color chart, with each gospel represented by a column, can adequately portray it. But in the case of John the parallels with the synoptics are much more scattered and diffuse, as well as much fewer, and the job of representing them on a chart would be very difficult indeed! With regard to such comparisons, one should note also the older work of E. A. Abbott, *Johannine Vocabulary: A Comparison of the Words of the Fourth Gospel with Those of the Three* (London: Black, 1905). (There is now also de Solages's work, reviewed in the preceding chapter.)

missing from Codex Beza as well as from some Old Latin manuscripts, although it is found in other witnesses. Aland originally relegated this verse to the apparatus (1963), but in the most recent edition it is included in the printed text.[16] (The United Bible Societies' text of the Greek New Testament gives it a D rating; in the editors' view there is a very high degree of doubt regarding its authenticity. The twenty-fifth edition of Nestlé relegated the verse to the apparatus.) In a similar instance Luke 24:36 has a more extensive verbatim parallel to John 20:19 (cf. 26) if the reading of all manuscripts except Beza and the Old Latin is allowed (i.e. καὶ λέγει αὐτοῖς εἰρήνη ὑμῖν). Also Luke 24:40 (καὶ τοῦτο εἰπὼν ἔδειξεν αὐτοῖς τὰς χεῖρας καὶ τοὺς πόδας), the whole of which has the same attestation, shows extensive verbatim agreement with John 20:20. To the degree that these verbatim parallels between Luke and John may be regarded as original, the case for John's use of the Lucan narrative per se appears stronger. The converse is also true. One may cite other variant readings in the parallels between Mark 14:3 and John 12:3 or Mark 2:9 and John 5:8. Few as they may be, they suggest an element of textual fluidity involved in matters of verbatim agreement. Moreover, the most ancient manuscript witnesses are subsequent to the period of greatest fluidity in the text, namely the second century. Probably this was a period of considerable textual assimilation among the gospels, including John. Assimilation may have resulted in the loss of an original reading on one side or the other. If so, some instances of verbatim agreement between John and the synoptics would be the result of assimilation. To what extent this may be so is in the very nature of the case uncertain, although it seems likely that the tendency of ecclesiastical textual history would be to bring gospel texts into agreement with one

16. K. Aland, ed., *Synopsis quattuor evangeliorum,* 9th ed. (Stuttgart: Deutsche Bibelstiftung), p. 497 (para. 352). The growing tendency to regard Luke 24:12 as a part of the original text is a reflection of recent text-critical work. H. Thyen, "Aus der Literatur zum Johannesevangelium (3. Fortsetzung)," *ThR* 42 (1977): 252: "der Vers [ist] Bestandteil des ursprünglichen Lukastextes und als solcher zugleich die Grundlage für die gesamte Konstruktion unserer Lieblingsjünger-Episode." In a following note Thyen cites the relevant literature (Jeremias, Aland, Snodgrass, Neirynck). This and other readings of D and the Old Latin in Luke 24 involve the question of "Western non-Interpolations," highly valued by Westcott and Hort, but more recently fallen out of favor.

another (i.e. to assimilate them) rather than the reverse.[17] In cases where John and the synoptics have verbatim agreement but there is a textual problem, one can only underscore the importance of making text-critical judgments on some basis other than a prior view of the relation (or lack thereof) between them.

SOURCE AND TRADITION CRITICISM

The problem of the relationship of John and the synoptics is by definition a source-critical problem insofar as it is a question of whether John knew the synoptics and to some extent drew upon them as sources for his own narrative. (If he did not employ Mark in as obvious a way as Matthew did, this does not necessarily mean that Mark was in no sense a source.)

But other sorts of source and tradition-critical considerations will also be involved in any thorough canvassing of this problem. Did John use sources parallel with, or similar to, the synoptics? If so, are the verbatim agreements with the synoptics, agreements in content generally, and agreements in order of events or pericopes to be attributed to the sources of John rather than to the evangelist's use of the synoptics? If so, one would suppose that the sources of John and those of the synoptics, whether oral or written, overlapped, were related, or had a common ancestor. It is not even unthinkable that the sources of John, rather than the Fourth Evangelist himself, were somehow influenced by one or more of the synoptics. In any case, the affinities between John and the synoptics may be at the

17. On the possibility of assimilation of Luke to John in the resurrection narratives, see F. C. Grant, "Was the Author of John Dependent upon the Gospel of Luke?" *JBL* 56 (1937):285-307, esp. 300-4. Grant thinks such assimilation likely. On textual fluidity and the tendency to harmonize parallel gospel accounts in the second century and earlier, see also J. N. Birdsall, "The New Testament," *The Cambridge History of the Bible*, vol. 1: *From the Beginning to Jerome*, ed. P. R. Ackroyd and C. F. Evans (Cambridge: Cambridge University Press, 1970), 336-37, 344. He writes (p. 344): "It is also clear that a tendency existed from the first to harmonize the parallel accounts of the gospels: the earliest instances of this are perhaps better explained by the hypothesis of parallel *oral traditions* than by that of harmonization of written documents." Birdsall goes on to mention the likelihood of harmonization in several second-century figures, including Marcion, Justin, Irenaeus, and of course Tatian.

level of sources, on one side or both, rather than at the level of final redaction or authorship.

Theories of written sources behind the Fourth Gospel have probably enjoyed greater favor on the Continent and in North America than in Great Britain.[18] Written sources would appear to accommodate the evidence of verbatim agreement better than oral tradition—at least to modern, Western eyes. Nevertheless, recent research in oral tradition outside the biblical field suggests that such verbatim agreements as exist between John and the synoptics may be explained by parallel or related oral tradition, without recourse to written sources, much less direct literary dependence. In fact, the kinds of verbatim agreement we find between John and the synoptics do not seem to me unlike (or more extensive than) those that appear in different versions of oral compositions that have been recorded under observable and controllable conditions by modern

18. It is difficult, and in all probability not very important, to substantiate the geographical point. Suffice it to say that the elaborate source theory set forth by Bultmann nearly forty years ago in his commentary was a landmark in at least two senses. Not only did Bultmann stimulate discussion of the sources of John; his work was also the harvest of a generation of such source-critical work. More recently other Continental scholars have struck out in new directions. W. Langbrandtner, *Weltferner Gott oder Gott der Liebe: Der Ketzerstreit in der johanneischen Kirche: Eine exegetisch-religionsgeschichtliche Untersuchung mit Berücksichtigung der koptisch-gnostischen Texte aus Nag Hammadi,* Beiträge zur biblischen Exegese und Theologie 6 (Frankfurt am Main: Lang, 1977), under the influence of H. Thyen develops a new view of the Johannine *Grundschrift* (esp. pp. 1-106). No longer a *semeia*-source, it is a proto-gospel of a Gnostic type. M.-E. Boismard and A. Lamouille, *L'évangile de Jean,* vol. 3, *Synopse des Quatre Évangiles* (Les Éditions du Cerf, 1977), present the latest, and presumably final, version of an elaborate source and recension theory involving the synoptics as well as John. Neither is derivative from Bultmann. In America my monograph *The Composition and Order of the Fourth Gospel: Bultmann's Literary Theory,* Yale Publications in Religion 10 (New Haven: Yale University Press, 1965), made Bultmann's source-critical work and the Continental discussion more readily accessible, especially to an Anglo-Saxon audience. Robert T. Fortna, *The Gospel of Signs: A Reconstruction of the Narrative Source Underlying the Fourth Gospel,* SNTSMS 11 (Cambridge: Cambridge University Press, 1970), represented an advance upon, or refinement of, Bultmann's theory insofar as the narratives were concerned. B. Lindars' sharp critique of Fortna, *Behind the Fourth Gospel,* Studies in Creative Criticism 3 (London: S.P.C.K., 1971), was not atypical of the English scene, where earlier on Dodd, Barrett, and Gardner-Smith had evinced little interest in written sources behind John.

scholars.[19] However that may be, increased interest in, and awareness of, the possible existence of oral tradition or written sources behind our canonical gospels has called in question the necessity of seeing the affinities between John and the synoptics as the result of a direct relationship between them. The lines of connection between writings now found in the New Testament are not necessarily given in the New Testament itself. When R. P. Casey chided E. R. Goodenough who, following Gardner-Smith, invoked a hypothetical oral tradition to explain the points of contact between John and the synoptics, Goodenough responded that the hypothesis was well founded and that it was better to adopt it than to ignore reality.[20]

The question of whether to look for common sources, written or oral, or direct dependence is nowhere more acute than in the passion accounts, and for good reason. Obviously the most extensive agreements in content and order occur there. The prospect of explaining these far-reaching similarities, as well as the others, without recourse to direct dependence was, of course, strengthened with the advent of form criticism and the interest in oral tradition which it spawned. Closely related to the rise of form criticism was a theological interest in the primitive tradition, or in the theological factors shaping that tradition. Thus the widely observed centrality of the message of the cross and resurrection in early Christianity. Given the centrality of the event of the crucifixion as an item for apologetic and theological explanation, and given the prevalence of oral composition and transmission, it seemed natural that the early communities should have composed and circulated accounts of the passion of Jesus.[21] As a matter of course, such narratives would have been

19. See Albert B. Lord, *The Singer of Tales,* Harvard Studies in Comparative Literature 24 (Cambridge, Mass.: Harvard University Press, 1960), pp. 63-64, 223-34; idem, "The Gospels as Oral Traditional Literature," *The Relationships Among the Gospels: An Interdisciplinary Dialogue,* ed. William O. Walker, Jr, Trinity University Monograph Series in Religion 5 (San Antonio, Tex.: Trinity University Press, 1977), pp. 33-91, esp. 87-89.

20. Goodenough, "John: A Primitive Gospel," *JBL* 64 (1945): 145-82, was criticized by R. P. Casey, "Professor Goodenough and the Fourth Gospel," *JBL* 64 (1945):535-42; Goodenough responded, "A Reply," *JBL* 64 (1945):543-44.

21. Cf. M. Dibelius, *From Tradition to Gospel,* trans. B. L. Woolf (New York: Scribner's, 1935), p. 178: "In no respect is that remarkable. For what we know of the Christian message makes us expect a description of the whole Passion in the course of a sermon, at least in outline. Every formulation of the message as preached

committed to writing. Not surprisingly, the existence of a traditional pregospel passion narrative or narratives came to be widely accepted.[22] On these terms, if John did not know the synoptics, but rather some common or overlapping traditions or sources, one would expect the most extensive agreement or overlapping in the passion accounts. And that is precisely what is found. If nothing is thereby proven, the prima facie case for John's dependence on the synoptics seems somewhat eroded.

It is worth observing that whereas synoptic studies, with the advent of form-critical method and perspective, moved from an interest in problems of literary relationships and sources, generally regarded as resolved, to oral and other tradition, no such clear movement was evident in Johannine research. Interestingly enough, it was in Great Britain and Scandinavia that form criticism aroused interest in the possibilities of oral tradition in John.[23] But form-critical interest in the Johannine miracle stories, for example, lagged behind such interest in the synoptic miracles. Rather, the Johannine miracle stories, obviously different from the synoptic, were attributed to separate cycles of tradition, and especially to a hypothetical *semeia*-source.[24] Inevitably, it was proposed that this miracle source and

---

mentions the facts of the Passion and Easter story." (The second German edition of this work, which contains this statement on p. 179, appeared in 1933.) So also R. Bultmann, *The History of the Synoptic Tradition*, 2d ed. of Eng. trans. by John Marsh (Oxford: Blackwell, 1968), pp. 262-91, esp. 275: "Unlike other material in the tradition, the Passion narrative was very early fashioned into a coherent form; indeed it can almost be said that the coherence was the primary fact in this case. For what led to a coherent narrative ... was above all the Kerygma, as we know it in the prophecies of the Passion and Resurrection in Mk. 8:31; 9:31; 10:33f. and in the speeches of Acts." (From second German edition of 1931, p. 297.)

22. Cf. the statement of Kümmel, *Introduction*, p. 77 n. 81: "It has been widely recognized since the beginning of form-critical investigation ... that the passion story was already a connected account in the old oral tradition." Kümmel himself agrees with this position, against Schreiber and Linnemann.

23. Aside from Gardner-Smith, see for e.g., C. H. Dodd, *Historical Tradition in the Fourth Gospel* (Cambridge: Cambridge University Press, 1963), and B. Noack, *Zur johanneischen Tradition: Beiträge zur Kritik an der literarkritischen Analyse des vierten Evangeliums,* Publications de la Société des Sciences et des Lettres d'Aarhus, Série de Théologie 3 (Copenhagen: Rosenkilde og Bagger, 1954).

24. Although this hypothetical source is now justifiably associated with Bultmann, who gave it wide currency, it was earlier proposed by A. Faure, "Die alttes-

the passion source had been linked, even before the composition of the Fourth Gospel, in what was called a Gospel of Signs.[25] Thus the stage was set for intensive redaction-critical study of the Gospel of John.

REDACTION CRITICISM

Actually, Bultmann's commentary on John was an extended exercise in redaction criticism, conceived and executed before the term was coined. The Johannine redactor, in the later sense of the term, was not the anonymous figure of rather limited talent who put the Fourth Gospel into its present order and brought it into line with dominant church tradition. Rather, the real redactor was the evangelist himself, who worked with written sources and other traditions, with which he did not fully agree, to produce a theologically sophisticated document embodying those very traditions but expressing a distinctly different point of view.

Of course, it has belonged to the very essence of redaction criticism to proceed by separating tradition and redaction and thus eventually to arrive at an understanding of an entire document through a grasp of how the evangelist or author has arranged, edited, and emended his materials. Such an enterprise is naturally on its surest footing when the source of the gospel being studied is known; for example in the case of Matthew, Mark and to a lesser degree the sayings tradition common also to Luke are known. With John the situation is more uncertain and the prospects less promising, except that much of the predominantly narrative material in the passion and elsewhere is either parallel or analogous to synoptic material. Either one or more of the synoptic gospels is the, or a, source in such cases; or John and the synoptics draw upon the same, or related, sources.

To take a concrete example, the Johannine and, let us say, the Marcan accounts of the cleansing of the temple are roughly parallel. If one holds Mark to have been John's chief source, he will need to explain the detailed differences in the text, not to mention the

---

tamentlichen Zitate im 4. Evangelium und die Quellenscheidungshypothese," *ZNW* 21 (1922): 99-121.

25. Cf. the work of Fortna by that name (n. 18 above).

difference in position, in terms of the Fourth Evangelist's intention. In fact, John 2:21-22 have a decidedly Johannine ring and could very well be understood as the evangelist's annotation of Mark or whatever source he was using. On the other hand, the charge that the temple shall not be made a house of trade is less obviously Johannine as compared with Mark's "you have made it a den of robbers." Moreover, John has unique details such as the whip of cords that serve no obvious purpose. The positioning of the account at the beginning is not hard to square with John's purpose or with his use of Mark. (Jesus as the crucified and risen one displaces the temple, a fitting motif for the beginning of the public ministry; cf. 1:11, 14, 51.) Yet the fact that John intentionally placed the cleansing here does not, of course, imply that he derived it from Mark. Conceivably it was an isolated piece of tradition; but it is equally possible that it was a part of, or associated with, a traditional passion narrative. Fortna quite reasonably suggests that in the Gospel of Signs the cleansing was associated with the passion narrative. A strong bit of evidence for this is the synoptic account, which Fortna takes to be traditional. Moreover, it is at least a plausible surmise that the association is historically authentic. Given the existence of other sources, it seems just as reasonable, some would say easier, to explain the Johannine account of the cleansing on the hypothesis that John did not use Mark as that he did. At the same time, one must acknowledge that John at least knew a tradition related to Mark (or to the synoptics) and must guard against the pitfalls of subjectivity in reconstructing John's *Vorlage* from within the Fourth Gospel. But this may not be a hopeless task.

Alternatively, it may be granted that the Marcan (or synoptic) cleansing story is not the principal or only source of John without conceding that John had no knowledge of Mark whatever. What if John simply chose in the main to follow another source with occasional side glances at Mark, whether literally, physically, or by way of memory? I know of no way to exclude such a possibility. John may have known Mark or the synoptics and preferred another source. This remains a viable alternative. It is, however, problematic at a couple of points, especially when set in the broad context of the comparison of both gospels as wholes. In the first place, one must ultimately take account of John's generally wide divergence from Mark in content and order (including Jesus' itinerary) as well as style. One cannot weigh only the positive evidence of points of similarity in parallel pericopes, but must hold them in the scales over against the wide divergences elsewhere. I run the risk of a general observation: those who believe John used one or more of the synoptics tend to be impressed most by the verbatim agreements and other similarities and points of contact within the clearly parallel materials and to see the divergences in content there and elsewhere as problems that must, but can, be explained. On the other hand, those who doubt or disbelieve that John knew the synoptics remain unconvinced by such positive evidence, not only because of a residue of unexplained divergences within the parallel pericopes, but also because of what they perceive as the very difficult problem of coming to terms with the far-reaching differences elsewhere. We are then already at the other, second problematic point. If John knew Mark but so largely disregarded or diverged from his and the other synoptic accounts, it is difficult to believe that he fully approved of them or to see how he regarded them as important. We are therefore pushed in the direction of Windisch. Conceivably John knew the synoptic gospels, but did not feel bound by or drawn to them.

An interpretation of John employing the method of redaction criticism must explain that entire document over against its proposed sources, whether hypothetical or extant. It is perhaps not surprising that as that method has gained adherents, relatively fewer commentators have undertaken to explain John on the hypothesis that he knew and used the synoptics. Although certain Johannine texts (e.g. the cleansing) are amenable to explanation on that basis, there are many others for which the synoptics seem remote or irrelevant. As the assumption of John's knowledge and use of the synoptics has been put in question, commentators have increasingly found it dispensable for their work.

If the considerations discussed so far weigh in favor of Johannine independence, the one now to be advanced may redress the balance. Quite recently, and from more than one quarter, has come the suggestion that a redaction-critical perspective should be able to furnish decisive data for the solution of the problem of John and the synoptics. The principle involved is quite simple and clear-cut. If elements of synoptic, let us say Marcan, redaction have found their way into the Fourth Gospel, then John must have known, not merely Marcan tradition, but the Gospel of Mark itself. Thus, for example, it is argued that the intercalation or interlamination of the trial before the Sanhedrin into the denial scene is the work of Mark himself, not tradition.[26] This being the case, the similar arrangement of these materials in John must be a consequence of John's knowledge of Mark rather than merely dependence upon common tradition. Moreover, redaction-critical study of Mark's passion narrative has convinced some scholars that it is entirely his own composition.[27] If so, and if there was no pre-Marcan passion narrative but only isolated traditions, a major underpinning of Johannine independence is knocked loose. The passion narrative, as well as the gospel form, may then seem to be Mark's invention, and other exemplars will be regarded as dependent upon him. The logic of this view of the evidence is seemingly impeccable. Traces of indisputably Marcan redaction in John should prove beyond reasonable doubt John's knowledge and use of Mark. (The same would, of course, be true *mutatis mutandis* of Matthean or Lucan redaction in John.)[28] The question is only the extent to which what

26. Perrin, *Introduction*, pp. 228-29. He writes: "A particular consideration is the fact that the trial before the High Priest (John 18. 19-24) is set in the context of the denial by Peter (18. 15-18, 25-7), as it is also in the Gospel of Mark. But there is a strong case that Mark himself originally composed this account of the trial at night before the Jewish authorities and then set it in the context of the story of Peter's denial. If this is so, the evangelist John must necessarily have known the gospel of Mark." In support of this view of Mark's redactional activity at this point in the narrative, Perrin is able to cite the excellent work of his student John R. Donahue, *Are You the Christ? The Trial Narrative in the Gospel of Mark*, SBL Dissertation Series, 10 (Missoula, Mont.: Scholars Press, 1973), the implication of which is to cast doubt upon the existence of a pre-Marcan passion narrative (pp. 239-40). Cf. also the essays in Kelber, *The Passion in Mark*, cited above (n. 8). Against this view of the bearing of Donahue's analysis of the redactional character of the Marcan sequence upon the question of the relationship of Mark and John, see Robert T. Fortna, "Jesus and Peter at the High Priest's House: A Test Case for the Question of the Relation Between Mark's and John's Gospels," *NTS* 24 (1978): 371-83.

27. See n. 26 above and especially the monograph of E. Linnemann, *Studien zur Passionsgeschichte*, FRLANT 102 (Göttingen: Vandenhoeck & Ruprecht, 1970), who was among the first to reject the consensus of a pre-Marcan passion narrative in a full-length monograph devoted to the subject.

28. In an important and thoroughgoing study A. Dauer has argued that traces of Matthean and Lucan redactional work turn up in the Johannine passion nar-

is indisputably Marcan (Matthean or Lucan) can be determined, but that may be a considerable question.[29]

E. J. Pryke's recent study of the language and style of Marcan redaction establishes what seem to me its outer limits.[30] When one canvasses the verbatim agreements between John and Mark to see whether on the Marcan side they fall in the area of redaction or of presumed tradition, he may be surprised to find that fully half are on this accounting within the (presumed) limits of Marcan redaction. This would seem to prove John's knowledge of such redaction and therefore of the Second Gospel. A second look, however, gives one pause. Of the linguistic and stylistic criteria used to establish redaction on the Marcan side, between 85 percent and 90 percent are missing from the Johannine parallels. The ones that are present are largely common Greek words or words without which a story could scarcely be told.[31] Possibly John screened out precisely the

rative, which he does not regard as based on Mark. See *Die Passionsgeschichte im Johannesevangelium: Eine traditionsgeschichtliche und theologische Untersuchung zu Joh 18, 1-19, 30*, StANT 30 (Munich: Kösel, 1972). Dauer takes up and develops insights of Nils A. Dahl, "Die Passionsgeschichte bei Matthäus," *NTS* 2 (1955-56): 17-32, esp. 22, and Peder Borgen, "John and the Synoptics in the Passion Narrative," *NTS* 5 (1958-59): 246-59, esp. 251. In his view the Johannine passion source reflects knowledge, perhaps indirect, of Matthew and Luke.

29. Lloyd R. Kittlaus, "John and Mark: A Methodological Evaluation of Norman Perrin's Suggestion," *Society of Biblical Literature 1978 Seminar Papers*, II, 269-79, abjures for the present the task of attempting to decide the question of the relationship of John and Mark on the basis of the determination of whether knowledge of specifically Marcan redaction is reflected in John, because we are not able to be sufficiently certain about what is, and is not, Marcan redaction.

30. *Redactional Style in the Marcan Gospel: A Study of Syntax and Vocabulary as Guides to Redaction in Mark*, SNTSMS 33 (Cambridge: Cambridge University Press, 1978). I am not, in fact, always convinced by Pryke's apparent reasons or evidence for assigning material to redaction rather than tradition. Moreover, in the case of the feeding of the five thousand (Mark 6:30-41), e.g., it is difficult to see how there could have been a traditional story at all, granted Pryke's far-reaching identification of redactional material (cf. pp. 159-60); cf. also the walking on the water (6:45-52; ct. p. 160). Nevertheless, if Pryke's assignment of material to redaction is provisionally accepted, nothing will be overlooked.

31. E.g. in John 1:23/Mark 1:3 ἔρημος, καθώς, φωνή; in John 6:16-17/Mark 6:45 ἐμβαίνειν, μαθητής, πλοῖον. Ibid., pp. 139, 142 respectively; cf. pp. 151, 160.

Marcan characteristics in writing, but is this likely? Alternatively, one could raise a prior question about the definition of Marcan redaction. Since the content of Marcan redaction appears without the Marcan hallmarks in John, is it redaction at all, or is it rather tradition? The hoped-for unambiguous evidence of redaction criticism seems at this point to contain a significant element of ambiguity still.

Yet there are also other factors that on broader redaction-critical grounds would seem to favor John's knowledge of the synoptics. Perhaps the Johannine allusions to matters otherwise known to us from the synoptics (e.g., Jesus' baptism, John's imprisonment, the Lord's Supper) suggest more strongly than the explicit similarities or parallels that John knew and took for granted that his readers would know the synoptic accounts. That John seems to view Jesus' ministry retrospectively implies that he assumes a more immediate and direct account of that ministry.[32] The question is whether such an assumption could apply, or likely applies, only to the synoptics as we have them. Such a consideration leads to yet a fourth dimension of our problem, one already touched upon, namely, the view of early Christianity which is presumed or involved.

HISTORICAL PERSPECTIVE

The so-called introductory questions pertaining to John have never been definitively answered, but there is nevertheless a measure of consensus on some of them. I skip over them, however, to go to a matter that seems to me of crucial importance. Most scholars would settle on a date near the end of the century for the composition of the Fourth Gospel in its present form, although a date as early as, or even earlier than, the Roman War is not without its defenders.[33]

32. In this respect the general position of E. C. Hoskyns, *The Fourth Gospel,* ed. F. N. Davey, 2d rev. ed. (London: Faber & Faber, 1947), and also C. K. Barrett, *St. John,* seems to me to be well taken.

33. The best known of whom is now J. A. T. Robinson; see *Redating the New Testament* (London: S.C.M., 1976), pp. 254-311. During the Durham SNTS meeting Bishop Robinson presented before the Johannine Seminar a vigorous defense of his position on the dating of John, contesting the validity of arguments for a date after A.D. 70 (or 80) based on the dating of the Twelfth Benediction (and

Given the later dating, a question that should give pause to any advocacy of John's complete independence of the synoptics is whether an evangelist composing a gospel in a major Christian center at the end of the first century could have been ignorant of all the others, and especially Mark. In the most widely held view both Matthew and Luke knew Mark, or a document closely approximating it, and a body of sayings tradition. Matthew and Luke seem to have worked independently of one another. Quite possibly these evangelists composed their gospels at about the same time at different places, and this would account for their apparent ignorance of one another. As one considers whether John could have been ignorant of the synoptics, it may occur to him that perhaps the most remarkable phenomenon of gospel relationships is Matthew's and Luke's independent use of Mark. What was there to commend Mark independently to both later evangelists? That it was the only gospel, or the only gospel approved in nascent orthodox circles? That it bore the authority of Peter or the Roman Church? Perhaps one of the strong points of the Griesbach hypothesis is that it undertakes to explain relationships among the synoptics without invoking the hypothesis that Matthew and Luke independently lit upon Mark as their principal narrative source. On that view Luke's use and disuse of Matthew (which he would have known) provides a closer parallel than is otherwise available for what seems to be John's erratic, eclectic, or at points almost capricious use and disuse of Mark and the other synoptics. But perhaps we have actually stated the question in such a way as to favor the view that John

---

therefore the synagogue controversy), c. 85. An animated discussion followed. It was suggested, and Robinson agreed, that his dating of John resolves the problem of Johannine-synoptic relationships in favor of John's independence only if the conventional dating of the synoptics (between 65 and 100) is accepted. On Robinson's own accounting the problem remains, although he is inclined to regard John as substantially independent for somewhat the same reasons I am. Thirty-five years ago the late Professor E. R. Goodenough of Yale, who had even less reason than Robinson to defend an early date on theological grounds, argued for a primitive (pre-70) origin of the Fourth Gospel (n. 20 above, noted by Robinson, p. 307 n. 218). Like Robinson, Goodenough was also unimpressed with arguments for dating Matthew and Luke, much less Mark, after the fall of Jerusalem, and delighted in debating the point with "critically orthodox" graduate students like myself, who were on the whole less astonished by his other heresies. Goodenough stated orally that John could have been written in Jerusalem before A.D. 40.

knew the synoptics by saying that the Fourth Gospel was composed in a major Christian center. This smacks of the traditional view of Ephesian origin. But what if John arose in a church or in Christian circles far from the synoptic and Pauline orbit? Furthermore, should it be assumed that the synoptic-Pauline axis, which so dominates the New Testament, is truly representative of first century Christianity, or Christianity at the end of the first century? Does the assumption that the New Testament canon and early Christianity are nearly identical or at least commensurate underlie the question just raised? How one views this matter will inevitably influence his perspective on Johannine synoptic relationships.

The circumstances under which John may have known, or not known, the synoptics are several and varied. Conceivably, when John wrote, the synoptics themselves were not so widely known or accepted. The sparsity of contact between the synoptics and the other New Testament writings is often observed. (There is no synoptic counterpart to the Johannine Epistles!) Different inferences may be drawn from this state of affairs. On the one hand, it may not be necessary to assume that John would have known any, much less all, of the synoptics when he wrote. If a number of gospels, or gospel-like documents, were current in the churches at the end of the first century,[34] the contacts between John and the synoptics may

34. That such documents existed is more than a matter of sheer speculation. The so-called apocryphal gospels are known only through patristic references and surviving fragments. W. Schneemelcher, *New Testament Apocrypha*, vol. 1: *Gospels and Related Writings,* founded by E. Hennecke, trans. and ed. R. McL. Wilson (London: Lutterworth, 1963), pp. 127-28, clearly reflects the widely held position that most such gospels are later than, and largely derivative from, the canonical gospels, in some cases obviously so. Yet he also remarks (p. 61): "For the earliest works of this kind still more can be said: they appear in part ... to be almost contemporary with the canonical writings and to have been written on the basis of the same traditions, and accordingly were valued in particular districts precisely as the canonical Gospels were in other churches." While granting that these earliest apocryphal gospels probably took their inspiration from Mark, Schneemelcher concedes that we cannot be certain of it. (Probably the Gospel of the Hebrews is the strongest candidate for independence of the synoptics, although little enough is known of it.) Further grist for the mill is the Fragment of an Unknown Gospel (Egerton Papyrus 2), as well as the discovery of a Carpocratian longer text of Mark claimed by M. Smith (n. 14 above). Quite possible the Fragment evidences acquaintance with, although not copying from, the canonical gospels (Jeremias,

be explained as arising from a common source or sources. On the other, if John knew one or more of the synoptics along with such other documents, he may not have deemed their authority so imposing as to require him to come to terms with any of them or to adopt them as his principal sources. He could scarcely have known which gospels (i.e. the synoptics) would eventually stand alongside his own in the New Testament.

Finally, we must consider the relevance of the question of the origin of the gospel genre to our problem. The priority of Mark over the other synoptic gospels is frequently taken to imply that Mark was necessarily the first gospel written and that the evangelist Mark was the inventor of the gospel genre. But it is by no means clear that the originality of Mark can be inferred from its priority even if Mark had no (unknown) predecessor. If the gospels are not unrelated to ancient religiously (or philosophically) motivated biography,[35] and if there was in early Christianity a reason or incentive for presenting the gospel message with reference to the historical object of faith, the appearance of more than one instance of the gospel form should not be surprising. The Jewish context in which Jesus lived presumably would not only have influenced the shape and character of his career, but to a considerable extent governed the perceptual and hermeneutical possibilities for its understanding and interpretation. To put matters succinctly, against the background of Jewish tradition and scripture, in which God makes himself known in history and, moreover, in historical narration, the claim that in the public activity of a particular man God had

---

in *New Testament Apocrypha*, 1, 95). This at least seems to be the predominant view. Yet G. Mayeda, *Das Leben-Jesu-Fragment: Papyrus Egerton 2 und seine Stellung in der urchristlichen Literaturgeschichte* (Bern: Paul Haupt, 1946), pp. 65–75, argues that precisely such linguistic and stylistic evidence as would demonstrate dependence is lacking. To mention the numerous proposals of hypothetical primitive gospels underlying John or the other canonical gospels (e.g., Fortna's Gospel of Signs) might appear to be arguing in a circle. Yet few if any of them were put forward with a view to proving or supporting John's independence of the synoptics.

35. Cf. Charles H. Talbert, *What Is a Gospel? The Genre of the Canonical Gospels* (Philadelphia: Fortress, 1977), who succeeds in showing significant affinities of the gospels with contemporary Hellenistic biographical literature. Whether, or in what sense, the genre itself antedates the canonical gospels may depend on how sharply, or narrowly, it is defined.

acted or revealed himself for the sake of human salvation would have quite naturally and understandably issued in the writing down of narrations of that man's career. Such considerations do not, of course, exclude the possibility that Mark was known to, and used by, John. They do, however, call into question the view, or the assumption, that if Mark was the first to hit upon the gospel genre he was its sole originator and the one from which all his successors must have derived the pattern. That view fits the obvious literary relationship between Mark on the one side and Matthew and Luke on the other much better than the relationship between John and Mark or any of the synoptic gospels.

THEOLOGICAL INTERESTS

Historical and other theological issues, insofar as they involve gospel exegesis, may be importantly shaped or influenced by one's answer to the question of whether John knew and presupposed the synoptics. One example will suffice.

The problem of John's position on the Lord's Supper has long agitated exegesis and theology attendant upon it.[36] The historical-exegetical task should begin with a decision as to whether or to what extent John presupposes the synoptic accounts. If he does, why does he not give more positive indication that he intends to affirm them, build upon them, or interpret them? Alternatively, if he knows the synoptic accounts, but does not wish to embrace the eucharist, or their understanding of it, why does he not give a clearer or more explicit indication of that intention? Because the baseline, the traditions or documents upon which John is drawing, remains unknown or disputed, it is difficult to agree about Johannine eucharistic theology and to relate it to other New Testament or early Christian traditions. Thus the wide divergence of opinion among informed exegetes.

How then can systematic theology or liturgics be expected to cope with this problematic situation? It goes without saying that the eucharistic tradition is so firmly anchored in the praxis of all major Christian churches that no exegetical discovery about John's

36. See the recent extensive *Forschungsbericht* and discussion of sacramentalism in John by Thyen, "Aus der Literatur zum Johannesevangelium," *ThR* 43 (1978): 328–59, and 44 (1979):97–134.

position vis-à-vis that rite is going to shake it. The only question may be whether or how Johannine texts should continue to be employed in relation to the eucharist. May the washing of the disciples' feet be understood as positively related to the institution of the eucharist, even if such a use departs from or contradicts the evangelist's knowledge or intention? Probably such a question is too simply put, but it draws the issue to the surface. To put the question in the broadest, and also the sharpest, terms, if John's Gospel stands in the New Testament because it was misunderstood in the early church as essentially agreeing with the synoptics and related traditions, if it is holy scripture by the error or man and the providence of God,[37] shall we assume that the former is the same as the latter and, equating man's error with God's design, proceed exegetically on the basis? Such a procedure would perhaps find a home in theological science, but it could scarcely fail to jar the sensibilities of exegetical science.

There are other important and difficult questions of the history of early Christian thought whose solution is related to the question of John and the synoptics. Is Johannine theology as represented by the Gospels and Epistles in a really historical sense the capstone of theological development in the New Testament period? I have long assumed so, with the impressive support of a phalanx of luminaries including Bultmann, Hoskyns, Dodd, and Kümmel.[38]

37. Cf. E. Käsemann, *Jesu Letzter Wille nach Johannes 17*, 3d rev. ed. (Tübingen: Mohr, 1971), p. 154: "Spiegelt sich im Evangelium historisch jene Entwicklung, welche von den Schwärmern in Korinth und von 2. Tim 2, 18 zum christlichen Gnostizismus führt, so ist seine Aufnahme in den Kanon der Grosskirche errore hominum et providentia Dei erfolgt."

38. While Bultmann would scarcely characterize John as the end product of a development, it is nevertheless clear from his *Theology of the New Testament*, trans. K. Grobel, 2 vols. (New York: Scribner's, 1951-55), that in his view Johannine theology is the high point of New Testament theology. Neither would Hoskyns subscribe to such language, but one could describe John as pivotal in his view (cf. *The Fourth Gospel*, p. 133): "The test that we must apply in the end to the Fourth Gospel, the test by which the Fourth Gospel stands or falls, is whether the Marcan narrative becomes more intelligible after reading the Fourth Gospel, whether the Pauline epistles become more transparent, or whether the whole material presented to us in the New Testament is breaking up into unrelated fragments." The sheer weight of Dodd's work (as of Bultmann's and Hoskyns') points in a similar

Or does it only appear so from a later perspective, after typically Johannine interests and emphases exercised their influence over the history of Christian thought, when in reality Johannine theology had originally seemed an isolated, if not aberrant, growth in the theological garden of early Christianity? Perhaps John struggled against the stream, only to be swept away, or co-opted, by it eventually. The possibility of interpreting John historically as the culmination or apex of theological development in the New Testament period is closely allied with, although not entirely dependent upon, the establishment of John's knowledge and acceptance of the synoptic gospels. If he deliberately stood apart from, or rejected them, such an interpretation is historically infelicitous. If he was ignorant of them, it cannot be wholeheartedly embraced, although it may perhaps be accepted with qualification (i.e., John knew and developed theologically a tradition related to the synoptic). In any event, there is at stake in the question of John and the synoptics a range of issues integrally related to the question of John's place in the development of theology in first century Christianity, as well as to the theological appropriation of Johannine thought.

SOME CONCLUSIONS

By looking at several significant dimensions of the relationship of John and the synoptics, we have attempted to lay out the present state of the problem. No solution having been promised, it should come as no surprise that none has been given. I conclude by mentioning two alternative possibilities.

I frankly still find it less difficult to explain the similarities between John and the synoptics on the hypothesis that the Fourth Evangelist did not know the others than to explain the wide divergences of several sorts on the hypothesis that he knew them. My reasons are principally redaction critical. It is easily possible

---

direction. See also *The Apostolic Preaching and Its Developments* (New York: Harper, 1936), pp. 73–75, esp. 75: "It is in the Fourth Gospel, which in form and expression, as probably in date, stands farthest from the original tradition of the teaching, that we have the most penetrating exposition of its central meaning." Cf. Kümmel, *The Theology of the New Testament According to its Major Witnesses: Jesus—Paul—John*, trans. John E. Steely (Nashville: Abingdon, 1973).

to see how Matthew or Luke understood and made use of Mark, given the two-source or Marcan hypothesis. Given John's knowledge of Mark, it is very difficult indeed to see how he (i.e. the evangelist or any comprehensive redactor) understood and made use of that gospel. Nevertheless, I am beginning to be able to conceive of a scenario in which John knew, or knew of, the synoptics and yet produced so dissimilar a gospel as the one which now follows them in the New Testament. I sketch it briefly.

The Fourth Evangelist represents somewhat independent Christian circles in which first the synagogue controversy and then a severe and not unrelated dispute over Christology (docetism, etc.) and related matters have been dominant issues. In this community an independent tradition of Jesus' miracles, especially healings, has circulated (perhaps a *semeia*-source),[39] and such tradition of his logia as has existed has been subjected to thoroughgoing reinterpretation or reminting in Christian preaching and in the controversies mentioned above so that it has become all but unrecognizable. Meanwhile, Mark, Luke, and Matthew, perhaps in that order, have become known to members of the Johannine community without having been fully appropriated into its traditions. Mark may have provided the inspiration for the drawing together of material into a gospel, although I remain unconvinced that this could not have been done independently or under the influence of a gospel now no longer extant. In any event, the life, interests, and controversies of the Johannine community provided the primary material and inspiration for the author of the Fourth Gospel. The influence of the synoptics was at best secondary and perhaps in some cases even

39. It cannot be said that there is any wide consensus in favor of such a source, despite its adoption by the students and followers of Bultmann (among whom Thyen is a notable exception), as well as others. The evidence for a *semeia*-source has been frequently rehearsed and need not be repeated here. Cf. Jürgen Becker, "Wunder und Christologie: Zum literarkritischen und christologischen Problem der Wunder in Johannesevangelium," *NTS* 16 (1970): 130–48. Fortna, *Gspel of Signs,* represents a distinct variation of this thesis, which in its general conception and bearing seems not at all implausible to me. Cf. my article, "The Setting and Shape of a Johannine Narrative Source," *JBL* 95 (1976):231-41, included in this present volume.

second-hand.[40] The Fourth Gospel would not have had any of the synoptics as its source(s), but neither did it take shape in complete isolation from them. Since it was composed with matters other than those which concerned the synoptics primarily in view, it does not reflect them in any consistent and coherent way, as Matthew and Luke can be perceived as embodying and reflecting Mark. But neither can it be said that John wrote to polemicize against or to displace other gospels. Windisch's position still suffers from the underlying assumption that John must be explained primarily with reference to the synoptics, an assumption which comes all too easily to anyone aware of their long common history in the New Testament canon. Possibly the Fourth Gospel can be adequately explained without primary or fundamental reference to the synoptic gospels, but also without denying the Fourth Evangelist's awareness of them.

If, however, one attempts to explain, in the sense of giving an exegesis of, the Fourth Gospel on this basis, how much different is that from explaining it on the basis of the theory of complete independence (i.e. ignorance)? It seems to me the answer is not necessarily as different as may at first appear. In neither case does one simply assume that the base line or material which John employs and from which he takes his departure is the synoptic gospels as such. In either case, the direction or development of his gospel is taken to be relatively independent of the synoptics. The Johannine Gospel would then reflect a distinct set of circumstances and perspective on them. In neither case is there warrant for treating any divergence from the synoptics as prima facie a deliberate and intentional departure. On the other hand, in neither case will it be possible to ignore the content of the synoptics in interpreting John, particularly in the parallel pericopes. This means in effect that on either side the question of the mode of the relationship should

---

40. This is, in effect, the position of a number of scholars, including Bultmann, Brown, Thyen, and Boismard. It is not, as becomes increasingly clear, the position being developed by Neirynck and his school. See his *Jean et les Synoptiques: Examen critique de l'exégèse de M.-E. Boismard,* with the collaboration of Jöel Delobel et al., BETL 49 (Louvain: University Press, 1979), which is as the subtitle implies a monograph-length examination of aspects of Boismard's work, esp. the third and final volume (n. 18 above). (See the immediately preceding chapter of this volume.)

remain open in principle. It may be that the nature of the relationship will appear increasingly to demand direct knowledge as the most adequate explanation, but the opposite may prove to be the case. That is, direct knowledge may become a dispensable hypothesis. However that may be, exegesis of the Fourth Gospel will rightly not be dominated by redaction-critical questions of its relationship to the synoptics or, indeed, by the question of its relationship to the synoptics narrowly conceived.

Part 3	Theology

The Presentation of Jesus in the Fourth Gospel

We speak of the presentation of Jesus rather than Johannine Christology. Obviously, christological teaching is implied, and even uttered, in the Fourth Gospel; Jesus teaches about himself. But to speak of Christology is already to put oneself one stage away from the Johannine presentation. Christology is second-order language about Jesus. John's Gospel is a first-order presentation of Jesus. It is not without significance that John wrote a gospel, and thus presented the story of Jesus, and not a theological tract. He does not talk about Jesus, but purports to describe how Jesus acted and talked about himself.

JESUS IN JOHN AND IN THE SYNOPTICS

Because John does this, his work invites comparison with other gospels, especially the synoptics. (Whether by coincidence or not, no surviving noncanonical gospel extant in its entirety presents a narrative of Jesus' ministry, although such gospels certainly existed.) In making this comparison one inevitably faces the question of whether John wrote with knowledge of any or all of the other gospels which have been canonized. Yet whether one decides pro or con, and even if he does not decide at all, he will find the comparisons and contrasts illuminating on both sides.

Jesus has been described as a healing, teaching, and suffering Messiah,[1] and in all four gospels he appears as a Messiah who performs miracles, teaches, and dies. Yet is it not correct to characterize the Jesus of John's Gospel as suffering, nor are his miracles best described as healings. Jesus is certainly designated a teacher in John, yet his teaching is not, and by its nature could not be, understood by his interlocutors. It is a teaching which can, however, be understood by the Christian reader. Although Jesus' suffering is not emphasized in the synoptic passion narratives, the passion predictions describe his death as suffering, and certainly Mark underscores suffering as characteristic of Jesus' ministry. John, on the other hand, does no more than hint that Jesus' death involves him in the suffering which the synoptics strongly suggest. The differences between the Johannine and synoptic portrayals of Jesus' miracles, teaching, and death are in large measure the differences between John and the synoptics, and the distinctive features of the former become all the clearer when set in contrast with the latter.

The miracles of the Fourth Gospel are, in contrast to the synoptics, referred to as signs.[2] Other miracles of Jesus which are not recounted are also called signs in this Gospel (2:23; 20:30). As such they point to Jesus as one sent from God and are acknowledged outside the immediate circle of his disciples (3:2). They have the express function of raising the question of who Jesus is and suggesting an answer. Those who are impressed by his signs do not for that reason only know who Jesus really is (3:2ff.), but they are on the right track. Those who want to reject Jesus are reluctant even to credit the authenticity and actuality of his signs (chap. 9). Faith in the Gospel of John is not simply belief in miracles, whether or not it was that in the source or traditions from which the Johannine miracle stories were drawn. Nevertheless, Jesus' miracles can only

1. This typology was suggested to, and adopted by, Robert A. Spivey and me by a former teacher, Paul W. Meyer. Simple though it is, it nicely and rather fully comprehends the Gospel's portrayal of Jesus (See *Anatomy of the New Testament: A Guide to Its Structure and Meaning*, 2d ed. [New York: Macmillan, 1974], pp. 187ff.).

2. Such nomenclature, as applied to miracles, is not entirely foreign to the synoptic gospels (Mark 8:11–13; Matt. 12:38–39), Acts (2:22), or even the Old Testament (Exod. 4:8–9f., 17). In the synoptics, of course, Jesus rejects the desire to see legitimating signs. Precisely such signs are offered in the Fourth Gospel.

be understood as events credited as historical which perform a positive function in the theology of the Fourth Gospel.[3] One can infer from their prominence that the miracle stories are taken up or recounted in the first instance because they aptly put the question of Jesus' identity (and thus create the possibility of genuine faith), not because the author wished to correct their erroneous theology. This use of miracles in John thus differentiates it from the synoptics, although there is a sense in which the miracle stories of those gospels perform a similar function. This is especially true of Mark. But what is explicit in John (i.e., the relationship of miracles to faith) is only implicit in Mark. Moreover, Mark more than John sets a question mark over the validity of miracles as propaedeutic to faith. This is especially true if Peter's confession of Jesus' messiahship, which Jesus all but rejects, is seen as the expression of a popular view of Jesus.

Be that as it may, the miracle tradition which John employs is itself quite different from that found elsewhere. It is often pointed out that none of the demon exorcisms common to the synoptics is found in John. Perhaps even more astonishing is the fact that no Marcan healing narrative has a Johannine parallel, although there are three or four Johannine stories of a similar sort. The one healing story that has a clear synoptic parallel, the ruler's son, is found in Matthew (8:5–13) and Luke (7:1–10) only, and is therefore a Q miracle, something of an anomaly. The Johannine miracle stories with clear Marcan parallels are not healings (6:1–15; 6:16–21). Thus one may say that the miracle traditions of Mark (and therefore also of Matthew and Luke), particularly the healings, are not found in John, while the healing miracles of John are also not found in Mark. For that matter, only four miracle stories in John qualify as healings, that is, only a fraction of the number found in Mark or in the synoptics generally.

Jesus is repeatedly called rabbi or teacher in the Fourth Gospel. In fact, "rabbi" is said to mean "teacher" (1:38). Somehow the knowledge that Jesus was a teacher, or that he taught, so prevalent in the synoptics, is still alive in John. But in John, Jesus' teaching

3. A view not accepted, or at least not assumed, by Rudolf Bultmann (*The Gospel of John: A Commentary*, trans. G. Beasley-Murray et al. [Philadelphia: Westminster, 1971], p. 119 n. 2). Bultmann appears to question whether the historicity of the signs was important to the evangelist.

has a very narrow focus. As we have noted, he teaches about himself and that teaching is distinctly Christian. While there may be, and likely are, authentic sayings and parables of Jesus in the Johannine discourses, the content, as well as the style, of his teaching can scarcely be historically authentic. Efforts to explain the Johannine Jesus' teaching as essentially authentic historically, whether by invoking the Qumran parallels or not, often end up appealing to well-worn hypotheses of a secret or esoteric teaching found only in John.[4] Such theories, reminiscent of the ancient Gnostics, can scarcely withstand critical scrutiny.

Quite apart from the christological content and emphasis, which is so dominant in the Gospel of John, one finds there another peculiarity. Aside from his discourses and disputes about himself and his own role, Jesus utters no teaching whatever during his public ministry. Only after he has withdrawn with his disciples, his own, does Jesus offer instruction regarding the conduct of life. Even then his instructions lack specificity. Rather, he commands his disciples to love one another as he has loved them (13:34). The character of his love for them, and therefore of the love to which they themselves are enjoined, is spelled out further in John 15:12. But such specificity as may be found there has to do only with the extent of love—it is to be limitless in its self-giving—not with concrete ways of living and acting in the world. Even the First Epistle of John, which dwells upon the necessity of love, does not elaborate upon the nature of love by referring to exemplary instances of loving acts.[5]

The richness, color, specificity, concreteness, and variety which characterize the teaching of Jesus in the synoptic gospels are by and large absent from John, as is his apparent willingness and intention to teach anyone who would listen the demands and will of God in view of the near advent of his kingdom. We have no parables, no pronouncement stories in John; therefore, we have none of the brief epigrammatic sayings which are so characteristic of the synoptic Jesus. Neither can much of Q or of the didactic elements of Mark,

4. See e.g., the proposal of Oscar Cullmann which introduces an element of speculation, or so it seems to me, into the otherwise well-argued presentation of his case (The Johannine Circle, trans. J. Bowden [Philadelphia: Westminster, 1976], pp. 93–94).

5. Cf., e.g., James 2. Although the author of James is not using the vocabulary of love, most of his examples would fit the exhortation of 1 John 4:7-12, 16-21.

M, or L be found. Instead, the Johannine Jesus expounds Christology and argues with his theological opponents, the Jews.

Any suffering of Jesus at his death can at most be imputed to the Fourth Gospel on the basis of other sources. In John, Jesus goes to the cross of his own volition and by his own decision. He decides when the hour for his departure in death has arrived, or rather he alone knows when the Father has decreed his hour has come. He lays down his own life; no one takes it from him (10:18). In John, Jesus' death is his glorification, not his humiliation.[6] No narrative typifies this more than the Johannine account of his arrest (18:1–11). There is no anguish of Jesus just preceding it. Gethsemane is at most alluded to in 12:27. Instead, Jesus seems to direct his own arrest even as later he will direct his own death (19:28–30). Jesus does nothing, and nothing happens to him, by chance; and this is nowhere more evident than in the account of his death, whether in the passion narrative proper or in the many references and allusions to it throughout the Gospel. In his conversation with Pilate at his trial Jesus explains what is going on, in contrast to the synoptics, where he remains silent throughout. Perhaps it is too much to say that Jesus interrogates Pilate, rather than Pilate interrogating Jesus; yet it is nevertheless clear that Jesus, not Pilate, is really in control of matters. Indeed, Jesus' own fixity of purpose is contrasted, probably quite deliberately, with Pilate's uncertainty.

By way of summary, in John as in the synoptics Jesus appears as miracle worker and teacher as well as the one destined for death. Yet in contrast with the synoptics the Jesus of John performs miracles expressly to signify who he is. Such works are not acts of compassion — only a few are healings — nor are they manifestations of the inbreaking eschatological power. The Johannine Jesus' teaching is explicitly, and rather narrowly, christological, lacking the diversity and specificity of the synoptics. Not surprisingly then, the tragic dimensions of Jesus' death, his own anguish and suffering in the face of it, are largely absent in John. He dies as man is scarcely known to die. If in Mark Jesus utters a cry of dereliction and in Luke a pious prayer, in John Jesus marks the end of his own

6. On this point I agree with the perspective of Ernst Käsemann, without necessarily endorsing his general view of the death of Jesus in John's Gospel and Johannine theology (*The Testament of Jesus: A Study of the Gospel in the Light of Chapter 17*, trans. G. Krodel [Philadelphia: Fortress, 1968], p. 19).

earthly ministry and work with the imperious pronouncement, "It is finished."

It should be possible to account for the obvious and significant differences in this broadly similar portrayal of Jesus, but this is not easy to do, as the history of the discussion of the problem clearly shows. Traditionally it has been suggested that John knew the other gospels and intended to deepen or supplement their presentation. Some critical scholarship, working on similar premises regarding the relationship of John to the synoptics, arrived at the view that John intended not to supplement, but to supplant, the other gospels.[7] Subsequently, the assumption that John knew the synoptics at all was seriously called into question.[8] Certainly it is now no longer possible to assume that John's differences from the synoptics can be accounted for by recourse to his alleged intention to augment or to alter them. If he knew one or more of them, he did not regard them as authoritative scripture. They were more or less at the periphery of his consciousness. The shape and character of the Fourth Gospel was apparently determined by other factors.

At this point it is relevant to indicate the hermeneutical issue raised by the question of John's historical relationship to the other gospels. Whether or not the Fourth Evangelist wrote with knowledge of the synoptics, and whatever his intention with respect to them, the church ultimately accepted John's Gospel as a part of the canon of scripture alongside and in conjunction with the synoptic gospels. Therefore, the interpretation of the Fourth Gospel in its original purpose and intent is one thing, but the interpretation of that Gospel in its canonical content may be something else. The possibility suggested by Käsemann, that the Gospel of John was accepted precisely because in the passage of time it was misunder-

7. This is the viewpoint of Hans Windisch, who answers, "Ersetzen" (*Johannes und die Synoptiker: Wollte der vierte Evangelist die älterer Evangelien ergänzen oder ersetzen?* UNT 12 [Leipzig: Hinrich, 1926]). It is also the position of E. C. Colwell, who argues that John seeks to allay objections about Jesus among readers offended by aspects of the synoptic portrayal (*John Defends the Gospel* [Chicago: Willett, Clark & Co., 1936]).

8. Here the seminal work has been P. Gardner-Smith, *St. John and the Synoptic Gospels*, a slim volume whose size belies its importance (Cambridge: Cambridge University Press, 1938). An impressive array of scholars, including Bultmann, Dodd, and R. E. Brown, has come to share substantially his position. But by no means all agree: C. K. Barrett and Kümmel, among others, remain unconvinced.

stood, cannot be ruled out a priori.[9] But if that is the case, is the interpretation of John in the church of necessity the continuation of that misinterpretation? On these terms a positive answer to this question can scarcely be avoided, at least in principle, but the sharpness of the question and the alternative it implies (historical or churchly exegesis) will be mitigated somewhat if it can be shown that the purpose and character of John is a function of historical circumstances different from those of the synoptics, rather than of a fundamentally antithetical theological insight or intent.

JESUS IN THE JOHANNINE MILIEU

A consideration of the origin of the distinctive Johannine presentation of Jesus is therefore germane to this question. It has frequently been proposed that John relies upon sources, otherwise unknown, which are different from, although not altogether unrelated to, the synoptic gospels.[10] In all probability he does, but this hypothesis only pushes the question of the Johannine milieu, and the influences shaping the Fourth Gospel, back one step farther. What sort of Christian community, subject to what influences, produced the substance, as well as the present form, of the Gospel of John?

The answer that this book is the product of a community of Christians who had undergone a traumatic exit or expulsion from the synagogue goes a long way toward explaining the distinctive character of the Fourth Gospel, if it does not answer every question

9. It was perhaps canonized "through man's error and God's providence." Cf. *The Testament of Jesus,* p. 75.

10. The most imposing and all-encompassing source theory is still that of Bultmann, *The Gospel of John,* passim. Cf. my article, included in this present volume, "The Sources of the Gospel of John: An Assessment of the Present State of the Problem," NTS 10 (1963-64):336-51 and book, *The Composition and Order of the Fourth Gospel: Bultmann's Literary Theory,* Yale Publications in Religion 10 (New Haven: Yale University Press, 1965). Bultmann discerned *semeia* (sign) and passion sources, among others, in the Gospel. Some more recent source-critical work, while less comprehensive than Bultmann's, is methodologically better grounded. Robert T. Fortna's *The Gospel of Signs: A Reconstruction of the Narrative Source Underlying the Fourth Gospel* is a painstakingly careful, and yet, bold effort in an area where source criticism is most likely to prove fruitful, i.e., the Johannine narratives (SNTSMS 11 [Cambridge: Cambridge University Press, 1970]).

about its provenance and purpose.[11] The miracles are signs, if not proofs, of Jesus' messianic dignity; and the discourses and dialogues of the first half of the Gospel concentrate upon the question of Jesus' identity and role. Just such a fixation upon the christological question fits the proposed church-synagogue milieu. That milieu in turn helps explain the eristic character of the first half of the Gospel especially, as well as its intense concentration on Christology. Jesus himself is portrayed as the origin of the dispute between Christians (Christ-confessors) and the synagogue, and his affirmations about himself become the warrant and justification for the Christian community's claims for him.

Doubtless those very claims are, in John, cast in the terminology of the Johannine community's confession. Yet at the same time, that community would insist that the christological claims and confession are rooted in and derive from Jesus himself.[12] (In this John is like each of the other evangelists, but he goes far beyond them in attributing explicit Christology to Jesus.) Whether that position is defensible is a good question, and one scarcely answerable in terms of whether or not Jesus actually said such things. Probably he did not.[13] The real question is whether John's presentation of him in

11. Certainly the leading recent proponent of this position has been J. Louis Martyn, *History and Theology in the Fourth Gospel* (New York, Harper, 1968). The article by Raymond Brown in *Interpretation* 31 (1977): 379-93, "Johannine Ecclesiology: the Community's Origins," which he kindly allowed me to see in typescript, indicates the importance of Martyn's proposals in contemporary scholarship. Before 1966 Brown himself saw the importance of expulsion from the synagogue as an issue in determining the date and provenance fo the Fourth Gospel. (See his *The Gospel According to John* (i-xii), AB 29 [Garden City, N.Y.: Doubleday, 1966], pp. lxx–lxxv, lxxxv.) Fortna's source theory is, of course, tied to Martyn's overall view of Johannine origins. The "Gospel of Signs" is the first gospel produced by the Christians who eventually gave us the Fourth Gospel.

12. This insistence is implicit in the narrative, gospel form itself. On the significance of this point see my *John*, Proclamation Commentaries (Philadelphia: Fortress, 1976), pp. 58–60; cf. 40–41, 54–56. Note also the sophisticated discussion of Franz Mussner, *The Historical Jesus in the Gospel of St. John*, trans. W. J. O'Hara (New York: Herder, 1967).

13. The view that he did not is, I believe, essentially correct and compelling, although certainly not universally shared. Cf. the view of Cullmann, *The Johannine Circle*, and the perspective of Leon Morris, *The Gospel According to John: The English Text with Introduction, Exposition, and Notes*, NICNT (Grand

these terms is on any grounds legitimate. Certainly it is not if one is seeking an "objective historical account," whatever that may be. It is understandable and legitimate only from a distinctively Christian perspective, that is, only on the confessional position that Jesus is the Christ. On that basis John's presentation is legitimate and becomes enlightening and suggestive. From any other perspective it is offensive, just as in the Gospel Jesus' claims for himself are offensive to those who do not share the belief of his followers.

That belief, its implicated hopes and uncertainties, becomes transparent in the so-called farewell discourses and final prayer (chaps. 13-17). There the presupposition of a community of his followers surviving more than a generation after his departure, with all the problems attendant upon their perilous situation in the unfriendly world, is plainly evident. It is such a community with its peculiar traditions and history, which through one of its gifted members has produced the presentation of Jesus found in the Fourth Gospel.

The possible influence of Gnosticism or Qumran upon the Fourth Gospel is certainly not to be discounted.[14] The evangelist and his community were as much influenced by the surrounding culture as any number of other ancient documents one might mention. Yet the similarity of outlook and terminology between John and some Gnostic and Essene writings may be as much a derivative of a similarity of

---

Rapids: Eerdmans, 1971), esp. pp. 44ff. Morris also has recourse to the theory of a private, more esoteric teaching found principally in John. Both Morris and Cullmann refer to the work of Riesenfeld and Gerhardsson.

14. Gnosticism and Qumran frequently figure in discussions of Johannine origins as if they necessarily represented mutually exclusive alternatives, although they do not, as Bultmann already saw. In fact, he claimed the discovery of the Dead Sea Scrolls supported, rather than refuted, his view of the Gnostic antecedents of the Fourth Gospel. See *Theology of the New Testament,* II, trans. K. Grobel (New York: Scribner's, 1955), 13; cf. *The Gospel of John,* p. 23 n.1. A representative collection of essays on John and Qumran is to be found in the book of that title edited by James H. Charlesworth (London: Chapman, 1972). The Gnostic position is not so well represented in the English literature on John, although one may with profit consult, for a judiciously sympathetic but critical presentation, Rudolf Schnackenburg, *The Gospel According to St. John,* trans. Kevin Smyth (New York: Herder & Herder, 1968), I, 135-52, 543-47. A recent statement of the case for the Gnostic origin and indeed, character of John is Luise Schottroff, *Der Glaubende and die feindliche Welt: Beobachtungen zum gnostischen Dualismus und seiner Bedeutung für Paulus und das Johannesevangelium,* WMANT 37 (Neukirchen: Neukirchener Verlag, 1970).

perspective on the community and outsiders as the expression of an actual direct influence, much less literary relationship. John, Gnostics, and the Essenes shared a similar sectarian attitude toward themselves and the world. This clear distinction between those who are in and those who are not, and the history of that distinction, is as much as anything else characteristic of the Fourth Gospel and determinative of its nature.[15]

JOHN'S UNIQUE METAHISTORICAL PRESENTATION OF JESUS

The historical circumstances which produced the Johannine presentation of Jesus are important for understanding it, but they do not really "explain" it, nor can they be substituted for it. John's presentation of Jesus comes alive in the narrative itself. He is the Jesus of the past, who lived and worked in first century Palestine among his fellow Jews. His conflicts with his contemporaries have been overlaid, but not lost, in the portrayal of him as the origin of his community's struggle with the synagogue.[16] His miraculous deeds are no longer harbingers of the power of the inbreaking kingdom of God, or even signs of the eschatological crisis precipitated by Jesus' ministry, much less deeds of love and mercy, but are signs of Jesus' messiahship and sonship. Yet in both cases the present role of Jesus and his followers is understood as based upon the historic work of Jesus of Nazareth, interpreted and refracted in the community's tradition and in the Gospel. Moreover, the death of Jesus, portrayed as the work of his Jewish opponents, was nevertheless a real event. Although John's portrayal represents a common early Christian tendency to blame "the Jews" for Jesus' death, at the same time it contains ample evidence pointing in alternative directions.[17]

15. Cf. Wayne A. Meeks, "The Man from Heaven in Johannine Sectarianism," *JBL* 91 (1972): 44–72.

16. Martyn does not in his two-level theory about the Johannine episodes emphasize what he calls their *einmalig* dimension, concentrating rather on the later level in which the church-synagogue dispute is reflected. Without unwarrantedly ascribing to him any views on the historicity of the incidents recounted, it is fair to say that on his terms the basic narratives could have been, and presumably were, regarded by the Johannine Christians as accounts of Jesus' actual deeds.

17. To give some obvious examples: It is only the high priest who decides and decrees that Jesus must die, when other Jewish leaders are uncertain what is to be

The Jesus of the Fourth Gospel is also the Jesus of the church's present and future. He is the source of the Spirit-Paraclete who abides with the church in its witness and especially in its adversity. Even as Jesus is depicted as present in the conflict with the synagogue which produced the Johannine community, so he is portrayed as the source of unity, stability, and purpose in the community's continued existence in the world. This presence of Jesus is not only given in the contemporary Johannine community, that is, contemporary with the author, it is given as an abiding assurance to the community about its own future: Jesus will continue to come to, and dwell among, his disciples.

The Spirit or Paraclete as the mode of Jesus' abiding with his disciples seems to be a felt reality, a presence regarded as given rather than imagined.[18] It is not, in other words, a mere theological idea of the evangelist or of his community. Exactly how the Spirit-Paraclete makes the presence of Jesus known and felt in the community is never stated in so many words. That is, the exact mode of his activity, the phenomenology of his presence, is not described, although his function is clear enough. Especially the emphasis on the Spirit's bringing to recollection and expanding upon Jesus' own teaching suggests that the Spirit-Paraclete worked through the leadership or ministry of the Johannine community. This does not necessarily mean that an ordained ministry of the Johannine church administered or dispensed the Spirit. Quite possibly the gift of the Spirit, especially in the functions described, authenticated the leadership of the church. The leadership of the Johannine church mediates the presence of Jesus to the congregation through the Spirit. But does the choice of leadership determine who shall possess the

---

done about him (11:50); a cohort of (Roman) soldiers participates in Jesus' arrest (18:3); there is in John no account of a trial and condemnation before the Sanhedrin; although it is said that Pilate wished to release Jesus, it is finally he who orders him crucified (19:16, 19:22) and takes responsibility for the execution (19:31, 38); finally, (Roman) soldiers crucify Jesus (19:23).

18. On the Spirit-inspired character of Johannine Christianity and the Johannine community, see George Johnston, *The Spirit-Paraclete in the Gospel of John*, SNTSMS 12 (Cambridge: Cambridge University Press, 1970), esp. pp. 127-48; also Käsemann, *The Testament of Jesus*, esp. pp. 36ff.; and Alv Kragerud, *Der Lieblingsjünger im Johannesevangelium; ein exegetischer Versuch* (Oslo: Osloer Universitätsverlag, 1959), esp. pp. 93–112.

Spirit? In all likelihood the other way around; the intervention and work of the Spirit determined the leadership of the church. Yet it is clear that the Spirit alone cannot authenticate itself (cf. 1 John 4:6). If the Spirit is nothing other than the continuing presence and revelation of Jesus to his followers, any continuation of that presence or revelation must bear a positive relation to the historical figure.[19] John's Jesus is intended to do just that, despite his Christian theological dress.

The conviction that this Jesus, who lived and died a half-century or more before and in his exalted state returns through the Spirit to abide with his church, is more than an important historical personage of continuing significance and memory is expressed in the recurring references to his preexistence, heavenly abode, and descent and ascent to and from the world of men. To say that these "mythological" concepts are exhausted in their meaning by their existential significance, that is, their expression of the importance of Jesus for the believer or the community, may be an unwarranted truncation of their scope. On the other hand, such an assertion is certainly not without foundation. Hazardous as it may be to claim that the evangelist did not take the language of preexistence and accompanying phenomena literally, it is nevertheless unnecessary to attribute to him the crudest kind of understanding of this constellation of mythological concepts. Surely he shows evidence of some sophistication, whether literary or theological, throughout his Gospel. If an existentialist, or other modern, interpretation of this Johannine language runs the risk of reading too much into the Gospel, or excluding certain dimensions of its meaning, it is not therefore necessarily wrong in principle. The simple yet mysterious character of Johannine language invites the reader to inquire about and explore its meaning.

The presentation of Jesus in the Fourth Gospel is multidimensional. He is still the Jewish man of Galilee. But he is also the spiritual presence with, and head of, the community of disciples

---

19. On Jesus and the Paraclete, see R. E. Brown, "The Paraclete in the Fourth Gospel," *NTS* 13 (1966-67):113-32, esp. 126-32. Cf. also R. Alan Culpepper's interesting observations regarding the parallel functions of the Paraclete and the Beloved Disciple, *The Johannine School: An Evaluation of the Johannine-school Hypothesis Based on an Investigation of the Nature of Ancient Schools*, SBLDS 26 (Missoula, Mont.: Scholars Press, 1975), pp. 267-70.

which we may safely call his church. He has been with the church in its past struggles and will continue with it into the foreseeable future. His nature is, however, never understood until his origin and destiny with God is truly comprehended. He and the Father are one; he goes forth from the Father and returns; not only he, but his followers, will abide with the Father for all eternity. There is no major aspect of this Johannine presentation of Jesus which is absolutely unique or foreign to other strains of early Christianity, even to the synoptic gospels.[20] What is uniquely Johannine is the way these aspects of, or perspectives on, Jesus are made to coalesce into a single narrative so that each is always present in almost every part of the narrative. For example, in the prologue the reader is reminded of the historical figure as well as the Jesus Christ who is the origin of grace and truth. In the account of his deeds one is similarly aware that the worker of signs is more than a miracle worker out of the past. In the account of his death one is, on the one hand, made cognizant of the overarching cosmic and historic frame in which that death is overcome; but, on the other, not allowed to forget that it was a real, historic death of a human being.[21] The farewell discourses are words of the exalted one; but he is still recognizably the person whose ministry has just been recounted, and the shadow of his death now looms in the foreground. It is the genius of the Fourth Evangelist to have created a gospel in which Jesus as the representative of the world above visits

20. Needless to say, however, John has his unique style, vocabulary, and emphases. John's Gospel is in some significant ways a strange and different book. Yet the main lines of his presentation of Jesus seem to be positively related to, even if they are not derived directly from, the portrayal of him which we find in the synoptics, and in other New Testament writings. E. C. Hoskyns wrote: "The test that we must in the end apply to the Fourth Gospel, the test by which the Fourth Gospel stands or falls, is whether the Marcan narrative becomes more intelligible after reading the Fourth Gospel, whether the Pauline Epistles become more transparent, or whether the whole material presented to us in the New Testament is breaking up into unrelated fragments" (The Fourth Gospel, ed. F. N. Davey [London: Faber & Faber, 1947], p. 133). This test is ultimately theological and cannot finally depend solely upon exegetical conclusions pro or con about literary and historical relationships. It is the question of whether John's presence in the canon makes theological sense.

21. For a balanced presentation of the significance of Jesus' death in John, see J. T. Forestell, The Word of the Cross: Salvation as Revelation in the Fourth Gospel, AnBib 57 (Rome: Biblical Institute Press, 1974).

and really lives in this world without depriving it of its verisimilitude and without depriving life here of its seriousness.

A CONCLUDING RESERVATION

Yet the presentation of Jesus in the Fourth Gospel should not be represented as the culmination of a development in the New Testament, or among the gospels, of such a sort and magnitude as to render all that came before it or stand beside it superfluous. If John Calvin rightly saw in the Fourth Gospel the key to the others, he did not for that reason regard it as rendering the others unnecessary.[22] The uniqueness of the Gospel of John, and indeed its theological worth, is enhanced when it is placed alongside the other gospels and seen with them. Apart from the synoptics the Johannine portrait of Jesus specifically, as distinguished from other characters such as the man born blind, the woman of Samaria, and Nicodemus, loses much of its depth and color. In fact, if we had had no synoptics, the Johannine portrait of Jesus would doubtless have produced a rather different configuration of Christian belief than has actually emerged historically. Whether or not John should be described as incipiently docetic,[23] whether or not it is in part the product of Gnostic influence, it is nevertheless the case that there is not in that Gospel a depiction of the man Jesus fully capable of standing guard over his genuine humanity. That depiction is present in the synoptic gospels, whether because of or in spite of the intentions of their authors.

Moreover, the valid spirituality of the Fourth Gospel would have been jeopardized if Jesus' statement that his kingdom is not of this world had been allowed to stand unbalanced by the synoptics' presentation of the kingdom as a reality breaking into this world. That Johannine statement about the kingdom is not wrong, even by synoptic standards, but standing alone and in the Fourth Gospel

22. "I am accustomed to say that this Gospel is a key to open the door for understanding the rest; for whoever shall understand the power of Christ, as it is here strikingly portrayed, will afterwards read with advantage what the others relate about the Redeemer who was manifested" (Calvin, *Commentary on the Gospel According to John,* trans. W. Pringle [Edinburgh, Calvin Translation Society, 1847], p.22).

23. Käsemann, *The Testament of Jesus,* pp. 26, 66, 70.

it opens wide a door to the temptation to make of Christianity a thoroughly otherworldly religion. In its canonical context, however, the potential thrust of such a statement is balanced, yes, blunted, by other statements about the relationship of God's kingdom (and Christ) to this world. Indeed, such statements do not really contradict the theological intention of the Fourth Evangelist, who portrays Jesus praying to the Father not to take his followers out of this world, but to protect them from the Evil One.

My personal history, first as a Christian, then as New Testament student, has revolved about a fascination with the Fourth Gospel. It is the greatest riddle of the New Testament and of Christian origins generally. When was this Gospel written? Who wrote it? Under what religious and cultural influences was it composed? What is its relationship to the other gospels? Indeed, what is its relationship to Jesus? Is the Jesus of John in any sense the Jesus of history? Or is that figure a construct arising out of the piety and theology of primitive Christian faith? I have not always been able to parse the riddle of the Fourth Gospel into so many subriddles. Yet for many years I have been aware of the problematic character of the Fourth Gospel as its stands alongside the other three.

THE RIDDLE OF THE FOURTH GOSPEL:
WHY IS IT SO DIFFERENT FROM THE OTHERS?

From childhood I can remember the oft-repeated claim of some preachers that Jesus was either whom he claimed to be (Messiah, Son of God) or the most colossal egomaniac and fraud the world has ever known. The posing of that alternative was a kind of evangelical tactic to eliminate the moderate middle, or all liberal or quasi-liberal, critical or quasi-critical, views of Jesus. They are excluded by virtue of Jesus' own claims. There was no gentle Jesus meek and mild, nor even a young and fearless prophet of ancient Galilee. There was and is only the strong Son of God, walking across the face of the earth performing astounding miracles and proclaiming, "I am the way, and the truth, and the life; no one comes to the Father, but by me."

Even before my mind was illuminated by theological training, I had become aware that this latter view of Jesus was largely the product of the Gospel according to John. Even the possibility of a more modest or restrained view of him could arise only on the basis of the synoptic gospels.

In a variety of ways John differs markedly from the other gospels. Yet there are enough similarities that the genre "gospel" seems to comprehend them all. John, like the synoptics, tells the story of Jesus from his encounter with the Baptist through his crucifixion and the discovery of the empty tomb. In all four gospels there is a scene with Peter near the center point in which the questions of Jesus' role and identity and the disciples' relation to him emerge as central issues. In each gospel Jesus gathers disciples, teaches, debates with opponents, performs signs or miracles, goes up to Jerusalem at a Passover, there encounters severe opposition, and—after a final meal with his disciples—is arrested, tried, crucified, and buried. On the third day women find the tomb empty. In addition, there are some instances in which the wording of the Fourth Gospel is exactly the same as in one or more of the synoptics, usually Mark. These are not nearly so numerous or extensive as the agreements among the synoptics, but they nevertheless exist. The character of Jesus' teaching in the Fourth Gospel, while different, is not necessarily incompatible with what is found in the synoptics. The famous love command of John (John 13:34; 15:12) has with good reason been regarded as an apt summation of Jesus' teaching. If Jesus talks much more about his messiahship and divine sonship in John than in the others, these theological convictions are not, after all, unlike those of the synoptic evangelists. What is latent in the synoptics is patent in John. Moreover, the general purpose of John's Gospel, as stated in 20:30-31, is not fundamentally different from that of the synoptics.

Yet alongside such significant affinities and similarities must be ranged a variety of substantial divergencies or differences. The ministry of Jesus in the synoptics takes place in Galilee and might well have occurred within a period of one year. In John the ministry encompasses about three years; there are three Passovers (John 2:13, 23; 6:4; 12:1), perhaps four (5:1). Jesus goes up to Jerusalem at least three times (2:13; 5:1, 7:10). After 7:10 he is no longer in Galilee at all, although there are subsequent periods when Jesus withdraws from public view (10:40–42; 11:54). In John, Jesus is portrayed in Jerusalem or Judea far more than in Galilee (2:13 to 4:3; 5:1–47; 7:10 to 20:31), so that one gains the distinct impression that he spent most of his time there during the period of his public activity. Thus the itinerary of Jesus, the structure of the Gospel, and the geographical location of Jesus' ministry in John differ from what we find in the synoptic gospels. But the divergencies do not end there. The substantial content of John (i.e., the specific stories, sayings, and controversies) is different. While much of the content of each of the synoptics is paralleled in the other two, most of what is found in John has no parallel in the synoptics and vice versa.

The parallelism or similarity of content between John and the synoptics lies mostly in the passion narrative. According to H. F. D. Sparks's gospel parallels, there are 93 pericopes or sections in the Fourth Gospel.[1] Of these, only 25 have synoptic parallels, while 68 do not. But in the passion-resurrection narratives (John 18–21), 14 of the pericopes have synoptic parallels, while only 11 do not. This discrepancy is really even broader than these figures reveal, for within the passion narratives the extent of verbatim agreement with the synoptics, especially Mark, is greater than elsewhere. Moreover, the order of events in the passion is very much the same, whereas in the prepassion parts of the gospel there is only the most remote or general similarity between John and the synoptics.

If one looks at the evidence from the standpoint of Mark, for example, the picture is similar. Of the 106 Marcan pericopes (again according to Sparks), only 21 have Johannine parallels, while 85 do not. But of the 24 Marcan pericopes in the passion-resurrection narrative (Mark 14–16) 15 have Johannine parallels and only 9 do not. The comparison of John with either Matthew or Luke would reveal even more striking discrepancies. Because John and the synoptics end on the same note, with the same general episodes of crucifixion

1. Sparks, *A Synopsis of the Gospels: The Synoptic Gospels with the Johannine Parallels* (Philadelphia: Fortress, 1964) and his *The Johannine Synopsis of the Gospels* (New York: Harper, 1974) were used in this analysis.

and resurrection and with many of the same individual narratives, one gets the impression that the gospels are more similar than they actually are. Of the prepassion narratives of Mark, which comprise most of that gospel, only a few (Jesus' encounter with the Baptist, the miracle of the feeding of the five thousand, the walking on the water, and the confession of Peter) have reasonably close Johannine parallels. It is true that John, like Mark, contains an account of Jesus' calling his disciples, but the actual call narratives are quite different in the two gospels. Moreover, the Johannine and Marcan narratives of the so-called confession of Peter (in Mark at Caesarea Philippi, in John not) are so different as to call in question our identification of them.

It is a striking fact that no Marcan healing miracles or exorcisms are found in John. The obverse is also the case, none of the Johannine healing miracles is found in Mark. Since, by and large, the Marcan healing narratives represent the bulk of the synoptic miracle tradition, it is fair to say that John and the synoptics contain different miracle traditions, which scarcely overlap.

Not only the miracle narratives or traditions differ, however. The style and tone of the Fourth Gospel, as well as the presentation of Jesus' message, are different. Nothing typifies this difference more than John's handling of the miracles. In the synoptics, especially Mark, Jesus admonishes his disciples to keep silence about his miracles, as if he is reticent about them or about their significance. But in the Fourth Gospel, Jesus demands faith in himself precisely on the basis of such miracles. They have become signs revealing who he is. Jesus' teaching and controversy are of a piece with his signs. With good reason it has been said that in the synoptics Jesus proclaims the coming kingdom of God, while in the Fourth Gospel he proclaims himself as king. In John, Jesus' teaching centers upon that subject which mostly is only suggested, or hovers in the background, in the tradition of the other gospels, namely Christology. Both to his opponents and to his disciples the Johannine Jesus expounds his messiahship and divine sonship openly. That is the principal content of his teaching. If in the synoptics awesome powers of human and supernatural evil seem to overtake Jesus, in John he goes to his death of his own volition and remains clearly in control, not only of himself but of those who seek his demise.

The Jesus of the synoptics was already the Christ of Christian confession in the hearts and minds of the gospel writers and the early congregations for whom they wrote. They are anything but value-free, objective, historical accounts. Yet the synoptics—or at least the synoptic tradition—breathe the air of first-century Palestine; that is, those gospels evoke the religious and cultural atmosphere in which Jesus worked in a way that the Fourth Gospel does not. It may be that it too breathes the air of first-century Palestine, but in a different sense. For in the Fourth Gospel, Jesus continually speaks of himself in the language of Christian confession, while in the synoptics he is much more restrained, and in Mark he appears reluctant even to accept the title of Messiah or Christ when it is proffered him by his followers.

I find it difficult to avoid the conclusion of two centuries of critical scholarship that a historical, or a historian's, view of Jesus must begin with the synoptic gospels or their content, i.e., the synoptic tradition.[2] By this I do not imply that everything in the synoptics is historically authentic, while nothing in John is. On the contrary, much in the synoptic gospels, including their outline or structure, is the creation of the Christian communities and writers which produced them. By the same token, it is most probable that there is authentic, historical data to be mined from the Fourth Gospel. (For example, John rather than the synoptics may be correct in having Jesus crucified the afternoon before, rather than the day of, the beginning of the Passover celebration.) But when all is said and done, I find it difficult to believe that the picture of Jesus which emerges from the synoptics and their several strands of sources or traditions does not take precedence over the Johannine, or that the synoptic gospels or traditions could have arisen *after* the one found in John had been widely disseminated among the early Christian churches. If the Johannine portrayal of Jesus had been the original, it would be hard to understand how and why the synoptic one ever developed—and not in one isolated gospel but in three gospels, each of

2. Recently C. K. Barrett has sharply rejected any too sanguine estimate of the historical value of the Fourth Gospel. Cf. *The Gospel According to St. John*, 2d ed. (Philadelphia: Westminster, 1978), p. viii: "I do not believe that John intended to supply us with historically verifiable information regarding the life and teaching of Jesus, and that historical traditions of great worth can be disentangled from his interpretative comments."

which represents multiple strands of compatible tradition. One may, of course, revive the venerable view that John represents an arcane, secret tradition, equally authentic historically, as Oscar Cullmann has recently once again proposed.[3] Yet this resolution of the matter is less than satisfactory. If Jesus talked in two different ways, why does one way appear in the synoptics and the other almost exclusively in the Fourth Gospel? Moreover, the literary style and vocabulary of the Fourth Gospel, even of the Johannine Jesus, finds its closest analogy not in the other gospels but in the Johannine Epistles.

If we are to consider the important matters comprehended by the title "Theology and Ministry in John," it is helpful to keep the relationship of John and the synoptics in view. The question is not which represents the point of view of Jesus. In important respects the synoptics are closer than John. But in every gospel Jesus' point of view is to be found only as it is refracted through the evangelist's prism. To be completely realistic, there is no possibility of going behind the gospels to recover a picture of Jesus and his message that is "objective" in the sense that it avoids their tendencies or perspectives. In fact, there is no distinctively Christian reason for deeming that desirable. All the gospels intend to be faithful and authoritative witnesses. John is no different in that regard. Yet John's distinctiveness, as compared with the differences among the other three, is substantial and significant. Our purpose, which will accord with the evangelist's, is to inquire how and to what extent John's portrayal of Jesus expresses his understanding of theology and ministry.

The problem of why John and the synoptics are so different, and yet at some points alike, will probably never be "solved" in the sense that an overwhelming majority of scholars will agree that John wrote either independently of the synoptics or with them in view, whether to supplement or correct them. It would be presumptuous even to suggest a solution in this context.

Yet a couple of things are clear. On the one hand, if John did not know the synoptics, he clearly knew a gospel tradition similar at many points, on the basis of which he offered his own theological elaboration. He at least knew, and presumably expected his readers

---

3. See Cullmann, *The Johannine Circle*, trans. John Bowden (Philadelphia: Westminster, 1976), p. 94.

to know, certain gospel facts and traditions (that Jesus was baptized by John, who Pilate was, etc.) in a form not unlike the synoptic. John could be read with understanding only by someone already imbued with the Christian tradition. Someone unacquainted with it, or outside it, would be as perplexed as Nicodemus or as offended as the chief priests and Pharisees by this strangely fascinating book.

On the other hand, if the Fourth Evangelist knew the synoptic gospels, they were not for him standards of orthodoxy in the sense of bearers of the only orthodox tradition, even to the extent that Mark seems to have represented standard tradition for Luke and Matthew. John goes his own way. Explaining how and why he does is a problem for the traditional view that John knew the synoptics.

In any case, the strange, extraordinary character of the Gospel of John must not be leveled off for the sake of a quick and easy compatibility with the others. His distinctive emphases deserve to be heard. If this presents a difficulty for Christian theology, it is somewhat tempered by this fact: The fathers of the church in their wisdom allowed both the synoptics and John to stand side by side in the Christian Bible. We have the obligation to take both seriously. When we are merely attracted and challenged by the still-human figure that emerges from the traditions embodied in Matthew, Mark, or Luke—especially Luke—we are brought up short by the Johannine Jesus, who demands that we decide who he is and whether or not we belong to him. But lest we become complacent about that lordly, divine figure and satisfied to repeat, "He is the way, the truth, and the life, no one comes to the Father but by him," those other gospels remind us of another and indispensable dimension of Christology and faith. There was a Jesus who lived a human life under the same conditions that oppress us, defeat us, but also offer us the possibility of meaningful, authentic life. To live as followers of Jesus is not just to say, "Lord, Lord," but to participate in that life and in those struggles as he did. Whatever may have been the case in antiquity, the riddle of the Fourth Gospel can finally be answered adequately only by those who know the other three.

Yet I want now, so far as possible, to regard the other three gospels as background, and on that basis address such questions as these: What are the distinctive aspects of Johannine theology? How do they determine or contribute to his view of church and ministry? Whatever may be said about John's relationship to the synoptics, it is clear that he intends to set forth an original, distinctive, and largely independent presentation of Jesus. We are on exegetically and theologically good grounds if we first ask about John's view of theology and church, theology and ministry. We shall then be in a position to see how it relates to the positions of the other gospels and New Testament witnesses.

JOHN AS CHRISTIAN PREACHING

In looking at the peculiar problem of the relationship of the Fourth Gospel to the synoptics, we noticed that there are similarities in form and content, as well in as their portrayals of Jesus, which justify the assumption that they are different representatives of a common genre. With reason they are all called gospels. Yet we have also observed that there are very great differences, which are often minimized or overlooked. Anyone brought up in the Christian tradition tends from an early age to assimilate the different gospels and to blur their differences. Therefore, it has become necessary and important to emphasize those differences.

Both the similarities and the differences come to light in a remarkable way in John 5. In this chapter the characteristic themes of Johannine theology find expression. By examining it we shall be able to see why the Gospel of John qualifies as distinctly Christian preaching, in a way that even the synoptic gospels do not.

The chapter begins rather abruptly. For good reason John has been called a seamless robe. The narrative moves with such clear intentionality, and often so smoothly, that the characterization seems apt. Yet at some points there are lacunae, breaks, abrupt stops and starts; and this is one of them. Jesus was last seen in Cana of Galilee, and while there he had caused the official's son, who lay at death's door in Capernaum, to become well. All of that, and whatever else may have been in the author's mind, seems to be summed up in the laconic "after this" of John 5:1. As the RSV renders it, "After this there was a feast of the Jews, and Jesus went up to Jerusalem." John then briefly recounts a miracle story in which Jesus heals a man whose illness is not clearly specified.

Now there is in Jerusalem by the Sheep Gate a pool, in Hebrew called Bethzatha, which has five porticoes. In these lay a multitude of invalids, blind, lame, paralyzed. One man was there, who had been ill for thirty-eight years. When Jesus saw him and knew that he had been lying there a long time, he said to him, "Do you want to be healed?" The sick man answered him, "Sir, I have no man to put me into the pool when the water is troubled and while I am going another steps down before me." Jesus said to him, "Rise, take up your pallet, and walk." And at once the man was healed, and he took up his pallet and walked. (John 5:2-9)

The story has some curious features. The name and location of the pool have long been matters of dispute. The names Bethzatha, Bethesda, and Bethsaida appear in different manuscripts. (The pool with its five porches may have been discovered recently by archaeologists. If so, the discovery illumines the historical background of the account more than John's purpose in recounting the story.) Even before Jesus speaks to the man, he knows that he has been ill for a long time. When Jesus asks the man whether he wishes to be well, he does not answer directly, but describes his problem in getting into the pool "when the water is troubled." Jesus pays as little attention to that response as the man apparently paid to Jesus' question. "Rise, take up your pallet, and walk," says Jesus. The word of Jesus exactly parallels Mark 2:9, where it occurs in quite a different healing narrative. Jesus may have said such a thing more than once, and it would be easily remembered. The man's remark about not being able to get down into the pool when the water was stirred up sounded so strange that some ancient copyist provided an explanation after John 5:3: "An angel of the Lord went down at certain seasons into the pool, and troubled the water: whoever stepped in first after the troubling of the water was healed of whatever disease he had." (That is v. 4, absent from modern translations.) This explanation may provide the legendary belief that underlies the story and makes sense of it historically, but it is not part of the original text.

The difficulties of the story do not prevent John's using it to portray Jesus and to say what in his view is crucially important about him. Probably the story was traditional, a story about Jesus' healing a person, very much like many such stories that circulated in the early church and are found now in the gospels. Possibly its traditional character accounts in large part for the peculiarities. Maybe the evangelist himself did not know where the pool was, exactly what illness affected the man, or why the movement of the waters was thought to effect a cure. Nevertheless, the story also has a Johannine character, whether imposed by the evangelist or found already in the tradition. Jesus knows, supernaturally and without asking, that the man has been lying ill for a long time. He does not wait to be approached (contrast John 4:47; Mark 2:2–4; 5:25–28; 7:25, 32; 8:22; 10:47) but initiates the healing. When the man responds to his question, Jesus seemingly takes no notice of what he has said, but gives a command that effects the healing suddenly and with no preparation. Such behavior is not uncharacteristic of the Jesus of the Fourth Gospel, who knows Nathanael before they meet, knows all about the Samaritan woman, who has never met him, and tells her about herself. He typically initiates the conversation or action. He often seems not to notice what has been said to him, but speaks at another level. (This is a characteristic of the Johannine technique of misunderstanding. Jesus' interlocutors do not have the theological knowledge to comprehend what he means. By the same token, he utters statements that seem to make little or no contact with what preceded.) None of these features may be entirely unique to the Fourth Gospel (cf. Mark 2:8 and 5:30). Yet they are certainly more frequent in John than elsewhere.

What we see so far is a miracle story that is not unlike a number of other miracle stories of the gospels except that it has certain Johannine features. It is likely that John draws upon tradition, and we shall find reason to infer that he builds upon that tradition in order to portray Jesus in a distinctive way. Indeed, he uses it to make clear what to him is most important about Jesus. There is, however, as yet only a hint of the course the narrative will take. First, the man manifests his healing; he takes up his bed at Jesus' command and walks. In a typical synoptic miracle story this would be the end of the account or nearly so. (There one sometimes finds a brief indication of the amazement of onlookers, but even that is absent.) In John, however, we are still near the beginning. The reader is next told that the healing had occurred on the sabbath (John 5:9). This is a motif familiar to the reader of the synoptics. Jesus becomes involved in controversy because he violates, or to many seems to violate, the sabbath. But in contrast to what is often found in the synoptics (e.g., Mark 3:1–6; cf. 2:23–28), the sabbath motif has not figured prominently, or at all, in the story itself. Only now is it introduced. Probably it was no part of the traditional healing narrative, but it is traditional at least in the sense that John gets it from tradition. He knows that Jesus was often accused of breaking the sabbath.

But it is the healed man, not Jesus, who now is accused of breaking the sabbath by carrying his pallet (John 5:10). (Similarly, in Mark 2:23, Jesus' disciples are attacked for plucking grain on the sabbath.) The healed man responds by saying that Jesus has commanded him to do it (John 5:11). The Jews then ask the healed man to identify the one who has commanded him. Nothing like this is found in the synoptic gospels. There it is no secret who works miracles and heals people, although Jesus may command people to remain silent about his miracles. We also observe yet another striking feature in the way this narrative is developing. The people who challenge the healed man are described as Jews. They doubtless were Jews; but in this setting everyone, including Jesus, presumably would have been a Jew. There is something odd about this.

Who is called a Jew, or when is a member of Israel called a Jew and by whom?[4] In the synoptic tradition it can be assumed that everyone is a Jew unless otherwise designated, so no one is ordinarily called that. Only when non-Jews appear is the term used. Thus the wise men from the East inquire about one born "king of the Jews" (Matt. 2:2) or Pilate designates Jesus "the King of the Jews" (Matt. 27:37 and pars.) after the Roman soldiers have mocked him, using the same title (Matt. 27:29 and pars.). When he hangs upon the cross, the Jewish chief priests, scribes, and elders, however, cry out, even in derision, "He is the King of Israel," not, "He is the King of the Jews" (Matt. 27:42). All this corresponds closely to first century Palestinian Jewish usage. Jews do not ordinarily refer to themselves in that way, except when assuming an outsider's

4. See the helpful articles by G. von Rad, K. G. Kuhn, and W. Gutbrod on *Israel* (Israel), *Hebraios* (Hebrew), *Ioudaios* (Jew), and related terms in Gerhard Kittel, ed., *Theological Dictionary of the New Testament*, III, trans. Geoffrey W. Bromiley et al. (Grand Rapids: Eerdmans, 1965), 356–91.

perspective. John's usage, on the other hand, does not conform to what we would expect from Jewish circles in first century Palestine. The narrator somehow stands outside the orbit of Judaism in that he seems no longer to consider himself, or even Jesus and his disciples, to be Jewish. Of course, John can have Jesus addressed as a Jew by the Samaritan woman (John 4:9), and Jesus can even imply that he is a Jew himself (4:22). The evangelist knows that Jesus is from Nazareth (1:45–46) of Galilee (7:41). Yet when Jesus or his retinue confronts hostile people, the latter are characteristically and routinely referred to as "the Jews." Moreover, these Jews can distinguish between disciples of Jesus and disciples of Moses (John 9:28) as if one had to choose between the two.

What we find in John is then clearly a departure from synoptic usage. Even there Jesus may set himself off from Moses in an unprecedented way. He calls the Mosaic divorce law a concession because of "your hardness of heart" (Mark 10:5). In the Sermon on the Mount he counterposes to Mosaic law his own, authoritative, "but I say to you," which characteristically radicalizes the Mosaic command. Yet all this occurs in a context of Jew talking to Jew, and on the assumption that the Jewish scriptures contain the word of God, which the Jews as such could understand, if they only would.

Jesus' original disciples did not regard themselves as having abandoned Moses any more than he himself rejected him, and the synoptic tradition reflects this state of affairs. When in a Q saying (Matt. 12:41–42; Luke 11:31–32) Jesus implies he is greater than Jonah or Solomon, it is perhaps noteworthy that he does not say he is greater than Moses. In John, however, Jesus says or implies that he is greater than Jacob (John 4:12–14), Abraham (John 8:56–58), and Moses (John 6:32–33, 49–51; cf. 5:45–47).

Both John and the synoptics were in all probability written in and for Christian communities which understood themselves to be such. That is, they were written in and for Christian churches as distinguished from the synagogue. Yet in the synoptics the tradition still embodies, to a recognizable degree, a time and a perspective different from the authors' own—whether it be the perspective of Jesus or that of the postresurrection Palestinian church, which lived in a Jewish environment where Aramaic was still spoken and people still looked for the coming redemption of Israel. (Cf. Luke 24:21

and Acts 1:6, which, although quite possibly compositions of Luke, are intended to convey the perspective of an earlier time.) On the other hand, John reflects an entirely Christian point of view, one in which it cannot be taken for granted that everyone is a Jew. Not only is this the evangelist's perspective, but it permeates the material of which the Gospel is composed. And in this respect John differs significantly from the synoptics.

By commonly referring to Jesus' interlocutors as "the Jews," John creates the impression that Jesus does not belong, or no longer belongs, to the Jewish community or world. By the same token, neither do the disciples (John 9:28), nor, indeed, does the evangelist himself. Not only John, but Jesus also, speaks from the perspective of a community separate and distinct from Judaism. Jesus, as well as the evangelist, talks like a Christian.

But we are getting ahead of our text. There follows upon the Jews' question to the healed man about the identity of his benefactor a rather strange interlude:

> Now the man who had been healed did not know who it was, for Jesus had withdrawn, as there was a crowd in the place. Afterward, Jesus found him in the temple, and said to him, "See, you are well! Sin no more, that nothing worse befall you." The man went away and told the Jews that it was Jesus who had healed him. And this was why the Jews persecuted Jesus, because he did this on the sabbath. (John 5:13–16)

Jesus is at first absent, but then he encounters the healed man in the temple and warns him. The warning goes unheeded, for apparently the evangelist would have us understand that the man betrayed Jesus to the Jews—that is, betrayed his identity—with the result that the Jews persecuted Jesus. The man had not known at first who Jesus was. Curiously, after the second encounter he knows, but the text never says Jesus told him! There may well be an intentional contrast between this man, who instead of affirming or confessing Jesus betrays him, and the man born blind, of chapter 9. The latter doggedly insists upon the reality of what Jesus has done for him in the face of severe questioning and even harassment, and finally confesses his faith in him (John 9:38). In any event, the fact of tension or opposition between Jesus and those who have been identified as the Jews is now established. They persecute him because of what he has done on the sabbath, namely, heal a man, and Jesus at length speaks in response.

Interestingly enough, Jesus speaks in answer to no direct question but to the presumed situation as a whole. "My Father is working still, and I am working," he says (John 5:17). Jesus never justifies his breaking of the sabbath with such an imperious statement in the synoptics, even though he may imply that he is "Lord of the sabbath" (Mark 2:28). There he appeals to the precedent of David (Mark 2:24–26), to common sense (Mark 3:4), or to commonly accepted practice (Luke 13:15; 14:5). Here he compares his working on the sabbath with God's working. I think it unlikely that Jesus actually said this about himself. More probably, here the confessing community speaks. If the Johannine church believed that Jesus was in the beginning with God (John 1:1–2; 17:24) and was at present with God in glory (17:24; 20:17, 26–29), it could believe that as the Father always worked Jesus continued to work, whether during the week or on the sabbath. (Of course, according to Gen. 2:3, God rested on the seventh—the sabbath—day. Yet contemporary Jewish exegesis of this passage did not unanimously take it to mean that God continued to rest every sabbath.[5])

Jesus' response actually goes far beyond what is called for by the situation. In fact, it injects an entirely new and disturbing element into it. A view of Jesus that does not arise directly out of the situation as previously described, out of the healing narrative, suddenly presents itself. It is a view well calculated to arouse the ire of any Jew who does not share the christological views of the Johannine community: "This was why the Jews sought all the more to kill him, because he not only broke the sabbath but also called God his own Father, making himself equal to God" (John 5:18).

It is probably significant that the Jews' persecution of Jesus is suddenly presented as already in progress, already attaining its full intensity (they were seeking to kill Jesus), without its development having been described fully in narrative form. Intense opposition between Jesus and the Jews dominates the Fourth Gospel from this

5. The evidence is marshaled by Barrett, *The Gospel According to St. John*, pp. 255–56.

point onward. Heretofore, the reaction of the Jews (John 2:13–22) and of their representative Nicodemus (John 3:1–21) has been more perplexity than hostility. The same is true of the Samaritan woman's reaction. Hereafter, although there may be moments of uncertainty or ambiguity, the Jews of the Fourth Gospel, including those who have believed in Jesus (John 8:31), are not only estranged from Jesus but hostile to him.

From this point onward John not only preaches Jesus as the Christ of Christian confession but presents him in a decidedly polemical way. This Jesus is the Christ of Christians but not necessarily the Messiah of Jewish expectation, although the evangelist continues to think that Jews should accept him as such. The christological preaching or teaching of John is from here on the occasion for offense on the part of the Jews. It is not just Jesus' claim to be the Messiah, a claim they reject. What Jesus claims for himself strikes the Jews as an intolerable offense against their religious beliefs, especially monotheism. Thus Jesus' claim to be working still with the Father (John 5:17) is construed by the Jews as a claim to be equal to God. In all probability this construction of Jesus' claim is in at least some sense correct, and is acknowledged by Christians to be so. Despite the fact that the claim that Jesus is making himself equal to God is a cause of profound offense, it is not denied or disclaimed outright. Indeed, it cannot be, for, rightly understood, it represents the distinctive christological claim that has arisen in the Johannine church.

Nevertheless, the claim is explained. Jesus does nothing that he has not seen the Father doing and claims nothing more than the Father has granted him:

> Jesus said to them, "Truly, truly, I say to you, the Son can do nothing of his own accord, but only what he sees the Father doing; for whatever he does, that the Son does likewise. For the Father loves the Son, and shows him all that he himself is doing; and greater works than these will he show him, that you may marvel." (John 5:19–20)

Yet at the same time Jesus presents himself as the revelation of God, the eschatological salvation-bringer:

> Truly, truly, I say to you, he who hears my word and believes him who sent me, has eternal life; he does not come into judgment, but has passed from death to life.
>
> For as the Father has life in himself, so he has granted the Son also to have life in himself. (John 5:24, 26)

The offense is qualified, explained, and later justified by appeal to witnesses: John the Baptist (John 5:33), Jesus' works (5:36), the Father himself (5:37), the scriptures (5:39), and therefore Moses (5:45–46). Yet offense it remains, for precisely what is the meaning of the Baptist? What do Jesus' signs or works portend? Where is the Father's witness to be sought? How are the scriptures and therefore Moses to be interpreted? All of these questions are at issue in the interchange between the Johannine Christians and those with whom they debate. Because there is agreement on none of them, there can be no agreement on the validity of the claims made by, or for, Jesus.

It is a matter of considerable historical import and interest whether, or to what extent, the claims made for Jesus in the first instance led to the polemical situation we find in the Fourth Gospel. Did the Christology expressed in the Johannine Gospel precede and give rise to the polemic? Or has that Christology evolved over a period of decades as questions and challenges to claims made in the name of Jesus resulted not in the moderation of those claims, but in their accentuation or perhaps their qualification in ways that heightened rather than reduced the offense? I think the latter is the case and that such a process is what we find reflected in John 5.[6]

Christology did not begin with Jesus' proclaiming himself, as he does in the Fourth Gospel. It did, however, begin with Jesus' announcing God's salvation, the advent of his kingdom or rule. However else Jesus may have conceived of himself, he was certainly conscious of his role as the herald of that kingdom. The earliest church, composed of his disciples and others, proclaimed him the messiah at his resurrection. (If Jesus thought of himself in such terms, he did not announce it publicly during his career.) Paul

---

6. For a fascinating description of how this polemical situation may have developed, see Raymond E. Brown, *The Community of the Beloved Disciple* (New York: Paulist Press, 1979), esp. pp. 25–58.

argues that in Jesus Christ, God acts to pronounce the ungodly righteous while at the same moment revealing his wrath against human sin. The synoptic authors rework and arrange traditions originating in Jesus' historic ministry to present him as the fulfillment of emerging Christian conceptions of messianic expectation. These conceptions originated in Judaism and were mined out of the Old Testament, the early Christians' Bible. Yet by and large they represented a reformulation of those expectations in the light of Christian perceptions of the significance of Jesus' career. As we see these formulations, in the New Testament at least, they are fundamentally conditioned or shaped by belief in Jesus' resurrection and in the saving effect of his death.

There may have been forms of early Christian belief in which death and resurrection were not so prominent. For example, some early Christians may have lived out of eschatological hope for the establishment of that rule of God which Jesus proclaimed (Mark 13, Revelation, forms of Q?). It is an oversimplification, but not entirely misleading, to say that as such fervent eschatological orientation and expectation of an imminent consummation waned, the thought and preaching of Christians, centered increasingly on Jesus himself as the eschatological salvation-bringer. More and more, salvation is found and proclaimed in him. There is a sense in which John represents the culmination of this tendency. Thus the Johannine Jesus is portrayed as performing those acts of judgment and salvation, i.e., the giving of life, which had been the prerogative of God. They had been the primary object of expectation and hope for the eschatological future:

> Truly, truly, I say to you, the hour is coming, and now is, when the dead will hear the voice of the Son of God, and those who hear will live. For as the Father has life in himself, so he has granted the Son also to have life in himself, and has given him authority to execute judgement, because he is the Son of man. (John 5:25–27)

Not surprisingly, Jews, and quite possibly also Jewish Christians, found such talk dangerous and blasphemous. Jesus makes himself equal to God. Therefore, Jesus responds at length in John 5:30–

47 to possible objections to the claims made for him, and his words sound like a rejoinder to objections already raised against him:

> You search the scriptures, because you think that in them you have eternal life; and it is they that bear witness to me; yet you refuse to come to me that you may have life. I do not receive glory from men. But I know that you have not the love of God within you. I have come in my Father's name, and you do not receive me; if another comes in his own name, him you will receive. How can you believe, who receive glory from one another and do not seek the glory that comes from the only God? Do not think that I shall accuse you to the Father; it is Moses who accuses you, on whom you set your hope. If you believed Moses, you would believe me, for he wrote of me. But if you do not believe his writings, how will you believe my words? (John 5:39–47)

Curiously, the Jewish objections to which Jesus speaks or the situation of opposition he describes here have not yet appeared in the narrative, but in the following chapters (esp. 6–10) they will be heard increasingly. It is almost as if we had dropped in on the middle of the dispute. The fundamental objection boils down to this: The Jesus of Christian confession and proclamation (not the historical Jesus) is an imposter for whom blasphemous claims are made (John 7:47; 8:48, 52; 10:20). "You, being a man, make yourself God" (10:33). The Johannine Christian answer to this objection is virtually to fly in the teeth of it:

> Jesus answered them: "Is it not written in your law, 'I said, you are gods'? If he called them gods to whom the word of God came (and scripture cannot be broken), do you say of him whom the Father consecrated and sent into the world, 'You are blaspheming,' because I said, 'I am the Son of God'? If I am not doing the works of my Father, then do not believe me; but if I do them, even though you do not believe me, believe the works, that you may know and understand that the Father is in me and I am in the Father." (John 10:34–38)

Yet the bold accusation that Jesus makes himself equal to God, or makes himself God, is not allowed to go unchallenged. At one point that is crucial for the Johannine Chrisitans it is qualified. "I can do nothing on my own authority," says Jesus (John 5:30); "as I hear, I judge; and my judgement is just, because I seek not my own will but the will of him who sent me."

This qualification will not, of course, satisfy the objectors, whether Jewish, pagan, or Christian. It is very interesting, and I think significant, that in the history of Christian doctrine the Jewish objections to the boldness, or the baldness, of Johannine Christology reappear, if in less overtly hostile form. The Ebionites, the Antiochene Christology, the Arians, and others shrink back from the identification of Jesus with God that is the dominant, if not unqualified, thrust of Johannine Christology. Modern liberal Christianity shares in this reservation. Even the ancient church did not ignore it. By embracing the Chalcedonian "truly God" the church seemingly endorsed an interpretation of Johannine Christianity that accentuates this most distinctive, or offensive, aspect. Yet it nevertheless allowed for a larger chorus containing some mellower and less shrill tones. It affirmed Jesus to be "truly man" as well. Moreover, in its canon of scripture the church preserved voices and traditions that balance the Johannine proclamation. John's Gospel may be said to be Christianity or at least Christology taken to a logical or illogical extreme, an extreme case of being Christian. It needs balancing out.

Two things, however, need to be remembered about the Johannine Christology. First, it arose in a polemical setting. In all probability the denial of more modest or traditional claims led, not to their withdrawal, but to the advancing of more sweeping and offensive claims. Second, the Johannine Christology lays bare what is involved in distinctively Christian confession and preaching. So as an extreme case of being Christian, it is also a valuable exploration of the depth and character of Christian conviction, hammered out under pressure, probably under threat. At the same time it represents a very narrow view, theologically and existentially. If, as seems likely, the Johannine community felt "hemmed in" by a hostile world, that narrowness is reflected in its doctrine and ethos.[7]

7. Klaus Wengst, *Bedrängte Gemeinde und verherrlichter Christus: Der histo-*

John's is a Christianity for tough times. It may, and I think does, contain its moment of eternal truth (if one wishes to speak in that way), but it does not provide a complete or adequate perspective for all seasons.

Having looked at the Johannine preaching, which is profoundly christological, let us now explore more closely the Johannine setting, and along with it the conception of church and ministry.

CHURCH AND MINISTRY IN JOHANNINE PERSPECTIVE

The theology of John did not arise in a vacuum. Probably the development of that theology was related to a polemical situation that had led to the separation of Johannine Christians, or the embryonic Johannine church, from the synagogue. Such an understanding of the setting of John's Gospel owes a great deal to the seminal work of J. Louis Martyn,[8] who construes the debate over whether Jesus was the Christ, first within the synagogue and then between the sundered communities, as the motive force that gives the Fourth Gospel its distinctive character.

It may be hazardous to infer too much about specifics of the setting of the Fourth Gospel from its portrayal of the conflict between Jesus and the Jews or Pharisees. Nevertheless, the thrice-repeated reference to expulsion of those who confess Christ from synagogues (John 9:22; 12:42; 16:2), if it reflects a historical situation at all, points to a period well after the historical ministry of Jesus. The question of confession of Jesus as the Christ was scarcely the issue constantly confronting and troubling his contemporaries. That this question became acute at the time of the Roman War and thereafter is probable, although its roots go back earlier. It is interesting to

---

rische Ort des Johannesevangeliums als Schlüssel zu seinen Interpretation, Biblische-Theologische Studien 5 (Neukirchen: Neukirchener Verlag, 1981), makes an interesting suggestion about the date and place of origin of the Fourth Gospel. On the basis of his analysis of Jewish-Christian tensions in the Fourth Gospel and his search through contemporary sources for a time and place to match the conditions implied, he concludes that the Gospel was written c. 80–90 in the southern portions of the kingdom of Agrippa II, i.e., in Gaulanitis and Batanaea, better known nowadays as the Golan Heights.

8. Martyn, History and Theology in the Fourth Gospel, 2d ed., rev. and enl. (Nashville: Abingdon, 1979). The first edition, from which the revision does not differ essentially, appeared in 1968.

observe that Jewish authorities are portrayed as already hostile to the proclamation of Jesus as Christ in Acts 1–5, i.e., at the earliest period. But this may be anachronistic. At the time of the arrest of Paul in Jerusalem (Acts 21) the issue between Paul and the Jewish authorities in Jerusalem seems to be observance of the law (Acts 21:24–25). That Paul had been persecuted by synagogue authorities is clear (2 Cor. 11:24–25). Before that, Paul himself persecuted the church, as both he (Gal. 1:13; 1 Cor. 15:9; cf. 1 Thess. 2:14–15) and Acts (chap. 9) attest. But also in Acts (5:33–42) the Pharisee Gamaliel urges the council to take a wait-and-see attitude to the claims made for Jesus. Not until John's Gospel is the question of whether Jesus is the Christ presented so unequivocally as the single issue dividing Christian believers, whether Jewish or Gentile, from "the Jews." If the Gospel of John seems to emerge from a dispute over Jesus that led to the separation of church and synagogue, then it is itself a kind of by-product of the birth of a distinctly Christian community.

A polemical setting of Johannine Christianity would account for the vigor, and even vehemence, of the Fourth Gospel's christological affirmation. If John is, so to speak, "hemmed in," the result is a narrow focus on what the community thinks is essential, the confession of Jesus as Son of God which constitutes its raison d'etre. This confession is deepened beyond what is otherwise known in early Christianity, or certainly in the gospel tradition. The cosmic significance of Christ, already suggested in Paul (Phil. 2:5–11; Col. 1:15–20) and Hebrews (Heb. 1:2–3), is now expressed in a gospel, a narrative of Jesus' career (John 1:1–2), and by the Lord himself (John 17:24). That God has acted in a decisive way in Jesus (cf. Rom. 1:1–4, 16–17; 3:21–22), a cardinal theological tenet of early Christianity, is now taken to mean that Jesus is, at least functionally, equivalent to God. The equation of Jesus and God in revelation is complete:

> Jesus said to him, "Have I been with you so long, and yet you do not know me, Phillip? He who has seen me has seen the Father, how can you say, 'Show us the Father'? Do you not believe that I am in the Father and the Father in me? The words that I say to you I do not speak on my own authority; but the Father who dwells in me does his

works. Believe me that I am in the Father and the Father in me; or else believe me for the sake of the works themselves." (John 14:9–11)

How or why does this happen? What basic theological instinct or perspective finds expression in such christological claims? Exegetical answers range from the view that the Johannine Jesus is docetically conceived, that he authenticates himself as a revelation through the *doxa* of supernatural signs, knowledge, and word (Käsemann) to the position of Bultmann that "the revelation is present in a peculiar *hiddenness.*" Bultmann writes: "This is the paradox which runs through the whole gospel: the *doxa* [glory] is not to be seen *alongside* the *sarx* [flesh], nor *through* the *sarx* as through a window; it is to be seen in the *sarx* and nowhere else."[9] Bultmann comprehends and expresses the nature of this paradox perhaps better than John does. But it is not a sheer imposition upon the text. The same Jesus who tells the Samaritan woman all she has done also grew weary from a journey and sat down at the well to rest. It is not the intention of the Fourth Evangelist to present the revelation of God in Jesus in such a way as to negate his humanity or to make his experience foreign, and therefore irrelevant, to his followers. "As the Father has sent me," says the risen Jesus (John 20:21), "even so I send you." "If they persecuted me, they will persecute you; if they kept my word, they will keep yours also" (15:20). "I do not pray that thou shouldst take them out of the world, but that thou shouldst keep them from the evil one" (17:15). The author of the closely related First Epistle of John writes (1 John 2:5b–6): "By this we may be sure we are in him: he who says he abides in him ought to walk in the same way in which he walked." And again (1 John 3:16): "By this we know love, that he laid down his life for us; and we ought to lay down our lives for the brethren." In Johannine thought, the believer's life in the world recapitulates certain crucial aspects of Jesus' own ministry.

Now, at length, we can consider the question of the nature of ministry in John. At the outset we should be aware of the sheer lexical data. The word "ministry" or "to minister" *(diakonia/dia-*

9. Bultmann, *The Gospel of John: A Commentary,* trans. G. R. Beasley-Murray et al. (Philadelphia: Westminster, 1971), p. 63.

konein) is rare in John, and the word "church" *(ecclesia)* does not appear at all. But it would be wrong to infer from this that there is nothing in John answering to the concepts of church and ministry. We have already seen that in John the disciples of Jesus constitute a distinct and separate group over against the disciples of Moses. This situation does not correspond to the time of Jesus itself, when Jesus and his disciples stood within the Jewish community. Rather, it more likely reflects a tension between the synagogue and the emerging Johannine Christian church, probably in the latter part of the first century. There is then at least an implicit Johannine ecclesiology. What about a conception of ministry?

One way to pursue this question would be to ask about the understanding of church order in John, or about the actual church order in the Johannine community. It cannot be shown that either the Gospel of John or the Johannine Epistles evince a highly developed church organization. Because of the narrative, quasi-historical, or biographical nature of the gospels, it is difficult to infer from them the kind of church order they espouse or represent.[10] This is, if anything, especially true of John. But because the Twelve are seldom mentioned and never named, because Peter seems to be put down in favor of the Beloved Disciple, because the importance of direct access of the believer to Jesus is emphasized, because the risen Christ seems to preside over his church through the Spirit-Paraclete; for all these reasons it is widely held that John represents a "low" ecclesiology or a view of church order in which ministerial office has not developed, or has not been allowed to develop. Rather, every believer is related to Christ in the same way. There is no ministerial hierarchy, perhaps not even the distinction of ministry and laity. The downplaying of the Twelve would be commensurate with an ecclesiology in which the concept of apostolic authority was not espoused or emphasized as the touchstone of churchly ministry. Also, in the Johannine Epistles, probably later than the Gospel, no clear conception of ministry or church order appears. 2 and 3 John are the work of someone who styles himself "the Elder," and the First Epistle of John is presumed to be by the

10. Cf. the observations in my article (included in this present volume) "Johannine Christianity: Some Reflections on Its Character and Delineation," *NTS* 21(1975): esp. pp. 222–24 (above pp. 1–3).

same person, but this is not certain. (Obviously all the letters as well as the Gospel are from the same or related early Christian circles or schools.) Whether "elder" is even a title comparable to that found in Acts, Paul, and the pastoral epistles is not completely certain. Probably it is. From 3 John 9 and the mention of "Diotrephes, who likes to put himself first," one may infer that church organization and order has become a problem in the Johannine community. Beyond that it is impossible to say much with certainty. Who represents the nascent episcopal office and authority? Diotrephes? Or perhaps the Elder? There is scarcely sufficient evidence to decide. I should like, however, to prescind from these and related questions in order to approach the subject of ministry in the Fourth Gospel from a different angle.

If it is true that Jesus does not speak of himself as performing a ministry or ministering in the Fourth Gospel, by contrast the term *diakonein* (to minister, or serve) occurs in a crucial context in the Gospel of Mark. At the end of the pivotal central section (Mark 10:45) Jesus says, "The Son of man also came not to be served [ministered to] but to serve [minister], and to give his life as a ransom for many." Moreover, the concept of Jesus' ministering or serving, which is at home in the synoptics, seems at first glance to be foreign to John. The absence of the term would appear to suit John's high Christology.

Yet this is not quite the case. There is in John, and only there, a narrative that portrays Jesus performing the most humble ministry or service, although the words *diakonein/diakonia* are not used. It is, of course, the story of Jesus' washing the disciples' feet (John 13:1–20). This story stands in John's account of the last supper at about the point at which the synoptics would lead us to expect the institution of the Lord's Supper, which, of course, is not found in John. There is, however, in Luke an interesting "missing link" connecting the Marcan concept of ministry *(diakonia)*, the Johannine foot-washing story, and the institution of the Lord's Supper. In the Lucan narrative (Luke 22:25–27) there follows after the institution a kind of brief farewell discourse of Jesus in which he speaks of ministering or serving *(diakonein)* in terms similar to Mark 10:45:

> And he said to them, "The kings of the Gentiles exercise lordship over them; and those in authority over them are

called benefactors. But not so with you; rather let the greatest among you become as the youngest, and the leader as one who serves. For which is the greater, one who sits at table, or one who serves? Is it not the one who sits at table? But I am among you as one who serves." (Luke 22:25–27)

Probably Luke draws on Q material (cf. Matt. 23:11) as well as on Mark 10:45. Moreover, Luke 12:37 records another saying of Jesus about service *(diakonein)*: "Blessed are those servants whom the master finds awake when he comes; truly, I say to you, he will gird himself and have them sit at table, and he will come and serve them." Certainly this suggests the Johannine foot-washing scene.

On the assumption that John knew Luke, Barrett thinks that John has probably developed the Lucan sayings into the story which we find in the Fourth Gospel. This is not impossible. But as real as are the affinities between Luke and John, there is much to be said for Bultmann's proposal that John here employs a traditional apothegm, related to Lucan tradition, which he has annotated and edited to express his own point of view.[11] It is, after all, quite a jump from the sayings of Luke to the Johannine story.

John certainly used tradition related to the synoptic. Possibly he knew, or at least knew of, one or more of the synoptic gospels. But this story is found only in John, nowhere else. Yet its earthy character implies an origin not far removed from the synoptic tradition, if not the historical Jesus. The very obvious twofold interpretation also suggests that the evangelist is here working with tradition. According to John 13:6–11, the washing of the feet symbolizes Jesus' saving work, especially his death:

He came to Simon Peter; and Peter said to him, "Lord, do you wash my feet?" Jesus answered him, "What I am doing you do not know now, but afterward you will understand." Peter said to him, "You shall never wash my feet." Jesus answered him, "If I do not wash you, you have no part in me." Simon Peter said to him, "Lord, not my feet only but also my hands and my head!" Jesus said

11. Bultmann, *The Gospel of John*, p. 462.

to him, "He who has bathed does not need to wash, except for his feet, but he is clean all over; and you are clean, but not all of you." For he knew who was to betray him; that was why he said, "You are not all clean." (John 13:6–11)

Here the footwashing is clearly a ministry or service that Jesus performs for his disciples, his church. In vv. 12–17, however, there is another interpretation of the washing of the feet.

When he had washed their feet, and taken his garments, and resumed his place, he said to them, "Do you know what I have done to you? You call me Teacher and Lord; and you are right, for so I am. If I then, your Lord and Teacher, have washed your feet, you also ought to wash one another's feet. For I have given you an example, that you also should do as I have done to you. Truly, truly, I say to you, a servant is not greater than his master; nor is he who is sent greater than he who sent him. If you know these things, blessed are you if you do them. (John 13:12–17)

Bultmann quite reasonably takes this second interpretation to be traditional, a part of the apothegm the evangelist used. It highlights the moral demand implicit in Jesus' act.[12]

The first interpretation (John 13:6–11), which centers around Peter's misunderstanding of the event, seems to be the distinctly Johannine one. Certainly it accords more closely with Johannine theology and style. Peter evinces the kind of misguided loyalty and impetuousness attributed to him elsewhere in the gospels. He at first refuses to allow Jesus to wash his feet. When Jesus tells him he does not know now what he (Jesus) is doing, but he will know

12. I am not unaware of contrary analyses, according to which 13:12–17 represents an interpretation that has been interpolated at a late stage of the composition history of the gospel. See, e.g., R. Schnackenburg, *The Gospel According to John*, III, trans. D. Smith and G. A. Kon (New York: Crossroad, 1982), 12–13, 23. Schnackenburg regards the second interpretation of the footwashing as an addition by a later editor. Nevertheless, he also deems it "earlier" (i.e., from earlier tradition) and very close to the synoptic tradition.

"afterward" (the *meta tauta* surely refers to the crucifixion and resurrection), a typical Johannine motif emerges. The disciples do not understand now, but they will understand in retrospect (cf. John 2:17, 22; 12:16). Then Peter declares even more strongly that Jesus will never wash his feet (13:8*a*), and Jesus says to Peter that if he does not wash him, Peter will have no part in him. This elicits from Peter what the reader perceives as a typically Petrine expostulation: "Lord, not my feet only but also my hands and my head!" (v. 9). This is also a typical example of Johannine style: Peter misunderstands. Peter thinks Jesus speaks of a physical washing, when something more profound is at stake. Jesus then makes a rather enigmatic rejoinder: "He who has bathed does not need to wash, but he is clean all over; and you are clean, but not all of you," (v. 10). (I follow Bultmann and Barrett, who accept the reading of Codex Sinaiticus, in which "except his feet" is omitted.) The bathing is the washing of the feet, which symbolizes Jesus' service for the disciple, the saving work which he accomplishes. Bultmann equates this service with Jesus' word, but it can scarcely be separated from his death (John 3:16; 6:51; 10:11; 15:13–14).

Whatever their origin, John the evangelist has laid these two interpretations back to back in such a way that they make sense together. The service that Jesus performs for the disciples in washing their feet is his salvific work, culminating in his death. This work must be accepted by the disciples. Accept it is all they can do in the first instance. They dare not refuse it. Christ acts decisively for the salvation of his disciples. Yet the disciples' acceptance of this work of Jesus comes to fruition only as they recapitulate it on behalf of one another. This is the significance of the second interpretation (John 13:12–17). What Jesus says here accords rather well with the Marcan teaching about Jesus' service or ministry (*diakonia/diakonein*). According to Mark, what Jesus does for his followers they must recapitulate among themselves. The Johannine sayings actually have synoptic and other parallels: John 13:15 (1 Pet. 2:21); John 13:16 (Matt. 10:24; Luke 6:40); John 13:17 (Luke 10:37).

We have thus arrived at a cardinal tenet of Johannine theology. Jesus' love for his disciples is recapitulated in their love for one another. At the beginning of the last supper we learn that Jesus loved his disciples, who were in the world, to the end (John 13:1).

At the conclusion of the meal he gives them a new commandment, to love one another as he has loved them (13:34). This, not incidentally, is in John's view the most persuasive form of evangelism (13:35; cf. 17:21, 23). Jesus lays down his life for his friends (15:13), after having first enjoined his disciples to love one another as he has loved them. In 1 John this dual motif, the disciples' boundless love for one another recapitulating Jesus' love for them, is strongly reiterated: "By this we know love, that he laid down his life for us; and we ought to lay down our lives for the brethren" (1 John 3:16).

John understands faith in Jesus as belief in him that finds specific and concrete manifestation in the disciples' mode of life. This realizing of faith in life belongs to the essence of faith. The author of 1 John never tires of making this point. In fact, he makes it quite clearly and eloquently:

> Beloved, let us love one another; for love is of God and he who loves is born of God and knows God. He who does not love does not know God; for God is love. In this the love of God was made manifest among us, that God sent his only Son into the world, so that we might live through him. In this is love, not that we loved God but that he loved us and sent his Son to be the expiation for our sins. Beloved, if God so loved us, we also ought to love one another. No man has ever seen God; if we love one another, God abides in us and his love is perfected in us. (1 John 4:7–12)

The indissoluble connection between what we call theology and ethics is stated simply and beautifully, but also forcefully:

> If any one says, "I love God," and hates his brother, he is a liar; for he who does not love his brother whom he has seen, cannot love God whom he has not seen. And this commandment we have from him, that he who loves God should love his brother also. (1 John 4:20–21)

John's seemingly dogmatic, and somewhat strident, Christology has as its other side a vital, ethically pregnant conviction that in

Jesus, God expresses his love for the world, especially for believers. If there is a Johannine conception of ministry—and I think there is—it is grounded in the belief that God is love and his revelation is the expression of that love. To believe, to live in and by the light of God's revelation in Jesus, is to participate in that love, to love God, Christ, and one's brothers and sisters in faith. This broadly based conception of ministry or service is incumbent upon the disciple of Jesus. If there are specialized ministries, they must be grounded in this fundamental ministry.

Nevertheless, there is a narrowness about this grand conception that is perhaps more apparent in the Epistle than in the Gospel, but it is present in both. God loves the world and intends to save it (John 3:16). Yet the world is by and large rejecting the definitive expression of that love, Jesus Christ the Son of God. The result is judgment. The hostility and tension between the disciples and the Jews is only an archetypal instance of the polarity between Jesus and his disciples, i.e., the church on the one hand and the world on the other. There is a relationship of proportionality, if no polar duality, between Jesus, the disciples, and the church on the one side, and Satan, the Jews, and the world on the other. The well-known dualism of the Johannine literature is the linguistic, conceptual product of a profound sense of estrangement and hostility.

This sense of estrangement makes it difficult for the epistolary author to affirm, with the evangelist, that God loves the world.[13] In fact, it is interesting to compare the forthright statement of John 3:16 with 1 John 4:9: "In this the love of God was made manifest among us, that God sent his only Son into the world, so that we might live through him." God's Son comes into the world, but the love of God is made manifest "among *us*. . .so that *we* might live

13. I find myself in agreement with the now widely held view that the author of the Epistles was not the same as the author of the Gospel. Cf. Raymond E. Brown, *The Epistles of John*, AB 30 (Garden City, N.Y.: Doubleday, 1982), pp. 19–30, for a full and extremely judicious treatment of the evidence. Some recent interpreters argue that the latest layer of the redaction of the Gospel comes from the same hand as the Epistles, or at least reflects the identical church situation; e.g., Fernando F. Segovia, *Love Relationships in the Johannine Tradition: Agapé/Agapan in I John and the Fourth Gospel*, SBL Dissertation Series 58 (Chico, Calif.: Scholars Press, 1982), pp. 218–19.

through him." God's love seems only to benefit the Christian community.

I do not know that the author of 1 John, much less the evangelist, would want to be held to so narrow a construction of the effect of the saving work of God, if we were able to question him. Quite possibly the exigencies of expulsion from the synagogue (John 9:22; 12:42; 16:2) have given the Johannine church a dim view of the world as well as of Judaism. However that may be, the tendency to reject the world in favor of the beleaguered community, and thus to see God as rejecting the world in favor of that community, is strongly at work in the Johannine literature.

This is particularly evident in what seems to be the sharp limitation, whether intentional or not, of the realm in which the ethical imperative, the love imperative, is taken to apply. Whom are believers to love? The answer seems to be that they are to love other believers: "Love one another. . . .By this all men will know that you are my disciples, if you have love for one another" (John 13:34–35); "This commandment we have from him, that he who loves God should love his brother also" (1 John 4:21). Many interpreters are loath to concede that in the Johannine view Jesus' command to love is limited to the circle of his disciples, i.e., the church. Strictly speaking, this may not be the case. The synoptic Jesus' command to love your neighbor as yourself (Mark 12:31; Matt. 22:39; Luke 10:27) is not rejected in John, it is true. There is no injunction to love your neighbor and hate your enemy (Matt. 5:43). One may argue that the command to love the brethren really raises the question of who your brother is. If all men and women are brothers and sisters before God, the command to love one's brother is equivalent to the command to love all people. However true in principle that may be, it does not seem to be what the author of the Gospel (and the Epistle) had in mind. His concern was with relationships within the church. Love among the members of the community establishes its unity. This unity, the realization and manifestation of love, is the basis of the community's witness to the truth of Jesus as well as of its very existence:

By this all men will know that you are my disciples, if you have love for one another.

> I do not pray for these only, but also for those who believe
> in me through their word, that they may all be one; even
> as thou, Father, art in me, and I in thee, that they also
> may be in us, so that the world may believe that thou
> hast sent me. (John 13:35; 17:20–21)

Ministry in John is self-giving service. It is conceived, at least in
the first instance, as an intramural relationship. As Jesus lays down
his life for his friends, so they are willing to lay down their lives
for each other. Through this ministry, however, a positive relation
to the world may be established, i.e., people may be converted. As
to the concrete and specific form this ministry may take, it is usually
less dramatic than laying down one's life. Washing one another's
feet, of which a modern equivalent is difficult to produce, is neither
sacramental nor sentimental. It is the symbol of that practical ministry which defines the very life of the Johannine community. The
community lives in and for such mutual service. Apart from it there
is, effectually, no revelation, no faith, and particularly no ministry
and no church:

> Beloved, let us love one another; for love is of God, and
> he who loves is born of God and knows God. He who
> does not love does not know God; for God is love.
>
> No man has ever seen God; if we love one another, God
> abides in us and his love is perfected in us.
>
> If any one says, "I love God," and hates his brother, he
> is a liar; for he who does not love his brother whom he
> has seen, cannot love God whom he has not seen. (1 John
> 4:7–8, 12, 20)

In conclusion, we return briefly to the problem of John and the
synoptics, not as an interesting literary and historical conundrum,
but as a matter germane to theology and preaching in the church.
The origins of the distinctly Johannine theology, particularly Christology, lie not in the synoptic tradition or in a direct line of development from Paul, but rather in the peculiar polemical situation
of the Johannine community. The claim that Jesus was the Messiah
was confronted by rejection within the Jewish community. The

resulting controversy, now reflected in the Fourth Gospel's accounts of Jesus' conversations and debates with his contemporaries, led to schism and alienation. Out of it the Johannine Christian community emerged. In some measure the high Johannine Christology with its dogmatic overtones, as well as the Johannine church, is a product of polemic. Yet at the same time that Christology does not contradict the other gospels or the theological developments evident there. Certainly John knew a gospel tradition similar to what is found in the synoptics, if not the synoptic gospels themselves. His gospel, although not deliberately written to supplement them, nevertheless makes sense and takes on an added dimension of depth when read alongside them. The Fourth Gospel by itself might well have led to a heretical form of Christology and Christianity that the author himself did not intend. For theological, specifically Christological, purposes John needs to be read with the synoptics. It is not wrongly construed as making explicit what is mostly latent or implicit in them.

Moreover, the Johannine interpretation of Jesus' teaching as fundamentally the command to love one another is also not foreign to the synoptic tradition. Interpreters have not erred in perceiving in John's "new commandment" the epitome of Jesus' teaching. In all likelihood the inwardness of this command ("love one another" as contrasted with "love your neighbor") to which we have pointed has something to do with the polemical circumstances of the Gospel's origin and history. (There are some good reasons why Johannine Christianity has been referred to in recent scholarship as sectarian.) Interpreters are obligated to understand and appreciate this history as best they can. When we begin to speak of the concept of ministry in John, however, we have not only the right but the obligation to think of a somewhat broader context or picture. In and of themselves the Johannine writings warrant the depiction of Christian ministry as the expression of love, not only in a general disposition but in concrete and specific acts on behalf of one's brother or sister in Christ. Mission then comes about as, so to speak, an overflow from the world's observation of such expressions of love. When put alongside the other gospels and the New Testament writings generally, once again John is found to bring to very pointed expression the teaching of early Christianity, of the New Testament, and indeed of Jesus himself. This last judgment may belong to the realm of faith as much as to that of historical criticism, but it is not a judgment devoid of historical integrity.

Index

MODERN AUTHORS

223

SCRIPTURE